Greece's (un) Competitive Capitalism and the Economic Crisis

Spyros Sakellaropoulos
Department of Social Policy
Panteion University
Athens, Greece

ISBN 978-3-030-14318-3 ISBN 978-3-030-14319-0 (eBook)
https://doi.org/10.1007/978-3-030-14319-0

Library of Congress Control Number: 2019934109

This Palgrave Macmillan imprint is published by the registered company Springer Nature Switzerland AG
The registered company address is: Gewerbestrasse 11, 6330 Cham, Switzerland

To Faye

Contents

List of Tables

Introduction

The October 2009 parliamentary elections held in Greece were won by the social democratic party PASOK (Panhellenic Socialist Movement) with 44% of the votes. PASOK succeeded the Conservative New Democracy party, which had received just 33.5%. The prime ministership was assumed by the president of PASOK G. Papandreou. The general feeling in Greek society was that despite the emergence of some unfavourable signs (notably the increase in the public deficit), the new government would not only manage to avoid austerity but would also strengthen the social state in Greece. This was anything but the way things turned out. It soon became clear that the country's economy was in very bad state and that it could not meet its obligations to service the public debt. It is for this reason that the Papandreou government applied to the European Union (EU) and the International Monetary Fund (IMF) requesting their help. And indeed, the EU, the IMF and the European Central Bank proceeded with the grant of a €130 billion loan to Greece in the context of implementation of draconian austerity defined by the contents of a Memorandum signed by all parties concerned. Since then, May 2010, Greece has entered upon a period of crisis for the economy, protracted for years, with very serious consequences for Greek society, contributing to its profound transformation.

This book aims to interpret the causes of the Greek crisis, to present its results and to highlight the reasons why there could not be an alternative policy—even when SYRIZA, the party that had been the vehicle for many hopes, inside and outside Greece, formed a government. The basic position that is asserted is that the Greek crisis cannot be seen independently of the 2008 world crisis. The latter is a result of the fact that it has not been possible to reverse the consequences of the 1973 crisis, while at European level the situation is being made worse by the reality that the euro has not succeeded in becoming the main global reserve currency, in conjunction with the fact that European productivity continues to lag behind that of the United States. What is peculiar to Greece is that the post-war regime of accumulation began to be problematic from the moment that the country joined first the European Economic Community (EEC) and then the European Monetary Union (EMU): the chronic competitiveness problem of Greek capitalism, deriving from the production of low-technology products, led to a rise in the trade deficit, but given that the other variables in the current account balance (tourism, transfers from the EU, remittances from the shipping sector) did not present similar problems, the situation remained manageable. But when difficulties arose there too, the crisis generalized, gross domestic product (GDP) contracted, the government deficit and public debt mushroomed and, in a turbulent international economy, Greece appeared to be on the verge of bankruptcy. Both for the Greek ruling class and for international capital the situation constituted a risk and an opportunity simultaneously: the risk was that the country would go bankrupt and the prevailing confusion would be uncontrollable. Foreign investors who had invested in Greek bonds could lose their money. The opportunity was that, given the absence of a clear alternative to the policy of the Memoranda, it became conceivable that another model of accumulation might be introduced, based on very low wages, the violent transformation of labour relations and the liquidation of non-competitive capital. A successful implementation of this strategy could make possible its subsequent extension to other Western countries. Application of such policies naturally presupposed necessary changes in the State. This is where the updated form of *authoritarian statism* comes in. It is a practice that was mentioned in the Marxist literature of the 1970s, but now it presents a more authoritarian context sealed by a *state of emergency*. Its basic characteristics are attempted elimination of the elements of political representation within the State; the proliferation of decision-making centres inaccessible to popular control; the hardening of repressive practices. This is in line with the policy of the EU and the EMU, where through a variety of agreements the powers of non-elected bodies are strengthened and the role of representative institutions is substantially limited. This does not imply "autonomy of the bureaucracy of Brussels". The EU is not an independent structure of supranational power mechanisms but an alliance of national formations designed to promote the goals of the most powerful monopoly fractions operating within them to the detriment of the interests of the lower classes. The fall of so-called really-existing socialism in conjunction with the retreat of the Left and labour movements made it possible for a number of reactionary ruptures to be put into effect. In the Greek case in particular, it was all made worse by the presence of the creditors' organization within the Greek state and its direct intervention on issues of national sovereignty, resulting in the transformation of Greece into a quasi-protectorate. This came into effect with the consent of the strongest sections of the Greek ruling class. On the one hand, they ceded elements of national sovereignty to the creditors but on the other hand they benefited from a policy that contributed to the reduction of labour cost, the erosion of labour rights and the liquidation of non-competitive capital.

Of course, the policy being pursued in Greece also had consequences and provoked reactions. The consequences were very serious: a great part of the country's productive fabric was destroyed, unemployment soared to 27%, inequalities widened, poverty spread, several businesses had gone bankrupt. But there were also sections of capital that saw their profitability rise, thanks to the fall in labour costs and on the other hand to the fact that some sectors began to channel their activities to countries outside the monetary union and often also to countries outside the West. The reactions not only include the various mobilizations that took place in the period 2010–2013 (a large number of nationwide strikes, the squares movement, interruption of parades, occupations of ministries, the movement of support for Hellenic Radio and Television, social solidarity practices) but also the collapse of the tacit two-party consensus and the emergence of SYRIZA as first party in the 2014 European elections and its assumption of the government (in coalition with the Independent Greeks) in January 2015.

Developments in and after January 2015 are of great interest: they transcend the boundaries of Greece, acquiring symbolic status internationally. A radical Left party wins national elections, underpinned by the deluge of social mobilizations that had preceded. There was the prospect of an *alternative* mode of governance, of a government of the Left. The whole development apparently signified interest in social experimentation that seemed to be challenging the power of the international markets and the ideology of neo-liberalism. The fact that very soon the Greek government proved unable to impose its will and exit the Memoranda not only exposed the overall picture of the international correlation of power but also the limits of a policy based on the belief that articulating a coherent argument within a given negotiating framework is enough to deflect it, if not overthrow it. In other words, the SYRIZA government's defeat in the summer of 2015 with its signing of a third Memorandum was nothing more or less than the final phase of a strategy from which the missing element was construction of clear alternative strategy for breaking with the policies of the lenders in conjunction with the conclusion of international alliances and the activation of the subordinate classes through a network of social support within the Greek social formation. In contrast, devotion to the end in itself of negotiations with insistence on the positive character of the European idea was to lead to the corresponding impasse. In the final analysis, it was a development that would clarify the meaning of the concept "weak link", reinstating interest in probable radical turns of events within the so-called capitalist metropolis.

This book was written for two reasons: The first was to provide a radical positioning against the dominant interpretations of the crisis in Greece, shifting the parameters of discussion away from the ideological discourse on the "lazy Greeks", the "over-inflated public sector" and the "high wages that torpedo economic productivity" to real content of the class policies being elaborated under the hegemony of international capital and its representatives in alliance with the most powerful sections of the local bourgeois order and against the interests of the popular majority. The second is that the enormity of the stakes that appeared to be revealed in the Greek social formation was so conspicuous that for the first time in many decades the Greek bourgeoisie and the imperialist centres gave every sign of being seriously concerned about the repercussions that could be triggered by further extension of the social dynamic. Nevertheless, the failure to come up with any different development as an alternative to SYRIZA's capitulation, and the weakness of the remainder to the Greek Left, exposed some significant limitations, and the need to interpret them.

These two parameters permeate the entire book, which is divided into ten chapters. The first chapter deals with the international crisis of 2007 at both global and European level. In the second there is an examination of the causes of the Greek crisis, which is presented as a product of the combination of Greek capitalism's chronic problems and the impact of the global crisis on the Greek economy. In the third there is an account of the eight austerity packages that ensued from the signing of the three successive Memoranda. The fourth highlights the economic impact of these policies, with emphasis on the historically unprecedented rapid fall of many indicators, not only the destruction of a wide range of productive units but also the existence of businesses and sectors that withstood the assault and displayed a remarkable dynamic. In the fifth there is a description not only of the very serious social consequences brought about by implementation of the Memoranda policies, but also reference to the social categories that benefited from the crisis. In the sixth we see the changes in the country's social stratification, one of the side effects of the economic crisis. The seventh emphasizes the concept of authoritarian statism, within which the "regime of exception" has been taking shape in recent years, marking a qualitative change in the configuration of representative democracy. It is reinforced by the changes brought about by the neo-liberal shift of the institutions of the EU, which in conjunction with the Greek crisis has led to the emergence of a hybrid form of Greek state, a quasi-protectorate. The eighth examines the reactions of the dominated classes towards the Memorandum policies, both at the level of social mobilizations and at that of creating structures of solidarity. In the ninth there is a discussion of the transformations in the party system from May 2010 up to the elections of September 2015, followed by an account of developments in the second period of SYRIZA-ANEL government. The tenth and final chapter presents an evaluation of why the SYRIZA-ANEL government failed to cancel the Memoranda, followed by a discussion of the question of whether there is a new strategy on the part of the ruling class, implementation of which will not bring back the pathogens of the past.

Before proceeding to the main content of this study, I feel the need to thank all those who assisted, each in his own way, to make this book a reality. To begin with, I would like to thank Palgrave who agreed to the publication, and in particular Rachel Sangster who greatly encouraged the idea of pursuing publication. Then there is Vangelis Georgakakis, my editor in Greece, who was not only encouraging during the writing but also took the initiative of proposing it to Palgrave. Much gratitude is also owed to Giannis Karahalios for his insightful observations and Panagiotis Sotiris not only for our years-long shared intellectual trajectory but also for the important comments he offered on the content of this book. Petros Papaconstantinou with his always straight-from-the-shoulder critique and Giorgos Grollios, Karolos Kavoulakos and Babis Kouroundis with their pertinent reflections on an earlier version of the text have also helped immensely.

The book is dedicated to my partner Faye Retsa in minimum recognition of her contribution to my life to date.

Athens, Winter 2019

1

The International Economic Crisis

Introduction

The basic thesis of this book is that the Greek crisis is not to be disconnected from the international financial crisis. In the first chapter, we propose to deal with the causes and the form of the global crisis that started in the United States due to the so-called real estate bubble and then expanded into Europe and the rest of the world. As we shall see at the end of this chapter and in the second chapter, the way the crisis was dealt with by the European economic elites was to afflict Greece in particular, this country for a number of internal reasons being destined to become the weak link of the European and the international economy.

Failure to Overcome the Crisis of 1973

The 2007–2008 housing bubble in the United States and its effects on the financial sphere are symptomatic of the fact that it was never possible completely to contain the consequences of the global economic crisis of 1973. This is shown by the steady decline in a series of indicators. As showing in the following two tables are characteristic (Tables 1.1 and 1.2):

S. Sakellaropoulos, *Greece's (un) Competitive Capitalism and the Economic Crisis*,
https://doi.org/10.1007/978-3-030-14319-0_1

Table 1.1 Rates of change of GDP per capita, developed economies, 1970–2011

	1970–1980	1980–1990	1990–2000	2001–2011	2005–2011
United States	2.35	2.66	2.48	0.63	−0.40
Japan	2.82	3.89	0.76	0.64	−0.41
United Kingdom	1.92	3.14	2.60	0.80	−0.51
France	2.98	1.65	1.45	0.52	−0.09
Germany	2.82	2.00	1.22	1.14	1.11
Italy	3.28	2.42	1.51	−0.52	−1.27
Greece	3.42	0.25	1.37	1.20	−1.36
Europe	2.66	2.15	1.85	0.96	0.11
Developed economies	2.58	2.61	1.97	0.83	−0.07

Source: Maniatis (2013: 44)

Table 1.2 Rates of change in private real nonresidential capital stock and in total economy labour productivity

Private real nonresidential capital stock (plant and equipment)					
United States	3.9	3.7	3.0	2.9	1.8
Japan	12.5[a]	9.4	6.1	2.9	1.1[b]
Germany	6.7	5.2	3.3	2.4	1.2
Industrial	5.0	4.2	3.1	3.3	2.1
Total economy labour productivity (GDP/worker)					
United States	2.3	1.2	1.3	1.7	1.7
Japan	8.6	3.7	3.0	1.1	1.8
Germany	4.2	2.5	1.3	2.5	1.5
Euro12	5.1	2.9	1.8	1.9	0.9
G7	4.8 (60–73)	2.8 (73–79)	2.6	1.9	1.0

Source: Brenner (2009: 7)
[a]Gross stock
[b]2006

It is observed that in all three variables (gross domestic product [GDP] change, capital stock, productivity), the trajectory is one of steady decline in all countries, leading to the conclusion that a major problem is emerging in the modern capitalist organization of production. This problem does not seem to be solvable, either, by adoption of low wages or curbs on private consumption, as shown in Tables 1.3 and 1.4.

The figures in Tables 1.3 and 1.4 show that wages and private consumption are indeed steadily declining. This indicates that the problem of profitability that has created the crisis is not a matter of high wages, and if it continues to exist this is due to the fact that all the policies

Table 1.3 Annual, per capita income growth rate, 1960–2004

	Annual growth rate (%)				
Countries	1960–1979	1979–2004	1979–1989	1989–2000	2000–2004
United States	2.2	1.9	2.1	1.9	1.3
Japan	6.6	2.0	3.1	1.5	0.8
Germany[a]	3.3	1.7	1.8	2.0	0.6
France	3.4	1.6	1.9	1.7	1.0
Italy	5.0	1.7	2.3	1.5	0.7
United Kingdom	1.7	2.1	2.2	2.0	2.1
Canada	3.0	1.6	1.7	1.6	1.4

Source: Melas (2011: 389)
[a]West Germany until 1991

Table 1.4 Real personal consumption expenditure

	1960–1969	1969–1979	1979–1990	1990–2000	2000–2007
United States	4.4	3.2	3.5	3.5	2.9
Japan	9.0	4.7	3.7	1.6	1.4
Germany	5.1	3.4	2.1	2.2	0.3
EU-12	5.6	3.7	2.3	2.1	1.6

Source: Brenner (2009: 7)

pursued in recent decades have failed to restore the profitability of strong capitalist formations to pre-1973 levels.

In particular, there have been a number of guidelines that have ultimately proven to be ineffective in solving the problem: (a) real wage increase at rates below the corresponding increase in labour productivity (intensification of exploitation), (b) liquidation of less competitive capitals, (c) increase of chronic and mass unemployment to reduce the bargaining power of labour, (d) increasing rates of concentration and centralization of capital, (e) a broad change in labour relations (part-time employment, flexible work relationships, fixed-term contracts, hiring out of workers) and (f) development of a parallel labour market (including mainly women, young people, immigrants) thus circumventing labour legislation (INEG SEE 2009: 100). The problem was not soluble either by reducing the cost of mechanical production systems, raw materials and energy, or by introducing so-called new technologies into the production process. All of the above is indicated in Table 1.5.

Table 1.5 Profit rates and the growth of compensation: United States, Germany, Japan (business cycle averages)

	1960–1969	1970–1979	1980–1990	1991–2000	2001–2007[a]
Private business sector					
US-non-financial corporate profit rate	0.146	0.105	0.098	0.108	0.100
Germany profit rate	0.177	0.132	0.128	0.094	0.095
Japan profit rate	0.190	0.126	0.119	0.035	0.086
Manufacturing sector					
US profit rate	0.245	0.134	0.118	0.164	0.141
Germany profit rate	0.189	0.124	0.104	0.052	0.122
Japan profit rate	0.364	0.297	0.198	0.103	0.083

Germany-West Germany thru 1990
Source: Brenner (2009: 10)
[a]2001–2006 for Japan

It is observed that in all three major capitalist countries in *both* sectors, profitability rates never reach the levels of the 1960s. A recovery is of course observable for some periods as a result of the policies mentioned above. It is, however, either temporary or does not reach the levels of the 1960s. We are led to corresponding conclusions if we take into account the data reported by Maniatis: the rate of profit (*r*) decreases in Japan from 0.25 in 1973 to 0.20 in 2007, in Britain from 0.25 in 1973 to 0.17 in 2007, in Italy from 0.21 in 1970 to 0.17 in 2007 and in Spain from 0.30 in 1973 to 0.22 in 2007 (Maniatis 2013: 62–63).

What is interesting is that the period from the 1973 crisis until the beginning of the new century was marked by a series of positive developments for the capitalist system. It had been the dissolution of the Soviet bloc, the reduction in the power of trade unions and the retreat of the national liberation movements. These developments would perhaps be expected to work positively and increase profitability, but this has not happened. What happened was that they fostered reproduction of the capitalist mode of production as a whole or as a capitalist dynamic. This means that while profitability in the capitalist metropolises does not re-attain its previous dynamics, the entry of other countries into the capitalist/imperialist chain (either with a high level of skill of the collective worker as in former socialist countries in Europe, or with low wages, as in some Asian countries, or with a combination of both) created pressure because competition intensified and shares in the international market were redistributed.

The Financial Sphere's Choice (Public Borrowing and Financialization)

All of this was leading to the need to adopt a new model of accumulation. The response attempted was to shift to the financial sphere through so-called financialization. The specific characteristic of the financial sphere is that of concentrating and managing money which is stagnant and untapped, anticipating the dynamics of capital accumulation by functioning as a network of requirements for future profitability, allowing for a rapid shift of capital from one sector to another where the level of profitability appears to be higher, continuously assessing the fixed assets of businesses that are out of circulation, creating a risk management system and, finally, contributing to the gradual convergence of the most variegated forms of asset yields (Milios 2006).

In this context, in times of crisis, stagnant funds seek higher profitability towards the financial sphere and when they find it they are channelled into it. The peculiarity of the post-1973 era is that, above and beyond its "traditional" activities, the financial sphere is characterized on the one hand by increased public borrowing and, on the other hand, by the phenomenon of financialization.

Increased public borrowing is part of an attempt to maintain a high proportion of public spending that could not be covered by tax revenues. To put it somewhat differently, the State did not want to tax companies that were already suffering a decline in profitability, but it was also not easy to fill this gap by taxing workers whose incomes had declined even more sharply. And it did not want to reduce public spending, which to a

Table 1.6 Public debt as a percentage of GDP

	Germany	France	Italy	Japan	Great Britain	United States
1975	19.02	15.42	56.21	18.87	46.68	33.08
1985	49.69	30.58	85.12	68.27	46.02	43.06
1995	55.60	55.43	121.55	92.43	46.30	66.52
2000	59.74	57.27	109.18	133.79	40.87	54.69
2005	67.97	66.44	105.82	191.64	40.23	61.60
2009	73.51	67.55	115.7	217.60	68.49	84.26

Source: Melas (2011: 372)

significant degree involved purchases of capitalist commodities and so tended to counteract further declines in profitability. This is why Western States have resorted to increasing public debt. As can be seen from the figures in Table 1.6, both in the United States and in the developed countries of the West, there is an escalation in public debt over the period 1975–2005.

This led to the expansion of the bond market and made public debt an important parameter of the whole development process.

This said that the phenomenon of financialization has three distinctive features: (a) the ability of large companies to finance investments on the basis of undistributed profits and their ability to participate in financial markets on their own account, (b) the orientation of banks towards securing profits from transactions in the financial markets as well as from lending to individuals and (c) the increasing participation of workers and households in the financial markets both to borrow and to make available their savings (Lapavitsas et al. 2012: 155).

As a result, in the last 30 years, the ratio of financial assets to global GDP has tripled from 1.5 to 4.5 (Fine 2011: 21).

Characteristic in this respect is the evolution of both the composition of the US debt and its relationship to GDP (Table 1.7).

The so-called liberalization of the banking markets—a consequence of the dominance of neo-liberalism—was a prerequisite for the development of the financial market. But other factors also contributed, such as the utilization of insurance fund reserves, the creation of new financial products, the increase in the cumulative volume of interest, the rise in share prices and the increased distribution of dividends to shareholders.

Table 1.7 Domestic debt and GDP (US$ billion) in the United States

	GDP	Total debt	Debt/ GDP ratio	Households	Financial corporations	Non-financial corporations	Government
1970	1.0	1.5	1.50	0.5	0.1	0.5	0.4
1980	2.7	4.5	1.66	1.4	0.6	1.5	1.1
1990	5.8	13.5	2.33	3.6	2.6	3.7	3.5
2000	9.8	26.3	2.70	7.0	8.1	6.6	4.6
2007	13.8	47.7	3.70	13.8	16.0	10.6	7. 3

Source: Melas (2011: 390)

Consolidation of financial sector dominance started from the relationship between banks and individuals of all kinds (corporations, households). Having first deposited their profits,[1] businesses purchased financial products at a second stage to increase their profitability; households took out consumer and home loans because they could not buy houses and other products with their wages. One contributing factor to this trend was the low-interest-rate policy adopted by the US Federal Reserve in the 2001–2003 period, which was to a certain extent also due to the fear that spread in the markets after the attack on the twin towers. The result was a bubble, reinforced by the inflow of capital from developing countries which, under the pressures of the global market, kept their reserves in dollars (Lapavitsas et al. 2012: 155–156).

At first banks lent to trusted customers, but then lending was extended to certain types of precarious loans. This was made possible by changing the way in which the loans were provided. Formerly a loan was the result of a personal relationship between the bank and the borrower. Then this arrangement was replaced by the establishment of certain objective criteria (the so-called scientific credit capacity rating) and the banks designated the loans they had granted as their assets, guaranteeing the

[1] As noted in the JP Morgan Securities report: "The real driver of this saving glut has been the corporate sector. Between 2000 and 2004, the switch from corporate dis-saving to net saving across the G6 [France, Germany, the US, Japan, Britain and Italy] economies amounted to over $1 trillion ... The rise in corporate saving has been truly global, spanning the three major regions—North America, Europe, and Japan." In other words, "Instead of spending their past profits, [US] businesses are now accumulating them as cash" (Papadimitriou et al. 2005 as cited by Harman 2008).

repayment of interest-bearing instalments to their holder. For a while this was seen as the apex of the modern financial outlook, but, as it will be shown, the delegation of valuation to third parties, to non-bank entities, created gaps and omissions that led to erroneous estimates (Lapavitsas 2013: 319).

In any case all the preceding would result in a huge increase in borrowing and the conversion of loans into special bonds purchasable by a number of depositors (businesses, insurance funds, other banks) and some financial institutions began to use cheap credit to purchase new guarantee titles (i.e. securities giving the right to receive instalments deriving from separate loans). Some other financial institutions then merged these guarantee titles so as to utilize more complex "composite titles" called debt guarantee debts, also known as collateralized debt obligations (CDOs) which gave their holders the right to collect cumulative interest from previous guarantee titles (INE-GSEE 2009: 111). These are packages of hundreds of loans of different quality that are created by rating agencies, which are paid for this and then assess them. Those with high ratings allow the banks that own them to minimize liabilities on their own funds. In this way rating agencies were of course also changed into players and referees of the global economy, with the consequence that instead of functioning to calm the climate of excessive economic optimism they reinforced it even further. The result was a new form of transaction where there is no guarantee from those issuing them that there will be payment at any specific time, given that CDOs are made up of housing and consumer loans along with consumer card debts originating from unknown entities and with unknown repayment ability (Metaxas 2016: 87). Besides CDOs, there was another class called mortgage backed securities (MBS).

Derivative financial products on the property market, such as MBS and CDOs, belonged to a broader category of securities called asset backed securities (ABS). The total of ABS securities skyrocketed in the United States from $549 billion in 2001 to $1687 billion in 2006, the vast majority of them related to mortgages (from $315 billion to $908 billion in the corresponding years) (Dumenil and Levy 2011: 189).

These innovations[2] were regarded as especially promising because if some businesses encountered difficulties this would not be a burden on a credit institution given that the risk was shared between different buyers. In other words, private investment banks turned into securities loans they had bought from banks or other credit institutions and so exempted themselves from the risks entailed in these loans. The bulk of the interest (the portion not retained by investment banks) was converted into dividends by buyers of the securities, thus limiting the cost of non-repayment of the loans (Tompazos 2010: 41–42; Metaxas 2016: 86). With this new system, the lender's profit is a function of the volume of loans sold and not the riskiness of the loan, the lender is not primarily concerned with investigating the borrower's solvency, nor does the lender need to monitor the evolution of the borrower's finances, resulting in a "depersonalization" process that makes it even more rigid. In the end, there are no longer the older security rules, for example, the correlation of the equities with the amount of the loan (Tompazos 2010: 42–43).

As a safeguard against any of the above not working well, credit default swaps (CDS) were created to compensate their holder for the numerous cases when another person meet his/her obligations (e.g. a State cannot pay a bond) (Varoufakis et al. 2011: 33–34). But the point is that in some cases the CDS insured for much greater amounts than the specific debt so that finally, an eventual bankruptcy would be disastrous for the issuers of the CDS (a characteristic example is that of Lehman Brothers) (Tompazos 2018: 32–33).

In any case, the result was that while the financial system in 1971 accounted for 3% of the US economy, it reached 42% in 2007. At international level in 2001, global income was $49 trillion and financial derivatives reached $85 trillion. In 2007, global income had reached $85 trillion, while the value of derivatives had rocketed to $670 trillion (Varoufakis and Missos 2012: 103–105).[3]

---

[2] There were even more daring investment banks that broke down CDOs and repackaged them, resulting in the creation of squared or cubed CDOs (Soros 2008: xviii).

[3] The value alone of the previously mentioned ABS securities leapt from a few tens of billions in 1980 to $2000 billion in 1993 and $11,000 billion in 2006 (Tompazos 2018: 31).

The Crisis of Financialization

A decisive role in developments was played by the real estate market, in the United States, but not only there (e.g. in Spain). Experiencing a decline in their incomes, ordinary people were induced to start borrowing, on the one hand to acquire private homes, on the other to cover the deficit in consumer products created by austerity policies. It is characteristic that in the United States in the 1980s an average household owed an average of $40,000 but in 2010 it had reached $130,000. At the same time in the late 1990s lending was extended to low-income people,[4] some of whom may not have had stable employment. The result was that aggregate credit card debt, which had been 135% of GDP in 1984, reached 335% in 2006 (Harvey 2010: 17–19).[5]

In the field of real estate, once credit became so freely available, prices began to rise[6] and the same policy was followed with consumer loans. The parameter that was ignored was that the credits were granted on the

[4] It was for this purpose that various forms of precarious loans were created. The first of these were the subprime loans, which were characterized by the fact that their borrowers did not meet the conditions for some kind of "conventional" loan (unsound credit record, bankruptcies, low income, non-permanent work, lack of necessary documents for justifying a loan). These are high credit-risk loans with higher interest rates and commissions that are generally targeted at the poorer strata. Another type was the Alt-A loan, also of high credit risk but lower than that of subprimes with interest rates and commissions fluctuating between subprimes and conventional loans (Lapatsioras and Milios 2008). It was postulated that this categorization would facilitate its deployment as a rescue procedure in the event of risk of non-payment of debts when the toxic securities collapsed first, putting in place procedures to prevent the crisis from spreading to other categories of securities. But the point is that the rate of diffusion of the crisis was such that it quickly spread even to highly rated titles (Tompazos 2010: 43–44).

[5] This whole situation explains why Americans had less and less savings from a certain point onwards: From $168.5 billion in 2000 (2.3% of disposable income), the figure had fallen to $42.7 billion in 2007 (0.4% of disposable income) (Lapavitsas 2013: 274), with total household debt rising from $5000 billion in 1995 to $13,975 billion in 2008 (Tompazos 2010: 50). This is due on the one hand to low real wages and on the other to a habit of consumption through borrowing that was not conducive to private savings, thus creating a situation where wage earners consume the surplus value that entrepreneurs either do not invest or do not consume privately (Tompazos 2010: 105).

[6] Indicatively, between 1997 and 2006, the price of a typical American home increased by 124%. Also, between 1981 and 2001, the average price for a house nation-wide ranged from 2.9 to 3.1 times the income of households. This ratio rose to 4 in 2004 and 4.6 in 2006. Of course, above and beyond the national average there were also areas such as Los Angeles where the corresponding ratio was 10 to 1 or Miami, where it was 8.5 to 1 (Melas 2011: 272).

basis of the valuation of the borrower's assets at current market prices. When a private person requested a loan and mortgaged his home, the loan was granted to him on the basis of the current price of the property. The debt levels therefore appeared to be low because high value property was available as collateral. Banks therefore began to grant more and more loans and in a self-reinforcing way their profitability grew steadily as owners mortgaged their property and took out new loans for other types of consumption (Lapavitsas 2013: 273). In this situation some of the owners had no intention from the outset of keeping the house, they simply took advantage of the very low interest rates projected for the first years in the relevant loan contracts so as to live through this period paying a cheap "rent" and then either abandon it or sell it and profit from the difference between the purchase price and the selling price (Tompazos 2010: 49). There were even some who bought a second house in the hope of multiple profits. Banks cannot be regarded as totally unconnected with the mindset generated among the borrowers, who for their part saw the home as a money-producing machine given that through buying property they acquired an asset the rate of change of whose price was higher than the interest rate paid for its purchase. But it was not clear to buyers/borrowers that a drop in property prices and/or an increase in interest rates would work against them. In 2007, both of these occurred (Gogas and Takli 2014: 323).

The rise in interest rates[7] impacted in three ways:

The first is that in a chaotic system (in the mathematical sense), the Fed's interest rate increase of 0.25% had multiplier effects on the loan of the individual borrower, whose interest rate went from 6.3% to 11.25% (Tompazos 2010: 51). This happened because of leverage, which in good times can ensure a geometric growth of profit but in bad times a correspondingly geometric increase in losses. This is because leverage is the use of borrowed funds in order to secure a return on the same equity. The use of foreign capital brings higher returns but also produces the opposite effect when the return on assets is less than the cost

[7] The rise in interest rates is attributable to the fact that many developing countries have converted their reserves into dollars and started investing in the US economy (Lapavitsas 2013: 271).

of the borrowed capital. Similarly, chaotic results were registered with the assets of banks, which were largely based on the securities held.
The second impact had to do with the more than doubling of subprimes (from 7.9% of the total in 2003 to 18.2% in 2004) and Alt-A (from 2.2% to 6.3%), a change due to decline in the proportion of conventional loans. This dynamic continued with the consequence that in 2006 35% of the loans (about one trillion dollars) consisted of the former two types of loans.[8]

The sharp decline in property prices is the third impact, because it has helped to make it clear that wage stagnation, coupled with rising interest rates, would have overloaded the servicing of credit—especially for the poorest Americans who were indebted with all types of loans (mortgage, consumer, card). Then it became clear that the system had a twofold problem: on the one hand, it was not clear who was in possession of the problematic loans, so the banks could not assess the solvency of each client and finally significantly reduced lending.[9] On the other hand, this generalized ambiguity caused the ratio of reserves to loans to lose its meaning, as it did the ratio of funds to loans, so banks were unable to monitor the rate of credit expansion (Garganas 2010: 40–41). Defaults on payment started from those who had the least ability to service mortgage debt,[10] with the result that banks became overloaded with possession of real estate,[11] depressing its value, making it very difficult to sell property at prices which were now securitized prices, and shifting the problem to banking derivatives. In November 2007, 16.5% of precarious loans

[8] Also see the data in Table 11.2 of the Appendix in Chap. 11.

[9] This has to do with the fact that in the period of the financial rise many of the transactions that were concluded were bilateral, a by-product of the effort by investors to circumvent restrictions from the regulating institutions. The result was that the range of information would be much smaller than in the Stock Exchanges and that third parties would not know details of the content of such transactions, so that one bank would avoid lending to another (Laskos and Tsakalotos 2012: 123).

[10] It is typical that foreclosure procedures were initiated in 2007 on 1.3 million households, 2.3 million in 2008 and 2.1 million in 2009 (Metaxas 2016: 149).

[11] As was absolutely to be expected, given that while 7575 thousand existing homes were sold in 2005, only 5505 thousand were sold in 2009 (a 28% decrease) and in the corresponding years, of the 1285 thousand new homes only 372 thousand were sold (a 71% decrease) (Dumenil and Levy 2011: 184).

were already not being paid and very soon the crisis was spreading. In January 2008, problems emerged with the higher rated securities, precisely because the mortgages for the securitized properties had gradually lost a significant part of their initial value (Wolff 2011: 65). This is why the crisis started in the United States, where banks were more exposed to the various bank derivatives. The result was that 315 banking institutions of regional importance with total assets of $650 billion went bankrupt in the United States in 2008–2010. Overall, the IMF has estimated that between January 2007 and September 2009, the largest financial institutions in the United States and Europe suffered losses of more than $1 trillion due to exposure to toxic bonds and precarious loans (Melas 2011: 269–270). The cumulative effect was such that at the level of the US economy overall, it is estimated that between June 2007 and November 2008 Americans lost more than ¼ of their total wealth, an amount of $14 trillion. The value of real estate decreased from $13 trillion in 2006 to $8.8 trillion in 2008, and savings and investment assets lost $1.2 trillion in the same period. Corresponding pension assets lost a value equal to $1.3 trillion. Total capital assets relating to pensioners lost $2.3 trillion (Melas 2011: 270–271). Finally, between December 2007 and October 2009, 8 million jobs were lost in the United States.

In a very short period of time, the crisis moved to the so-called real economy. Global GDP fell by 0.6% in 2009, with developed countries suffering disproportionally great damage. Their total GDP fell by 3.2%: in the United States by 2.4%, in the Eurozone by 4.1%, in Japan by 5.2%, in Britain by 4.9%, in Germany by 5.0%, in France by 2.2% and in Italy by 5.0% (Selcuk and Yilmaz 2011: 55). Asian countries based on the export model of economic growth (Taiwan, China, South Korea, Japan) saw their exports fall by at least 20% in just two months, with world export trade falling more than 30% within just a few months (Harvey 2010: 5–6). Overall, 2010 saw the biggest decline in world trade since 1929. Debt of $1 trillion remained unpaid in the same year, with Western countries spending $8.9 trillion to support their banks (see below) (Metaxas 2016: 149).

So things seemed to be getting extremely serious. A mighty crisis appeared to be unfolding. It was for this reason, through the Paulson plan (Troubled Asset Relief Program-TARP), that $700 billion of toxic bonds related to the real estate bubble were purchased, with $250 billion of injected capital being provided to the banks (Laskos and Tsakalotos 2012: 131). The US Federal Reserve was then obliged to offer an amount unprecedented in history of low interest loans to commercial banks and other financial institutions (INE-GSEE 2009), as a way of managing the problem, hoping that as a next step there would be a gradual recovery. This policy, which was followed by other US central banks, included interventions in the open market, short-term borrowing programmes, direct lending to investment banks, the purchase of commercial securities by industrial and commercial companies and so on. (Lapavitsas 2013: 279). Finally, it is estimated that the Fed has granted as a whole $29,614.4 billion to United States and foreign banks as financial aid (Felkerson 2011: 32).

The European Crisis

What should be noted, and directly related to developments in the EMU and the EU is that financialization is linked to maintaining the dollar as global reserve currency, which is due to two factors: on the one hand, the United States has remained the country with the highest productivity among the G7[12] countries and on the other hand that it possesses undoubted military strength and corresponding geopolitical influence. This weight of the dollar explains why, despite the 2007–2008 crisis, the United States did not collapse. Not only did we not see orchestrated attacks against the dollar, but, on the contrary, there were coordinated efforts by countries that continued to keep it as a reserve currency to ensure that it kept its value (Fine 2011: 24). And this explains why the consequences of the banking crisis in the United States also had significant impact on the European milieu, causing a large drop in overall demand, in part investment-led and in part export-led. Germany, in particular, has suffered very seriously because of the reduction of its exports

[12] With a benchmark of 100 for productivity (GDP/working hours) in the United States, Italy is at 75.6%, Japan at 65.9%, Germany at 91.6%, France at 95.7%, Britain at 77.8% and Canada at 76.6% (OECD 2011).

to non-EU countries (due to the decrease in the value of the dollar but also of the yuan, which made the euro expensive and led to Germany losing to China its lead as an exporter of goods) and on the other hand because its banks were exposed to precarious debt securities (Lapavitsas et al. 2012: 156). This happened because the large trade surplus[13] reflected high productivity in some sectors—as a result of being specialized in products which are not merely price-competitive and which are accordingly not vulnerable to competition from emerging economies (Tompazos 2010: 216), not to mention the reduction in labour income, which has acted as an internal devaluation mechanism. The point at issue is that wage reduction has acted as an incentive for German workers to save a larger proportion of their income than other Europeans. This, coupled with the fact that domestic direct investment has been limited, has led to German banks finding themselves with increased liquidity and also a strong currency. A significant proportion of this liquidity was channelled into precarious banking derivatives in various countries, with the result that the outbreak of the crisis began to create serious problems for the German economy as well.

To understand, however, developments in the EU and EMU, we must go back a few years. By the end of the twentieth century, the EU had realized that it was having difficulty competing with the other Western economic poles (North America, Japan) not to mention the emerging economies (China, India, Russia, Southeast Asian countries). For this reason, the EU adopted the Lisbon Strategy, which aimed at a concerted effort to further implement neo-liberal policies internally. We recall that the "Lisbon Strategy"[14] aimed to make the EU in 2010 the most competitive and dynamic knowledge-based economy in the world, capable of economic growth with better jobs and greater social cohesion.

But the results were not what the European elites expected. Annual real growth of GDP in the United States is clearly superior to that in the

[13] We point out that in 1998, at a time when the E10 average (excepting Belgium-Luxembourg) was 2.09%, Germany characteristically had a trade surplus of 3.04% of its GDP. In 2008, the respective figures were 7.18% for Germany and 0.21% for EU12 (Vlahou and Lambrinidis 2011: 233).

[14] It was so named because the key decisions were taken in March 2000 at the Lisbon Summit.

EMU countries, which also lagged behind the corresponding British rates.[15]

In order to understand the central role of the United States on the international checkerboard and the inferior role of the rest of the Western countries, especially the European countries, we can cite the degree of imperialist power, which includes in absolute numbers the size of the GDP, military expenditure, volume of foreign direct investment, the share held by a country at international level in the largest banks, expenditure on military equipment and the amount of available foreign exchange reserves held by central banks in the currency of the country.[16]

Table 1.8 shows that the distance between the United States and the other powerful countries is from obvious to colossal. For Europe in particular, despite the Lisbon Strategy and/or the EMU, for the indicators under examination the United States enjoys a supremacy ranging from slight to very great. In the final imperialist power ratio, we need to add the strength of Britain, France, Germany and Italy all together to offset the strength of the United States.

Beyond that, the creation of the EMU and the use of the euro by the Eurozone countries have complicated the situation even more. This is because the very large productivity gaps between the Eurozone countries have been undermining most of these economies. Similarly, the advent of the crisis in the European economy hit most countries inside and outside the Eurozone, albeit in different ways. The problem was particularly exacerbated by the fact that European economies dealt basically with each other and the transmission of pressure from one to the other became rapidly apparent. At the same time, the development of new

[15] An important role in this is said to have been played by the lead that the United States has never lost in relation to the Eurozone countries, in areas such as private expenditure in research and technology, the value added of the information and communications technology sector in the total value added, the degree of employment of the ICT sector in total employment.

[16] Norfield constructs this table taking into account the five characteristics attributed by Lenin to the imperialist stage: (a) concentration of production and capital, (b) generation of finance capital, (c) the importance acquired by capital export, (d) establishment of international capitalist networks with monopoly status and (e) completion of the parcelling out of territories between the largest capitalist powers (Lenin 1916). But Norfield notes that the position of an individual country can only properly be understood by looking at its relationship to the imperialist system as a whole, not simply by examining whether its index value is higher or lower than another's (Norfield 2012).

Table 1.8 Imperialism index (US = 100)

	GDP (2011)	Military spending (2010)	FDI stock (2010)	Top banks (2009)	Central bank FX reserves (2011)	Total index
United States	100.0	100.0	100.0	100.0	100.0	100.0
United Kingdom	16.0	8.1	34.9	94.9	6.3	32.0
France	18.4	8.4	31.4	88.4	3.9	30.1
Germany	23.7	5.6	29.3	48.3	32.7	27.9
Japan	38.9	7.9	17.2	44.7	6	22.9
China	50.0	16.6	25.7	0.0	0.0	18.5
Italy	14.6	5.1	9.8	30.2	0.0	11.9
Spain	9.9	2.3	13.6	31.0	0.0	10.1
Netherlands	5.6	1.7	18.4	22.4	0.6	9.7

Source: Norfield (2012)

economic competitors (above all China, India, Russia) has made it hard to resolve the crisis through outwards expansion. The great ambition of elevating the euro into a world currency, which would thus be sheltered against speculative attacks, was not able to become a reality. In 2004, 19% of specific financial products (spots, swaps, outrights) were in euros, with the dollar predominating with 44%, the British pound at 8.5% and the yen at 10%. What is most important, though, is the euro's share in total global reserves. According to the relevant data, in 2007, 63.9% of the world's foreign exchange reserves were in US dollars; the euro accounted for 26.5%, pound sterling merely 4.7% and the yen 2.9% (Melas 2010: 35).

Faced with the prospect of situations spinning out of control, the European Central Bank (ECB) decided to implement a policy similar to that adopted by the Fed in the United States: that is to supply huge amounts of money to banks to get rid of the so-called toxic bonds. Thus, on August 9, 2007, the ECB made available liquidity of €98.4 billion and on August 13 another €48 billion. On February 17, 2008, England nationalized the Northern Rock Bank, and on September 30, 2008, the French and Belgian monetary authorities proceeded to nationalize the Dexia Bank. On October 5, 2008, Germany adopted a €15 billion rescue plan for the Hypo Real Estate Bank and decided to guarantee without limit all personal deposits in banks (Tompazos 2010: 56–58). On October 13, the big EU states announced that the planned amount of funding or guarantees for bank financing would reach €1700 billion (Tompazos 2010: 56–58). This meant an exchange of the toxic bonds held by banks with public bonds, in parallel with unrestricted liquidity provision from central banks to commercial banks. Overall, in the period between October 1, 2008, and October 1, 2012, the European Commission approved an amount of assistance to banks of about €5058.9 billion (Toussaint 2017: 130).

However, it should be noted that there were three major differences between the FED (Federal Reserve System, the central bank of the US) and the ECB: (a) the first was the fact that the dollar remained the world's reserve currency, which enabled the US government to issue "blank cheques" at least for the duration of the crisis without endangering the value of the dollar; (b) as a federal state, the United States could undertake internal redistribution from the states most in surplus to the states most in deficit. Europe's *sui generis* character precluded this from happening (Varoufakis et al. 2011: 32–33) and (c) Wall Street deleted the toxic CDOs through the parthenogenesis of a financial tool that shifted the costs to taxpayers. European banks, by contrast, in order to achieve the same effect adopted the following plan: a proportion of the public money they had received was used to bet on the possibility that a State would be led to bankruptcy, because of international pressure. Such was the shift to CDS risk insurance contracts.

This latter factor explains the difference in degree of intensity of the crisis experienced by the countries of the European periphery. Specifically, following all the interventions and through deleveraging,[17] banks started to improve their budgets, but this overall evolution led on the one hand to a reduction in lending to the countries of the periphery and on the other to a halt in the purchase of long-term securities through a preference for short-term instruments (cheques, bills of exchange, letters of guarantee etc.). This led to credit shortage and growing recession through-

[17] Remarkable as it may seem, the leverage ratios were clearly higher in Europe than in the United States. Characteristically, at the end of 2007 the Bank of America was at 11.7, Citigroup at 19.2 and Deutsche Bank and UBS at 40.8 (Metaxas 2016: 82).

out the Eurozone. The countries that had spent large sums rescuing banks were impelled to increase public lending and the easier availability of State bonds exerted an upward pressure on yields (Lapavitsas et al. 2010: 7–8). The weakest economies of the South (Greece, Portugal, Spain) were in the eye of the storm, finding themselves facing significant deficits in their current account balance and as a result being perceived as vulnerable to bankruptcy. (Ireland was added to this list, but for different reasons, because of the involvement of its banking system in the housing bubble.)

And so we arrived at the onset of the crisis in Greece. But in order to be able to understand the link between the international crisis and its manifestation in Greece, it is necessary first to give a comprehensive presentation of the situation of the Greek economy in the run-up to 2009.[18]

References

Brenner R., 2009, "What is good for Goldman Sachs is good for America. The origins of the current crisis", pp. 1–76, file:///C:/Users/user/Desktop/spiros%20back-up/Spiros/epistimi/arthra/BrennerCrisisTodayOctober2009.pdf, accessed on 19/1/2018.

Chesnais F., 2016, *Finance capital today. Corporations and banks in the lasting global slump*, Leiden-Boston: Brill.

Dumenil G. and D. Levy, 2011, *The crisis of neoliberalism*, Cambridge Massachusetts: Harvard University Press.

Felkerson J., 2011, *$29,000,000,000,000: a detailed look at the Fed's bailout by funding facility and recipient*, Levy Economics Institute, Working Paper no 698, pp. 1–36.

[18] Obviously since 2009 there have been very significant developments in crisis management at both the European and the global levels: in the United States there has been evidence of a marked recovery, with GDP increasing cumulatively by 34% between 2009 and 2017, while in the Eurozone countries from 2014 onwards there has been a return to, low, growth rates (1.4% in 2014, 2.4% in 2017). At the same time, whereas public debt in the European Union increased from 60.7% of GDP in 2008 to 86.5% in 2014, by 2017 it had fallen to 81.6%. But the character of this book precludes presentation, let alone interpretation, of these developments. For more on this subject see Tompazos 2019, Chesnais 2016, Roberts 2016.

Fine B., 2011, "Beyond financialization", in Vlahou A., N. Theoharakis and D. Mylonakis (eds.) *Economic crisis and Greece*, Athens: Gutenberg, pp. 19–36 (in Greek).

Garganas P., 2010, "Crisis: from the banks to the whole economy, ideology and politics", in M. Stylou et al. *The Greek Capitalism, the Global Economy and the Crisis*, Athens: Marxistiko Bibliopoleio, pp. 38–50 (in Greek).

Gogas P. and E. Takli, 2014, "The framework of the World Economic Crisis", in S. Roukounas and P. Sklias (eds.) *The Greek Economy from the EMU to the Bailout*, Athens: Livanis, pp. 321–338 (in Greek).

Harvey D., 2010, *The enigma of capital and the crisis of capitalism*, New York: Oxford University press.

INE-GSEE (Institute of Labour—Greek General Confederation of Labour), 2009, *The Greek Economy and Employment. Annual Report 2009,* Athens: Institute of Labour—Greek General Confederation of Labour (in Greek).

Lapatsioras S. and G. Milios, 2008, "Financial Crisis and 'economic regulation'", Second Part, Theseis no 104, http://www.theseis.com/index.php?option=com_content&task=view&id=1042&Itemid=29, accessed on 23/1/2018.

Lapavitsas C. et al., 2010, Eurozone Crisis: Beggar thyself and beggar neighbor, Research on Money and Finance, http://eprints.uwe.ac.uk/23045/1/fullreport.pdf, accessed on 7/5/2018 and not Lapavitsas 2010.

Lapavitsas C. et al., 2012, *Crisis in the Eurozone*, London: Verso.

Lapavitsas C., 2013, *Profiting without producing, how finance exploits us all*, London and New York: Verso.

Laskos C. and T. Tsakalotos, 2012, *Without Return*, Athens: Kapsimi (in Greek).

Lenin V.I., 1916, *Imperialism, the highest stage of capitalism. A popular outline*, https://www.marxists.org/archive/lenin/works/1916/imp-hsc/index.htm, accessed on 23/12/18.

Maniatis T., 2013, "Accumulation of Capital and Crisis in Global and Greek Economy: a Marxist approach", in *Group of Marxist Researches, Marxism and the Greek economic crisis*, Athens: Gutenberg, pp. 42–87 (in Greek).

Melas K., 2010, "A first evaluation of the Eurozone and the common currency", *Monthly Review* no 64, pp. 22–39 (in Greek).

Melas K., 2011, *Contemporary crises of the global financial system (1974–2008)*, Athens: Livanis (in Greek).

Metaxas G., 2016, *Crisis?*, Athens: Ekdoseis ton synadelfon (in Greek).

Milios G., 2006, "A Marxist Analysis of Finance and the Question of Commodity Money", Theseis no 97, http://www.theseis.com/index.php?option=com_content&task=view&id=961&Itemid=29, accessed on 23/1/2019.

Norfield T., 2012, "Imperialism by numbers" http://economicsofimperialism.blogspot.gr/2012/05/imperialism-by-numbers.html, accessed on 26/1/2013.
OECD, 2011, "Government at a glance 2011" http://www.oecd-ilibrary.org/docserver/download/4211011ec027.pdf?expires=1391032406&id=id&accname=guest&checksum=754DE0EB3673B1F2D74C139C1D4CE150, accessed on 29/1/2014.
Papadimitriou, Dimitri and Anwar Shaikh, Claudio Dos Santos and Gennaro Zezza, 2005, How Fragile is the US Economy?, Strategic Analysis, February 2005, The Levy Economics Institute of Bard College as cited by Chris Harman, 2008, "From the Credit crunch to the spectre fo the global crisis" International Socialism no 118, www.marxists.org/archive/harman/2008/xx/crisis.htm#f10, accessed on 10/3/2019.
Roberts M., 2016, *The long depression: Marxism and the global crisis of capitalism*, Chicago: Haymarket Books.
Selcuk B. and N. Yilmaz, 2011, "The effects of global crisis into Euro region: a case study of Greek crisis", *European Journal of Economic and Political Studies* vol. 4 no 2, pp. 49–72.
Soros G., 2008, *The new paradigm for financial markets, the credit crisis of 2008 and what it means*, New York: Public Affairs.
Tompazos S., 2010, *Centrifugal times. The global economic crisis 2007, 2008, 2009*, Athens: Papazisis (in Greek).
Tompazos S., 2018, *Global crisis 2007–2017 and patterns of capital reproduction*, Athens: Topos (in Greek).
Tompazos S., 2019, *Global crisis and reproduction of capital*, London: Palgrave.
Toussaint E., 2017, *The public debt. Its history and importance in today's crisis*, Athens: Red Marks (in Greek).
Varoufakis Y. and V. Missos, 2012, *Global Economic Crisis*, Athens: INE-GSEE (in Greek).
Varoufakis Y., T. Patokos, L. Tserkezis and C. Koutsopetros, 2011, *The economic crisis in Greece and Europe in 2011*, Athens: Institute of Labour—Greek General Confederation of Labour (in Greek).
Vlahou A. and G. Lambrinidis, 2011, "Crisis and uneven development in the context of the EMU: The External Trade Balance and the international competitiveness of the Greek Economy", in Vlahou A., N. Theocharakis and D. Mylonakis (eds.) *Economic crisis and Greece*, Athens: Gutenberg, pp. 229–255 (in Greek).
Wolff R., 2011, "A Marxist analysis of the crisis", in Vlahou A., N. Theocharakis and D. Mylonakis (eds.) *Economic crisis and Greece*, Athens: Gutenberg, pp. 52–72 (in Greek).

2

The Greek Crisis

Introduction

> The crisis has clearly shown that the pre-existing Greek growth model suffered from structural disadvantages. Over-indebtedness and overconsumption in the public sector fuelled overconsumption in the private sector, perpetuating significant deficits in competitiveness and productivity. During the 2000–2008 period, rising private and public consumption expenditure led to an ever expanding trade deficit, as domestic production did not suffice to meet demand, but the level of domestic and foreign investment was too low to enable production to be increased to the required levels. (MacKinsey and Company 2011: 11)

The above quotation is from a research firm, MacKinsey & Company, which conducted a study on the Greek economy on behalf of the Hellenic Federation of Enterprises (SEV). We quote it because we judge that it corresponds to the dominant elites' basic interpretation of the crisis in the Greek economy. It is a narrative that broadly advances the following claim: From the fall of the junta[1] (*metapolitefsi* in Greek) onwards, very

[1] The meaning of the term "metapolitefsi" is rather vague in Greek literature. Some employ the term to denote the "moment" of the fall of the Colonels' dictatorship (July 1974) and the assumption of

S. Sakellaropoulos, *Greece's (un) Competitive Capitalism and the Economic Crisis*,
https://doi.org/10.1007/978-3-030-14319-0_2

large increases have been granted to workers, and the public sector has been over-inflated. All of the successive governments bore a significant responsibility for this because, for reasons both demagogic and clientelistic, it was a policy they encouraged. But by the same token, the unions were not without their share of the responsibility, given the corporatist attitudes that induced them to demand greater benefits than the Greek economy objectively could withstand, until finally this developmental model came to the end of the road.

According to this narration, the "metapolitefsi" is stigmatized as a period where excessive concessions were made to the working classes, something which is seen as having had a disastrous effect on the country's development.

The position adopted by this book is that the end of the dictatorship was marked by a number of institutional concessions to the dominated strata (abolition of the monarchy, unimpeded functioning of parliamentary democracy, punishment of key figures in the dictatorship, adjustment of the army to the role played by every corresponding institution in Western parliamentary democracies, and legalization of communist parties and organizations). This was done to establish the domination of a hegemonic bourgeois strategy, which was, however, obliged to take into account the deep discontent of the dominated strata at the post-civil war state,[2] the seven-year-long junta and the partition

government by the leader of the Right K. Karamanlis. Others by "metapolitefsi" mean the first years after the fall of the dictatorship, marked by great mobilizations of workers and significant wage increases. Finally, some consider the "metapolitefsi" to be a period extending from 1974 to the present day, given that its basic characteristic is the functioning of the Parliamentary Republic, limitation of the role of the army and freedom of action of the Communist Left. Until the fall of the dictatorship, the constitution of the country was that of a monarchical republic; the army was very actively involved in political affairs (culminating in the imposition of the military dictatorship in 1967), and the Communist Left operated illegally (see below). As will become evident, the term is used here in consonance with the outlook of the dominant elites, combining the second and third interpretations (significant salary increases at the start and a culture of super-radicalization which then became a containment on economic growth).

[2] In the period between 1947 and 1949, a bloody civil war was waged in Greece, pitting the Right and the Centre on one side against the Communist Left on the other. The victory of the former resulted in consolidation of a regime characterized by a plethora of authoritarian measures: banning of the functioning of the Communist Party, executions, imprisonment and exile for its members and supporters, limitations on political rights, a key role for the army and the throne as against elected governments, etc.

of Cyprus.[3] As a counterbalance, approval was given to what has been called the super powers of the President of the Republic, transference of significant sectors of political authority from the parliament to the government and the administration, functioning of the dominant parties as mechanisms for integration and management of social dynamics (Sakellaropoulos 2013).

In the economic field, wage increases were awarded primarily in the period between 1974 and 1981 due to the growth of factory trade unionism but also to the strike movement in the public sector. The first four years of Panhellenic Socialist Movement (PASOK) government (1981–1985) were characterized by moderate increases for a large proportion of wage earners, but after 1985 this situation changed.[4] All the policies to be applied subsequently aimed at limiting the participation of labour in the GDP and gradually removing all the institutional gains of the lower classes that had been achieved in the early years of the "metapolitefsi". This was a slow and rather contradictory process. By the period immediately preceding the crisis, many grassroots achievements had already been revoked and substantial redistribution of wealth for the benefit of capital had taken place.[5] But the advent of the crisis was to bring the Greek social formation into a new era with great

[3] The military dictatorship imposed on April 21, 1967, through intervention by the army put an end to the wave of protests (political and labour mobilizations) that continued from 1960 to 1967 and aimed at the democratization of political life and improvement of social conditions. The dictatorial regime was kept in power until July 1974 when a coup was launched in the Republic of Cyprus, resulting in military invasion by Turkey. Cyprus is an island inhabited by a Greek majority and a Turkish minority. When the island was occupied by the British, Greek Cypriots for decades demanded unification of Cyprus with Greece. Finally, in 1960, after lengthy negotiations between Great Britain, Greece and Turkey, there was a jointly accepted compromise and the island went from British occupation to being an independent State. In July 1974, the Greek dictatorship tried to overthrow the legitimate President of Cyprus Archbishop Makarios, and set up its own man, N. Sampson, to promote union with Greece in a second phase. This provoked the reaction of Turkey and occupation by the Turkish army of the northern part of the island, a situation which has continued since 1974. Faced by the danger of a Greek-Turkish war, the Greek military leadership handed over the government to political leaders.

[4] By October 1985 (PASOK having won re-election the preceding June), it had become clear that there had been an excessive increase in the current account deficit. Austerity measures were accordingly imposed and lasted for two years.

[5] Typical examples are the privatization of large public companies such as Olympic Airways and the Telecommunications Organization of Greece, the spread of flexible labour relations and the reduction in the share of wages in GDP.

changes that were light-years removed from whatever conservative reforms had taken place in the country in the previous period.

We will accordingly approach the Greek economic crisis as the crisis of a specific accumulation model that had been chosen by the Greek bourgeoisie, a crisis triggered both by the emergence of internal contradictions in Greece's capitalist economy and by pressures internalized by the Greek social formation as a result of the global crisis and the crisis of Europe (a parameter that is totally absent from the narrative of the ruling classes, since they regard the crisis as an exclusively Greek phenomenon for which the responsibility is shared between Greek citizens, who have made excessive demands, and Greek governments, which have indulged them).

On the Bloated Public Sector, Excessively High Wages and Other Such

One of the recurrent arguments of the dominant elites is that the country was drawn into crisis by the "over-inflated" public sector that generated continuing deficits, creating a steady rise in public debt. As for what happened to the deficits and how we arrived at this increase in public indebtedness, this will be dealt with a little later. For the moment, let us examine the numbers of civil servants, according to Organisation for Economic Co-operation and Development (OECD) data (Table 2.1).

The findings that emerge are that Greece in 2000 had the smallest narrowly defined public sector of all the countries under examination and in 2008 the second smallest after Japan. On the other hand, at the level of the broader public sector, in both of these years, it presented the highest number of employees. But on the whole, the average was in the vicinity of 20%, a figure lower than that of five OECD countries and higher than that of eight others. At the same time, in these eight years, there was a 1.4 percentage-point increase in public employment, a development that can in no way be represented as a cause of economic disaster, given the modesty of its dimensions.

Nevertheless the issue does not pertain to the number of civil servants, but rather to the amount of public expenditure and the money spent. If

Table 2.1 Employment in general government as a percentage of the labour force

Country	2000 General government	2000 Public corporations	2000 Total	2008 General government	2008 Public corporations	2008 Total
Norway	29.5	6.0	35.5	29.6	4.9	34.5
Denmark	29.7	3.5	33.2	28.7	2.8	31.5
France	21.8	3.3	25.1	21.9	2.5	24.4
Finland	22.2	0.0	22.2	22.9	0.0	22.9
Netherlands	12.7	7.7	20.6	12.6	8.8	21.4
Greece	6.8	12.5	19.3	7.9	12.8	20.7
Canada	15.9	1.8	17.7	16.5	2.3	18.8
United Kingdom	16.8	1.2	18.0	17.4	1.2	18.6
Australia	15.1		15.1	15.6		15.6
United States	14.8		14.8	14.6		14.6
Italy	15.3	0.0	15.3	14.3	0.0	14.3
Germany	11.1	5.4	16.5	9.6	4.0	13.6
Spain	12.2	1.3	13.5	12.3	0.7	13.0
Japan	7.7	0.0	7.7	6.7	1.2	7.9

Source: OECD (2011), *Government at a Glance* 2011

Table 2.2 Public expenditure as a percentage of GNP in Greece and in EU15 (1995–2009)

Year	EU15	Greece
1995	52.2	51.3
1996	49.8	49.4
1997	48.2	50.2
1998	47.3	49.6
1999	46.9	49.8
2000	44.8	46.7
2001	46.2	45.4
2002	46.7	45.1
2003	47.3	44.7
2004	47.0	45.5
2005	47.0	44.6
2006	46.5	45.4
2007	45.8	47.5
2008	47.4	50.6
2009	51.5	54.0
Average	47.6	47.9

Source: Eurostat

there are large numbers of civil servants but only limited total public expenditure, then public finances are not burdened (Table 2.2).

It is obvious that for the whole period, the average European public spending is in the same range as Greek public spending. So, there is no such thing as the Greek peculiarity of excessive public spending that has allegedly caused such a severe economic crisis. To this data should be added the fact that in the same period (1995–2009), the average salaries of civil servants in the EU15 as a percentage of GDP was 10.8% and in Greece 10.9% (Maniatis 2011: 209). Consequently, it is not in the salary of civil servants that the cause of the crisis can be found.

One variant of the over-inflated public sector theory is the stance that detects a high level of social spending. Between 1995 and 2008, social protection expenditure in Greece did indeed rise from 19.9% of GDP to 26%, but remained below the EU15 average of 27.5%. Merely mentioning this fact should by rights suffice to stop the discussion. In 1995, Greek social expenditure was 35% less than the corresponding European figure, and this deficit was quite correctly chosen to be covered, and still it was not fully covered. But above and beyond this there are other aspects that need highlighting. This growth only involved increases in pensions: other social transfers (family allowances, unemployment benefits, housing subsidies etc.) remained unchanged at 3% of GDP, which is the lowest percentage in the EU15.[6] This is of great importance because Greece, after paying pensions and before paying other social transfers, has one of the lowest poverty rates in the EU15 (22.8%). Nevertheless, when the other social transfers are added, the country records the highest poverty rate (20.5%) for the period under consideration. The conclusion is that in Greece there are a minimal number of universal allowances and they are also unevenly distributed due to the high levels of tax evasion (see below), obscuring who is and who is not entitled to a benefit. Added to this are the clientelistic networks that make it difficult to provide access to social resources for legitimate beneficiaries, not to mention perpetuating very large inequalities in the distribution of pensions (Dafermos and Papatheodorou 2011: 3–4[7]). At the socio-political level this means that, rather than the rise in social spending favouring the popular strata, the benefit accrues on the one hand to elements of the administrative and trade union bureaucracy in the public sector and broader public sector and, on the other hand, to self-employed professionals and entrepreneurs

[6] This is happening despite the fact that spending on pharmaceutical products jumped from 1.1% of GDP in 1998 to 2.7% in 2009. This was due to overpricing by drug multinationals using Greek medicines as a basis for costing their products at the pan-European level, resulting in inflated prices, first, in Greece and then throughout Europe. The Novartis scandal arose out of this practice.

[7] The increase in pensions, which in 2007 amounted to 11.7% of GDP, as against the EU27 average of 8.9%, can be attributed to four factors in this period: The first was described by Dafermos-Papatheodorou as the high pensions being paid to members of the State bureaucracy—"state" in the broader but also in the narrower sense of the term. In this connection, it is characteristic that according to the OECD data for 2011, 20% of the richest Greeks received social benefits approximately 3.5 times higher than the economically weakest 20% (OECD 2014: 5). The second factor has to do with the fact that the average retirement age in Greece in 2010 was 57 years for men and women, whereas in the OECD countries, the average age was 63 for men and 61.9 for women (Institute of Labour—Greek General Confederation of Labour 2014: 390–392). The third is that there has been a tendency in Greece for the ageing of the population to proceed faster than the EU27 average. Thus in 2000, residents of Greece over the age of 60 comprised 23.3% of the population, compared to 20.9% for the EU27. Some years later, in 2009, the figure had reached 24.4% for Greece and 22.9% for the EU27. The fourth factor is that in Greece, private insurance has not become as prevalent as in the rest of Europe, and in a way the targeting of Greek pensions also had that dimension to it: to increase the market shares of this business.

perpetrating extensive tax evasion. This is another aspect of the social alliance that has dominated the country in the last few decades (see below).

Let us move on now to the question of wage costs: If we stick to one side of the coin then the dominant argument since to be confirmed. The increase in unit labour costs in 2001–2008 among the 35 countries most competitive with Greece was high, in the vicinity of 20%. But relevant studies by the Labour Institute of the Greek General Confederation of Labour (INE-GSEE 2010; Ioakeimoglou 2011) have shown that this increase in relation to the non-European Monetary Union (EMU) countries can be explained by the appreciation of the euro during the same period. Trade relations with non-Eurozone countries have consequently not experienced any significant internal change that might account for the depth of the current crisis. On the contrary, such problems as these are due to the country's participation in the Eurozone.

As for the differences from the Eurozone average for the period 1995–2009, there is a cumulative increase in real labour costs in the order of 30%. While this is a significant change, it should not be overlooked that there was an equally remarkable change in labour productivity between 1995 and 2004, when it increased by 30%, which is the second-highest figure among the 18 most developed European Union (EU) countries, coming after Ireland. After that (between 2005 and 2009), the growth rates in productivity corresponded to the average of the EMU countries, but with real wages continuing to grow more in Greece than in the other EMU countries. They, nevertheless, were parallel to the growth rates in productivity in contrast to the other EMU countries were these is a divergence between wage increases and growth in productivity (Ioakeimoglou 2011). It is therefore difficult to see how such a crisis could have erupted because in the 2000–2009 period, salaries in Greece increased proportionately with the increase in productivity, whereas in the EMU countries, this was not the case. The conclusion is that the decline in productivity in the Greek economy cannot plausibly be cited as a factor that led to the crisis.

But even if we restrict ourselves to the labour cost parameter, this is not enough to explain a crisis of this magnitude. There are two reasons for this: The first is that despite wage increases at rates higher than the corresponding rates in the Eurozone, the differences in the units of purchasing power remained very high (2009). On the basis of 100 for Germany, Greece was at 94, the Netherlands 140, Belgium 139, Ireland 123, Austria 122, France 119, Spain 113, Italy 112, Finland 106 and Portugal 74 (the only country behind Greece) (Ioakeimoglou 2011: 78). If indeed we make the comparison in purchasing power units when we compare the differences between average annual earnings and labour productivity, we see that while average labour costs in Greece amounted to 83% of the EU15 average, labour productivity in the country rose to 95% of the EU15 average (Institute of Labour—Greek General Confederation of Labour 2010: 181). The second reason has to do with the structure of wage costs. In 2009, in the business sector of the economy, 1% of gross earnings exceeded €7220 and 5% were over €4200 per month. The gross earnings of the remaining 95% were €1610 on average, and 24% earned less than €1000 (Institute of Labour—Greek General Confederation of Labour 2010: 179). So what is more significant is not how much salaries have increased overall but how great the difference between them remains.

In conclusion, the crisis cannot be explained through the increase in unit labour costs, given that there has been a corresponding increase in productivity. Yet, the differences between the Greek wages and the EU-15 average remained significant, constituting a standing competitive advantage for Greek capitalism, which had not previously experienced any profitability problems.

The above findings are further enhanced by data of a different kind focusing on the great wealth transfer from the lower classes to the ruling class between 1990 and 2007. In 1990, Greece's GDP was €38 billion. By 2007, it had reached 208 billion, a 550% increase. By contrast, the basic wage of the unskilled worker in 1990 was €15; in 2007, it was €30, so it had only doubled. Correspondingly, corporate earnings (SA and LLC) in 1990 amounted to €575 million, but in 2007, they had increased to €16 billion, amounting to a 28-fold increase (Bogiopoulos 2011: 302). The taxable profits of all legal persons (public limited companies, limited liability companies, general partnerships, limited partnerships) increased from €11.7 billion in 2002 to €13 billion in 2003 (+10.6%), €14.3 billion in 2004 (+10.5%), €14.8 billion in 2005 (+2.9%), €14.4 billion in 2006 (−2.3%) and €17 billion in 2007

(+17.8%), with a total rise of 44.9% for 2002–2007 (Pelagidis and Mitsopoulos 2010: 235). The profitability index (return on capital, i.e. net operating surplus as a percentage of net fixed capital stock) shows a sharp rise between 1991 and 2007 from 67% to 115% (Institute of Labour—Greek General Confederation of Labour 2011: 146–147). As a result, the share of labour in GDP fell from 70% in 1990 to 61% in 2008 (Institute of Labour—Greek General Confederation of Labour 2013: 153). Arguably one of the problems of Greek capitalism was not the high wages; it was Greek entrepreneurs' practice of not investing their high profits in technological modernization (see below) and instead saving their capital, hence the liquidity that Greek banks had for a long time and hence also the Greek public sector's ability to issue bonds.

Another argument used by the dominant circles is that the level of private consumption in Greece in the period 2002–2009 was higher than that in the Eurozone countries (78% of GDP in Greece vs 58% in the Eurozone)[8] (Melas 2013: 125). In the early years of the twenty-first century, there was in fact a significant increase in private consumption.[9] It was encouraged further by financial institutions that were constantly promoting "new" financial products. In 2000, around 70 credit cards circulated in the Greek market. By 2009, there were more than 200 of them. In 2001, there were 2000 stores that accepted credit cards. A decade later, their number had reached 650,000. Housing credit as a percentage of GDP rose from 3.8% in 1994 to 33.9% by 2009. Consumer credit, which accounted for 0.9% of transactions in 1994, reached a figure of 16.5% in 2009 (Melas 2013: 128).

But describing the developments of a decade cannot be a substitute for analysing a phenomenon that has many causes. One reason for the increase in home loans is that increases in real wages have been limited, falling short of the amounts needed for the purchase of a home.[10]

[8] Of course it is often conveniently forgotten that public consumption for the same period was in the vicinity of 17%, while the corresponding European figure was 20%. Probably the reason is that this is not readily compatible with the theory of the over-inflated state.

[9] According to relevant data, in the 1980s, gross national savings stood at 22.9% of GDP (EU12: 21.6%), in the 1990s, 17.3% (EU12: 21.2%), between 2001 and 2006, 13.5% (EU12: 21.4%) and between 2007 and 2009, 6.4% (EU12: 21.2%) (Giannitsis 2013: 161).

[10] Home ownership in Greece is a form of investment and defence against the absence of a social state. In developed European countries where inflation was low and the welfare State developed,

Borrowing therefore became virtually obligatory (as opposed to what had been the usual practice in the 1970s and 1980s).

Another reason for the lack of savings is that the low interest rates offered by Greek banks, in conjunction with the deindustrialization process and the lack of trust in the stock market (after the events of 1999–2000),[11] induced potential investors to shift towards consumption. Another reason for it is that increases expressed in units of purchasing power provided no additional consumer capacity of any significance, with the result that some of the popular strata turned to private borrowing.

But it is important, too, to examine the structure of consumer expenditure per quarter of consumption. The 25% of households with the lowest consumer expenditure spend 87.8% of their total consumer outlay on necessary goods (food, beverages, tobacco, clothing and footwear, housing, durables, health, transport, communications). The second lowest 25% spend 79.8%, the second highest 75.5% and the highest 68.5% (Laskos and Tsakalotos 2012: 145). So, the increase in consumption acquires completely different characteristics depending on the income category. The poorest categories simply try to cope with consumption costs much higher than in the past (e.g. more expensive food costs due to increased food imports, Internet and mobile telephone costs, rent increases due to the increase in real estate's prices) whereas the rich strata turn to the luxury goods market, though admittedly these may, again, be for food or durable goods (electrical, home appliances, furniture, private cars).

Last but not the least, what happened between 2002 and 2009 in Greece is something that had *already happened* in most Western countries, precisely because of the abovementioned financialization (Table 2.3).

Among the 18 countries surveyed, Greece in 2010 comes 13th in terms of household debt. But in 2000, Greece ranked last (18th), and the

---

social inequalities were not sharpened as in Greece. It is obvious thus that a tendency towards savings was more intense.

[11] From early 1999 until September of the same year, there was a rapid rise in the indices at the Greek Stock Exchange, resulting in hundreds of thousands of Greeks investing their savings there. The continuous fall that was to start from the end of September and last for years resulted in the loss of savings for a large part of the Greek population.

Table 2.3 Household debt as a percentage of GNP

Country	1980	1990	2000	2010
United States	52	64	74	95
Japan	60	82	87	82
Germany	59	61	73	64
United Kingdom	57	73	75	106
France	27	46	47	69
Italy	6	21	30	53
Canada	56	63	67	94
Australia	42	46	74	113
Austria	41	41	47	57
Belgium	35	38	41	56
Denmark			95	152
Finland	29	48	35	67
Greece	8	9	20	65
Netherlands	43	49	87	130
Norway			64	94
Portugal	15	23	75	106
Spain	24	41	54	91
Sweden	53	61	51	87

Source: OECD

shift towards consumption in the first decade of the twenty-first century, for the reasons explained, led to a rise in indebtedness from 20% to 65%. The particularity of Greece is that it became part of the financial market relatively late. The previous level of household debt (relatively low) cannot explain the magnitude of the economic crisis. If it could, many Western countries would have been in a much worse position for a long time.

Finally, there is an argument that is articulated primarily in the international public sphere, but also finds receptive ears in Greece. According to it, Greeks do not work long enough hours, and this has led to the current situation. But this widespread view suffers from a lack of documentation, as shown in the following table (Table 2.4).

It is obvious that salaried workers in Greece are working at an average of 1803 hours a year and they work harder than those in all the countries under examination, with the exception of Poland and the Czech Republic, putting in significantly longer hours than workers in Germany, France or Britain. If we also take into account data on employees as a whole, we find that in Greece, people work more than their counterparts in any

Table 2.4 Hours of self-employment, whether dependent or not, in OECD countries (2008)

Austria	Belgium	Czech Rep.	Denmark	Finland	France	Germany	Greece	Ireland	Netherlands	New Zealand	Poland	Portugal	Spain	United Kingdom	United States
Dependent working hours															
1483	1489	1923	1576	1610	1461	1352	1803	1522	1301	1731	1940	1686	1619	1638	1797
Total (dependent and non-dependent) working hours															
1631	1568	1992	1610	1728	1542	1432	2120	1601	1389	1753	1969	1745	1627	1653	1792

Source: Pelagidis and Mitsiopoulos (2010: 180)

other of the countries mentioned. This perhaps helps explain how between 1990 and 2008 labour productivity in Greece increased by 50% as opposed to 40% in Germany, 35% in France, just over 20% in Spain and Portugal, and 15% in Italy (Laskos and Tsakalotos 2012: 175–176).

The Real Problem: The Lack of Competitiveness of Greek Capitalism and the Aggravation of This Phenomenon in Times of Crisis

Having examined various arguments of the ruling elites, we shall focus on our position concerning the root cause of the current crisis: When Greek capitalism in 1981 joined the European Economic Community (EEC), it had a significant problem of competitiveness in relation to European capital, except the shipping capital and some sectors of the Greek economy (construction, cement and steel). But the choice was made by the Greek bourgeois state which followed the direction of the long-term reproduction of the capital relation and thought that the competition of the most dynamic sections of European capital would contribute to the internal restructuring of the Greek production structure through eliminating non-competitive capital and the empowerment of the most competitive. On the other hand, the Left, since the 1960s, has continued to argue that Greece's entry into the EEC would have devastating effects on the country's economy (Iliou 1962).

Finally, the problem of competitiveness persisted, despite some internal restructuring, but the course of the Greek economy until 2009 did not reveal any catastrophic problems. This paradox is due to a number of factors that have managed to keep Greek capitalism on a European trajectory, postponing the emergence of its structural problems for later. Specifically:

(a) The existence of a national currency until 2001 allowed exchange rates to fluctuate in accordance with the intention of each government to stimulate exports.
(b) The relatively low wages paid in the Greek economy helped maintain this advantage of Greek capitalism.

(c) The massive entry of immigrants after the fall of the Eastern bloc has also been added to point (b), resulting in the existence of a cheap and to a large extent uninsured labour force that has reduced the real production costs.
(d) The continuation of the development of shipping, tourism and construction as key components.
(e) The development of the financial system and the stimulation of the market through new financial derivatives.
(f) The utilization of the various European Community Structural Funds both as forms of support for productive and commercial activities and as a material basis for the creation of ties of social consensus.

Why is it claimed that the competitiveness problem persists?

It is quite simply because there was no planning and no strategy for the qualitative change in the abovementioned characteristics to those of a competitive high-tech capitalism. Accordingly, at an early stage, in 2003, investment in venture capital was barely 0.007% of GDP in Greece, as against a EU15 average of 0.021% (Stasinopoulos 2005: 150). Correspondingly, investment in venture capital for expansion and replacement in 2003 barely reached 0.007% of GDP in Greece, compared to a EU15 average of 0.088% (Stasinopoulos 2005: 152). At the same time, in Greece investment in research was carried out essentially by the State: in the period 1999–2005, Greece's public sector expenditure on research and technology was 50.5% of the total, whereas in the private sector, it was only 28.3%. In the EU27, the corresponding figures were 35.1% and 56.8% (Labrianidis and Vogiatzis 2013: 536). Employment in the sectors of knowledge-intensive services was 1.7% of total employment in 2003, as against the EU25 and EU15 averages of 5.43% and 5.88% respectively (Stasinopoulos 2005: 155). The personnel employed in Greece in research and development (R&D) activities between 1995 and 2007 comprised 0.37% of total employment compared to 0.63% for the EU15 (Argeitis and Nikolaidi 2014: 66).[12]

[12] For corresponding data, see Labrianidis and Vogiatzis 2013: 532–533, where it is eloquently shown how, apart from the small number of researchers employed in all sectors in Greece (reaching

Expenditure on research and technology in Greece in the 1998–2007 period amounted to 0.50% of GDP. In the EU15, it was 1.84% (Argeitis and Nikolaidi 2014: 64). The business sector in Greece spent only 0.18% of GDP on R&D (2005) as against the EU27 average of 1.15%, the EU15 average of 1.20% and the EMU16 average of 1.16% (Lykos 2012: 168). The result was that processing companies in Greece in the 1988–2007 period limited their expenditure on research and technology to 0.8% of gross added value, whereas in ten EU15 countries they were over 5%, showing lower rates compared to the total investments in other branches of the Greek economy; even in the high- and medium-to-high-tech sectors, the rate of investment was significantly lower than the EU15 average, second only to Portugal (Argeitis and Nikolaidi 2014: 68–70).

That said, employment in high-tech manufacturing sectors stood at 17.8% for the 1995–2009 period (EU15 average: 32.8%). The contribution to production of added value for the 1980–2009 period was 17.5% (EU15 average: 36.4%). The number of patents per million inhabitants registered in 2008 at the three patent offices (America, Europe, Japan) was 1.2 for Greece and 29.7 for the EU27 (Argeitis and Nikolaidi 2014: 65). The Innovation Index in 2005 was 0.2, ranking Greece 29th among 33 European countries. The annual expenditure on the purchase of PCs, software, among others, as a percentage of GDP in 2003 stood at 1.20% for Greece and 3% for the EU15 (Stasinopoulos 2005: 163). Similarly, there were 4.65 broadband network users per 1000 inhabitants in 2004 in Greece, putting Greece in second-last place, before Romania, in the EU26 (excluding Luxembourg), whereas in terms of Internet users, it ranked last with 177 users per 1000 inhabitants (Melas 2009: 198).

This technological lag points to a rigidity that operates against the possibility of a technological transformation of Greek capitalism, something indispensable for competitiveness within the framework of the EMU. The timidity of the orientation towards technology also had corresponding effects both on the structure of production and on that of exports, where the choice of investing in medium- and high-tech industries proceeded at a snail's pace (Table 2.5).

4.4 per 1000 persons in 2007, compared to 7.4 for the OECD average and 6.0 for the EU27) just 1.31 are working in the private sector (compared to 4.81 for OECD countries).

Table 2.5 Structure of added value in production, employment, industrial units and investments based on technological classification of the manufacturing sectors

	1994	2006
Structure of added value in production		
High-tech industries	6.6	6.3
Medium- to high-tech industries	13.9	11.8
Medium- to low-tech industries	26.4	37.5
Low-tech industries	53.1	44.4
Total manufacturing industries	100.0	100.0
Employee structure		
High-tech industries	5.7	6.4
Medium- to high-tech industries	13.5	14.0
Medium- to low-tech industries	23.5	27.7
Low-tech industries	57.3	51.9
Total manufacturing industries	100.0	100.0
Branch number structure		
High-tech industries	2.7	2.7
Medium- to high-tech industries	12.7	14.6
Medium- to low- tech industries	23.1	28.6
Low-tech industries	61.5	54.1
Total manufacturing industries	100.0	100.0
Investment structure		
High-tech industries	6.6	5.0
Medium- to high-tech industries	12.4	11.1
Medium- to low-tech industries	22.3	49.0
Low-tech industries	58.8	34.9
Total manufacturing industries	100.0	100.0

Source: Giannitsis et al. (2009: 44–45)

Note: (a) low-tech products: food, beverages and tobacco, textiles, leather and footwear, wood, wood and cork articles, pulp, paper, paper products, printing and publishing, industrial products not elsewhere classified, recycling; (b) medium- to low-tech: coke, refined petroleum products and nuclear fuels, rubber and plastic products, other non-metallic mineral products, basic metals, metal products (apart from machinery and equipment), construction and repair of ships and boats; (c) medium- to high-tech: chemical (other than pharmaceuticals), mechanical equipment not elsewhere classified, electrical machinery and equipment not elsewhere classified; (d) high-tech: aircraft and spacecraft, pharmaceuticals, office and automatic processing machines, radio, television and telecommunication equipment, medical, precision instruments, optical instruments

It is observed that over a period of 12 years (1994–2006), which include the country's entry into the EMU, there were changes in direction involving medium-to-high and high-tech: Some sectors recorded a retreat, while others a slight advance. Thus, in the creation of added value, *both* high-tech *and* medium-to-high-tech industries saw a reduction in their shares, and this was also the case in the field of investment structuring. There was similarly a reduction in the share of low-tech industries. On the other hand, medium-to-low-tech industries evidently gained ground. As for the employment structure and the articulation of the number of branches, here too the middle-to-low-tech industries were on a rising trajectory, whereas low-tech industries were in decline. High-tech and middle-to-high-tech industries were either stagnant or showing very limited growth.

The overall picture was one of retreat among low-tech industries. Yet what is missing from the picture is the fact that the real dynamics were expressed by medium- to low-tech industries. This becomes even more apparent when we examine the evolution of exports of high-tech and high-to-medium-tech industries (Table 2.6).

It is obvious that in 1995, Greece had the lowest percentage of high-tech exports of all the countries, which would later comprise the EMU and for which data is available. Only for Portugal was the percentage lower. Something similar applies to exports of high- and high-to-medium-tech products where, both in 1995 and in 2011, Greece had the lowest proportion of relatively high-tech exports of all the EMU countries. Similar conclusions emerge if we look at the proportion of low- and high-tech goods in all Greek exports: High-tech exports drop from 29.84% of the total in 2000 to 22.57% in 2009. Low-tech exports increase from 70.16% to 77.43% (Institute of Labour—Greek General Confederation of Labour 2016: 182). It is indeed quite characteristic that in 2008, the share of manufacturing exports in the total exports of Greece was 54%, while that of manufacturing exports in the total exports of the Euro Area 16 was 77% (Economakis et al. 2014: 189).

This situation also explains why the ratio of marketable[13]/non-marketable goods to net added value declines in the years prior to the

[13] Marketable goods: agriculture, mining, processing, hotels-restaurants, financial-insurance and other business services. Non-marketable: energy, construction, transport-storage-telecommunications, trade, the public sector, other services.

Table 2.6 Technological level of exports, Eurozone countries, select years

	Rate of HT exports to total exports (%)		Rate of HT and HMT exports to total exports (%)	
Country	1995	2011	1995	2011
Austria	9.46	13.18	46.97	54.22
Belgium	9.26	17.85	52.38	57.75
Estonia	10.95	15.45	32.55	41.91
Finland	15.00	11.12	40.23	43.52
France	18.98	25.82	59.81	62.73
Germany	15.06	18.56	68.31	69.02
Greece	4.30	8.72	16.54	21.98
Ireland	40.67	53.56	62.09	82.56
Italy	9.78	10.39	48.40	49.50
Luxembourg		9.26		32.05
Netherlands	21.31	22.97	52.15	53.88
Portugal	8.11	7.80	33.95	38.88
Slovakia		18.75		61.77
Slovenia	9.28	13.73	45.79	58.85
Spain	8.63	11.15[a]	56.08	53.55[a]
Cyprus	9.99	37.01	24.13	52.62
Malta	64.78	34.45	72.31	34.45

Source: Economakis et al. (2014: 188)
[a]2010

crisis: 2000: 0.866, 2001: 0.797, 2002: 0.777, 2003: 0.716, 2004: 0.695, 2005: 0.693, 2006: 0.666, 2007: 0.648, 2008: 0.661, 2009: 0.689. The decrease was much greater than in the EU27 countries, although there was a fall in the ratio of marketable to non-marketable goods in those countries also: 2000: 1.072, 2001: 1058, 2002: 1041, 2003: 1031, 2004: 1028, 2006: 1026, 2007: 1039, 2008: 1019, 2009: 0.977. The resulting conclusion is very well summarized by Economakis, Markaki and Anastasiadis: "for the entire period after the entry of Greece into the euro area the Greek economy based its development on productive sectors not exposed to the international competition, comparatively more than the EU-27 as a whole. Therefore, the type of development of the Greek economy neither presupposed nor led to the improvement of its international competitive position" (Economakis et al. 2015: 432).

The competitiveness gap becomes more evident if one takes into account the outward foreign direct investment (FDI) parameter. It is clear that Greece is making very little direct investment abroad, and when it does occur, it involves non-high-tech products, which are channelled mainly to neighbouring countries. Although, according to the Bitzenis and Vlachos survey, Greece saw an increase in the volume of FDI over the 20 years prior to the crisis (see fn 34): "Greece's OFDI stock in 2010 was higher than that of only two of the comparator countries—the neighboring EU countries Bulgaria and Cyprus, which had nominal GDPs that were approximately 16% and 8%, respectively, of the size of Greek nominal GDP. Austria with a nominal GDP in 2010 that was approximately 124%, and Ireland with about 67% of that of Greece, have more than four and nine times higher OFDI than Greece. Portugal and Spain also had larger OFDI stocks in 2010 than Greece: 1.7 times in the case of Portugal (with a GDP about three-quarters the size of Greek GDP) and 17 times higher in the case of Spain (with a GDP about four and a half times the size of Greece's GDP). In terms of OFDI performance over time, during 1990–2010, Greece's OFDI stock grew to 13 times its size in 1990—during 1990–2010, a growth rate higher than that of Bulgaria, but lower than that of the rest of the comparators" (Bitzenis and Vlachos 2011: 3).

Things could not be otherwise since, from the point of view of Greek companies, geographical proximity, low labour costs and the absence of potentially competitive European investments have played a key role in their decision to commence operations abroad. In the host countries, Greek multinationals supplied products and services that did not require further processing and were ready for consumption (Bitzenis and Vlachos 2011: 5). In 2009, 28.3% of the Greek outward FDI stock went to Cyprus, 12.3% to Turkey, 11.1% to Romania, 6.7% to Serbia, 5.1% to Bulgaria, 1.8% to Albania and 1.6% to the former Yugoslav Republic of Macedonia (FYROM). In other words, two-thirds was directed to the Balkan countries and Cyprus, with its own special relationship with Greece (Bitzenis and Vlachos 2011: 15). So Greek FDI played an important role only in countries neighbouring Greece: 51% of the total inward FDI stock in Cyprus, 24% in Albania, 14% in the FYROM, 13.3% in Serbia, 6.7% in Turkey, 6.6% in Romania and 4.2% in Bulgaria (Bitzenis and Vlachos 2011: 5).

Precisely within this framework, the pre-existing competitiveness problem that arose with the country's entry into the EEC would only intensify with the accession of Greece to the EMU and would lead to the crisis in the current account balance.

The Crisis in the Current Account Balance

To understand the exact meaning of the crisis in the current account balance, it will be necessary to present the evolution of its basic fundamentals and then focus on each of them (Table 2.7).

The general observations that can be made are that there has been a significant increase in the current account deficit since 2005, a more or less corresponding increase in the trade deficit and in the deficits of the fuel balance and in the balance of shipping. By contrast, the balance for services has stagnated in the same period, triggering a similarly increased deficit in the balance for goods.

On examining the current account balance in greater depth, we see that the first required stopping point is at the trade balance, which is the ratio of exports to imports. This is an indicator which, since the founding of the Greek state, has been in deficit but, as shown in the table, the situation has deteriorated considerably in recent years (Table 2.8).

It is clear that while until 1997, the index was steadily above 40%, between 1998 and 2001, it fluctuated between 35.1% and 36.8%, but

Table 2.7 Time series of the current account balance (2001–2008) (% GDP)

Year	Current account balance	Trade balance	Fuel balance	Shipping	Balance of services	Balance of goods (trade + services)
2001	−7.2	−14.8	−2.0	n.a	6.2	−8.5
2002	−6.5	−14.5	−2.2	0.3	6.9	−7.6
2003	−6.6	−13.2	−2.4	0.1	6.7	−6.5
2004	−5.8	−13.7	−2.4	0.1	8.3	−5.4
2005	−7.5	−13.9	−3.4	−0.4	7.8	−6.2
2006	−11.1	−16.6	−4.1	−1.6	7.2	−9.4
2007	−14.2	−18.2	−4.0	−2.4	7.3	−10.9
2008	−14.3	−18.0	−5.0	−1.9	7.0	−11.0
Aggregate 2001–2008	−9.1	−15.4	−3.2	n.a	7.2	−8.2

Source: Bank of Greece and Manassaki et al. (2010: 104)

Table 2.8 Time chart of import/export ratio

Year	Exports/imports	Year	Exports/imports
1980	48.8	2001	36.8
1985	44.5	2002	31.5
1990	40.4	2003	30.1
1995	43.0	2004	29.2
1996	41.4	2005	32.0
1997	41.0	2006	32.4
1998	35.9	2007	29.9
1999	36.3	2008	28.5
2000	35.1	2009	29.5

Source: ESYE

from 2002 to the beginning of the crisis, ranged between 28.5% and 32.4%. So this was essentially an incipient crisis in the trade balance, culminating just before the outbreak of the generalized crisis.[14]

The key issue that Greek capitalism had to deal with was the structure of Greek exports itself, as, for reasons already presented, it remained unfavourable compared with that of the EMU countries. This explains the country's poor export performance, which ranged between 8.6% and 10.6% of GDP throughout the 1996–2006 period, as against the EU15 average of between 23.3% and 29.3% (Athanasoglou et al. 2010: 167).

In order to overcome this structural difficulty, Greek entrepreneurs implemented a partial revision of their export destinations, as shown in the following table (Table 2.9):

This table leads to very important conclusions. We notice that in the 1980s, when the country entered the European communities, the vast majority of its exports were towards the EU15 countries (though they were fewer than half in 1981, they had risen to more than two-thirds by 1991) and this radical redirection took place at the expense of exports to North Africa and the Middle East, where from 25% they were reduced to less than 10%.

The intensified internationalization of the economy, the chronic presence of competitiveness problems in Greek capitalism, along with the

[14] In this connection, it is characteristic that whereas in 1976, Greek exports accounted for 0.257% of world exports, in 1991, this figure fell to 0.247%, in 1997 to 0.200%, in 2003 to 0.177% and in 2007 to 0.140%.

Table 2.9 Greek exports by geographical area

Region	1980	1981	1991	2001	2002	2005	2009
World	100	100	100	100	100	100	100
OECD	54.7[a]	57.8[a]	77.1	61.6	62.1	61.9	52.9
EE25			72.5	56.0	56.8	55.4	47.6
EE15	47.6	43.3	67.2	47.7	48.8	46.9	37.1
North America	6.1	9.1	6.3	5.9	5.4	5.,7	5.7
Other developed countries			1.5	1.0	1.0	0.9	0.7
Other OECD countries (excluding South Korea)			3.0	4.5	4.3	6.1	6.8
Balkans			4.0	16.6	15.2	14.6	17.2
Commonwealth of Independent States			1.0	3.9	3.6	2.7	2.8
North Africa & Middle East	25.0	26.1	7.1	6.2	6.6	7.4	8.9
Africa (excluding North Africa)			0.6	0.6	0.7	1.5	0.9
S.E. Asia			0.9	1.5	1.6	1.9	1.3
L. America			1.1	1.1	1.0	0.6	1.1
Other Countries			2.0	2.9	3.8	3.2	6.9

OECD: Austria, Belgium, Canada, Denmark, France, Germany, Iceland, Italy, Ireland, Luxembourg, the Netherlands, Norway, Portugal, Spain, Sweden, Switzerland, Turkey, New Zealand, Mexico, the Czech Republic, Hungary, Poland, South Korea, Slovakia

EU (27): France, Belgium, Luxembourg, the Netherlands, Germany, Italy, the United Kingdom, Ireland, Denmark, Portugal, Spain, Sweden, Finland, Austria, Malta, Estonia, Latvia, Hungary, Slovenia, Cyprus, Romania, Bulgaria

EU (15): France, Belgium, Luxembourg, the Netherlands, Germany, Italy, the United Kingdom, Ireland, Denmark, Portugal, Spain, Sweden, Finland, Austria

North America: The United States, Canada, Mexico

Other developed countries: Japan, Australia, New Zealand

Other OECD countries: Iceland, Norway, Switzerland, Turkey

Balkans: Romania, Bulgaria, Albania, Croatia, Bosnia-Herzegovina, Serbia-Montenegro-Kosovo, FYROM

Commonwealth of Independent States: Ukraine, Belarus, Moldova, Russia, Georgia, Armenia, Azerbaijan, Kazakhstan, Turkmenistan, Uzbekistan, Tajikistan, Kyrgyzstan

North Africa and Middle East: Morocco, Algeria, Tunisia, Libya, Egypt, Lebanon, Syria, Iran, Iraq, Israel, Jordan, Saudi Arabia, Kuwait, Bahrain, Qatar, Emirates, Oman, Yemen

African countries (excluding North Africa): Mauritania, Niger, Ghana, Nigeria, Gabon, Ethiopia, Kenya, Rep. of S. Africa

S.E. Asia: Taiwan, Indonesia, Singapore, the Philippines, Hong Kong, South Korea, Thailand

Latin America: Argentina, Brazil, Bahamas, St. Vincent, Honduras, Panama, Chile

Other Countries: India, China, remaining countries

Source: Pan-Hellenic Association of Exporters

[a]Switzerland is also included

powerful influence of China, India, Southeast Asia and Eastern European countries on international markets, would induce Greek capitalism in the 1990s to look for new markets. This was the period when exports to EU15 countries would fall (from two-thirds of the total in 1991 to less than half in 2001)[15] and would be diverted mainly towards the Balkans (from 4% to 16.6%) and secondarily to the countries of the former USSR (from 1% to 3.9%). This was due, on the one hand, to the geographical proximity of these regions and, on the other, to the strong presence of Greek companies and credit institutions in Southeastern Europe (Athanassoglou et al. 2010: 166). The sequel was to be determined by the creation of the EMU and the additional problems that the inability to use the weapon of devaluation created for Greek capitalism. Thus, the trend of the 1990s accelerated and up until the outbreak of the crisis, exports to the OECD, EU25 and EU15 countries decreased further by 10%. On the other hand, the level of exports to the Balkans stabilized. There was a 2.7% increase in exports to the North African and Middle Eastern countries and a 4% increase to the other countries.

This improvement in the share of total exports going to each region was as follows: of the total exports to EU countries, Greek exports accounted for 0.32% between 1996 and 2000 and 0.30% between 2001 and 2006. Of the total exports to the EU15, Greek exports stood at 0.51% in the 1996–2000 period and fell to 0.46% between 2001 and 2006. On the other hand, for the same periods, there was an increase in exports to the Middle East and Mediterranean countries from 1.09% to 1.14% of the total and to Southeastern Europe from 2.54% to 2.72% (Athanasoglou et al. 2010: 170).

We see this evolution as the manifestation of a defensive movement by Greek capitalism, which has difficulties surviving in the highly competitive environment of the Western countries, is burdened even further by comparatively higher inflation in the Greek economy and accordingly chose gradually to focus on national formations of lower productivity. In essence, it was a prelude to the crisis that would follow.

---

[15] It is characteristic that Greek exports to Germany comprised 23.9% of Greek exports in 1991 and just 10% in 2009.

It is interesting to see the structure of the Greek export share by technological level, as it shows that any shift in Greek exports to medium- and high-tech products has been welcomed in non-EU15 regions. Thus, in Southeastern Europe, Greek medium-tech exports increased from 1.42% to 3.69% of the total and high-tech exports from 0.71% to 0.89%, whereas there was a distinct fall in low-tech exports from 3.21% to 1.65%. It is interesting that in the Mediterranean region and the Middle East, the percentage of high-tech Greek exports more than doubled, from 0.26% of the total to 0.54%.[16]

Let us now turn to the issue of imports. Here the overwhelming majority comprises industrial products: In 1990–1994, 79.9% of imports were industrial products. In 1995–1999, this figure rose to 81.4% and in 2000–2004 to 83.8% (Vlahou and Lambrinidis 2011: 247). One important factor in this situation is the absence of an extensive domestic industry producing for the internal market. But above and beyond that, the importance of increased spending on imported fuels, even more so in times of high oil prices, is something that should not be overlooked. In 2003, fuel imports accounted for 48% of the total value of Greek exports, but that was to soar to 72.4% in 2006 and would reach 82.8% in 2008. So, more than four-fifths of the revenue earned by Greek exports went to the oil market (Vlahou and Lambrinidis 2011: 234). The reason for this was that between November 2003 and November 2009, the average price of Brent oil increased by 166.7%, or 109.2% in euros (Economou 2010: 10).

Another parameter that has made a negative contribution to the trade balance is the agricultural balance (food, beverages, tobacco, cotton, processed hides etc.). As soon as Greece joined the EEC, the balance for

[16] One of the factors that helped boost Greek exports was the move made by Greek capital to carry out direct investments in these regions. By 2009, more than 8000 businesses had become active in the region of the Balkans, investing over $6 billion in just three years. Investments were also made in African countries. The main players in this strategy were the financial and insurance institutions but also Hellenic Petroleum and food multinationals such as 3E and Chipita, along with other businesses such as Foli-Follie (fashion jewellery and accessories) and the Fourlis group (home furnishings and furniture). It is characteristic that Greece's direct investment abroad would rise from $8 billion in 2001 to reach $17 billion in 2006 and then skyrocket to $32 billion in 2010 (Kapaktsis 2012: 433–443). Essentially, like the reorientation of exports, it was an attempt to overcome the problem that Greek capitalism faced within the EMU.

agricultural products was dramatically transformed from a surplus to a deficit, and that deficit has increased sevenfold, at a time when the proportion of economically active farmers in the Greek population is more than three times higher than the corresponding figure for the Dutch, the British or the Germans, all of whom however present positive balances for agricultural products. Characteristically, we could mention that in the period between 1974 and 1980, the agricultural balance each year was a surplus of $45 million. By contrast, immediately after accession to the EU (1981–1985), the surplus turned into a significant annual deficit of $254 billion, to reach $1860 billion in 1997 (Fotopoulos 2010: 182) and $616 million in 2000. The export/import ratio went from 1.14 in 1981 to 0.81 in 2000 (Nikolaidis 2005: 98). As for more recent years (1994–2008), while the total trade deficit increased by 413.1%, the deficit in the agricultural balance saw a 529.12% rise (Petropoulos et al. 2010: 322) with the consequence that while in 1994, the deficit in the balance for agricultural products corresponded to 5.62% of the total trade deficit, by 2008, the figure had risen to 7.02% (Bilias 2014).

There are a number of reasons for this development. For a start, it is worth mentioning the phasing out of tariffs, State subsidies and price fixing through the operation of the Common Agricultural Policy (CAP). The CAP continually placed limits on crop cultivation and livestock breeding, and imposed reductions in areas under cultivation and agricultural production, not only for products in surplus but also for deficit products (e.g. tobacco and cotton) (Fotopoulos 2010: 183–184). It should be borne in mind, too, that the rule in Greece is for allotments to be small, unlike in the rest of Western Europe, something which objectively places limits on productivity per hectare. Characteristically, the utilized agricultural area per farm in Greece between 1990 and 2007 went from 4.31 hectares to 4.7 hectares, compared to from 68.44 hectares to 64.79 hectares for the United Kingdom, from 16.45 hectares to 25.54 hectares for Holland and from 5.62 hectares to 7.60 hectares for Italy (Tsiboukakis 2012). Moreover in this limited geographical area weak productive forces were employed. In 2003, in the Eurozone countries, 1154 tractors were used per hundred hectares of arable land; in Greece, the figure was 954.14. In 2000, in the other EU countries, 160.38 kilograms of fertilizer was used for 100 hectares of farmland; in Greece, the amount was just 118.7 kilograms. The result was that while cereal production per hectare in the Eurozone countries amounted to 5771 tonnes, the figure for Greece was 4338.5 tonnes. Wheat production per hectare in the countries of the EU was 70 tonnes, as against a Greek figure of 33 tonnes. Sugar production in Greece yielded 577 tonnes and in the countries of Western Europe 741 tonnes.

The upshot of all the above would be a trade balance in permanent deficit. This is not due to the fact that Greece is importing too much. Import penetration in the country between 1996 and 2006 fluctuated between 20.6% and 25% of GDP, as against the EU15 average of between 22.3% and 29.6% (Athanasoglou et al. 2010: 168). So there are proportionally fewer Greek imports. The central problem is the big gap between Greek imports and Greek exports, which is imposing continual downward pressure on the trade balance and consequently on the current account balance.

Tourism has been a mismatch in the trade deficit over time. But both the revaluation of the euro and the growth of other tourism-friendly tourist destinations as an alternative to Greece resulted in a decline in revenue. Greece's receipts from tourism between 2002 and 2007 fell from 2.02% of total global receipts to 1.81%, from 4.73% of all EU27 tourist receipts to 4.24% and from 6.01% of total Eurozone country receipts to 5.57% (Klouri and Karapappas 2010: 207). As a result, whereas in 2002 net receipts from tourism services covered 34.07% of the deficit in the trade balance, by 2008 this figure had fallen to 20.33% (Klouri and Karapappas 2010: 206).

Similar problems afflict ship-owning capital, which is the mainstay of Greek capitalism, but its dynamism has been in decline through the early years of this century. Whereas in 2002 the active Greek-owned fleet comprised 17.8% of the world's active fleet, this figure dropped to 16.9% in 2006 and 14.7% in 2009 (Panagiotou and Bragoudakis 2010: 227).

Another—until recently—favourable parameter for the balance of current accounts was the positive sign on financial transactions between Greece and the EU. But here too there was a decrease in real revenue. From 4.2% of annual GDP between 1990 and 1999, it fell to 2.4% for the period between 2000 and 2008 (Manassaki and Koltsida 2010: 239). The corresponding decrease in the proportionate cover of the balance of current accounts was from 21.1% in 2000 to 11.8% in 2008 (Asimakopoulos et al. 2010: 440).

In offsetting the current account deficit, a key factor was the fiscal transactions balance. The contribution of direct investment to it was very small: Cumulatively for the period between 2000 and 2008, the relevant balance was positive only to the extent of 0.5% of GDP. This is because FDI in Greece is limited. In the period between 2003 and 2006, it accounted for only 3.2% of total investment in Greece, whereas the corresponding figure for France was 12.8%, Italy 5.6%, the United Kingdom 29.4% and Spain 8% (Hardouvelis 2008: 88).

Unlike the situation with FDI, portfolio investment has played a key role both in the formation of the fiscal transactions balance and in the coverage of the current account deficit. Portfolio investment includes the liabilities of residents, that is, deposits by residents of other countries, primarily in shares and bonds issued abroad (capital inflow) and the claims, that is, the deposits, of residents of Greece in shares and bonds issued abroad (capital outflow). If debt claims are deducted from liabilities, a surplus of around €104 billion emerges in the GDP (Asimakopoulos et al. 2010: 428).

The most important source of financing was the deposits in bonds and Greek government treasury bills, amounting to €83.7 billion for the entirety of the 2000–2008 period, when inflows from shares came to €21.5 billion (Asimakopoulos et al. 2010: 435). This increase took the total sum of liabilities from €67.5 billion in 2000 to €208.9 billion in 2008, of which general government liabilities rose from €62.8 billion in 2000 to €191.9 billion in 2008 (Asimakopoulos et al. 2010: 437).

As a result "*this trend has impacted the current account deficit negatively, because interest payments on bonds held by residents of other countries are recorded as payments to the income account (a component of the balance of current accounts). In the period between 2000 and 2008 interest payments on bonds and treasury bills came to € 33 billion, of which about 3/5 were for the three-year period 2006–2008. The income account for Greece was therefore in deficit over this entire period, during which interest payments on Greek government securities held by foreigners were the main factor determining the amount and the evolution of the deficit in question. These interest payments, as a percentage of GDP, more than doubled in the period between 2000 and*

2008 and in 2008 amounted to 3.4% of GDP (referred to in Asimakopoulos et al. 2010: 439)".

As regards portfolio investment in shares listed on the Athens Stock Exchange, liabilities (capital inflows) from foreign investors' deposits increased by €26.6 billion in the 2000–2008 period, with corresponding outflows amounting to €5.1 billion, resulting in net increases in equity investments of €21.5 billion, covering 13.5% of the total current account deficit of the period in question (Asimakopoulos et al. 2010: 439).

Viewed overall, in the period between 2000 and 2008, the current account deficit came to €17.7 billion, corresponding to 9.1% of GDP. This is a very unfavourable development when one considers that in the 1980s it was no more than 1.1% and in the 1990s 2.7% (Giannitsis 2013: 173). Of the deficit, 65.8% was financed from a net inflow of funds for portfolio investment (52.5% in the form of bonds and treasury bills and 13.5% in shares), 14.7% from EU funds and 13.6% from other investments (mainly deposits and remittances by Greeks from abroad) (Asimakopoulos et al. 2010: 440). But this high level of borrowing led to an increasing income account deficit (from 1.1% of GDP in 1998 to 4.5% in 2008) owing to payments on interest, dividends and profits (Vlahou and Lambrinidis 2011: 235).

So the crisis has its origins in the early 1980s, when the country entered what was then the EEC. After that the trade balance gradually deteriorated and since the adoption of the euro as a national currency, things have got even worse. The result is that between 1981 and 2009, the total trade deficit with the EU countries was €254 billion (Bogiopoulos 2011: 361).

On the Question of Debt

The current account deficit was covered to a significant extent by the issue of bonds. Given the increase in the deficit of this balance as a percentage of GDP, this necessarily led to both a rise in debt and an increase in the interest paid. This was facilitated by the fact that joining the EMU enabled the Greek state to borrow at a lower interest rate and at the same time extend the repayment of loans over a longer period. The average time for

Table 2.10 Public debt as a percentage of GNP

Year	Public debt as a percentage of GNP
1970	17.9
1980	22.5
1990	71.7
1995	97.9
1996	100.3
1997	97.5
1998	95.4
1999	94.9
2000	104.4
2001	104.7
2002	102.6
2003	98.3
2004	99.8
2005	101.2
2006	107.5
2007	107.2
2008	112.9
2009	129.7

Source: Eurostat

repayment of debt increased from 1.6 years in 1994 to 10.5 years in 2005. At the same time, the average long-term nominal interest rate fell from 20.7% in 1994 to 3.6% in 2005 (Ioannidis 2013: 62). Consequently, on the one hand, there was a growing need for the Greek state to borrow and, on the other hand, very favourable conditions for borrowing.

But let take things one at a time, starting with the evolution of the relationship between public debt and GDP (Table 2.10).

It is obvious that there was a steep rise in indebtedness following the country's entry into the EEC, a broadly stable adjustment between 1995 and 2005, when the rate of growth in GDP was quite high, a significant increase between 2005 and 2008 and a sharp increase in 2009. Of course, the 22.5% increase (!) between 2007 and 2009 is *also* due to the fact that GDP fell 0.2% in 2008 and 3.1% in 2009.

That said, the figures in the following table show clearly how debt undergoes change in accordance with corresponding changes in GDP (Table 2.11).

It is noted that there is a continuous percentage increase in indebtedness, which, while negligible in the pre-EEC period, subsequently

Table 2.11 Debt change/GDP

Year	Debt change	Debt change/GDP
1976–1981	1.8%	38%
1981–1989	19.9%	77%
1989–1993	46.8%	154%
1993–2003	99.3%	109%
2003–2009	130.1%	161%

Source: Giannitsis (2013: 87)

Table 2.12 Interest payments as a percentage of GDP

Interest payments to GDP	2000	2001	2002	2003	2004	2005	2006	2007	2008	2009
Greece	7.4	6.5	5.6	5.0	4.8	4.6	4.6	4.8	5.1	5.1
Ireland	2.0	1.5	1.3	1.2	1.1	1.1	1.0	1.0	1.4	3.1
Portugal	2.9	2.9	2.8	2.7	2.6	2.4	2.7	3.0	3.1	3.0
Spain	3.2	3.0	2.7	2.4	2.0	1.8	1.6	1.6	1.6	1.9
Italy	6.4	6.3	5.7	5.2	4.8	4.7	4.6	4.9	5.1	4.4
Belgium	6.6	6.5	5.8	5.3	4.8	4.3	4.0	3.9	3.8	3.5
Germany	3.2	3.1	2.9	3.0	2.8	2.8	2.8	2.8	2.8	2.5
France	2.9	3.0	2.9	2.8	2.8	2.7	2.6	2.7	2.9	2.4
EU average	3.6	3.5	3.2	3.0	2.8	2.8	2.7	2.7	2.8	2.7
Eurozone average	3.9	3.8	3.5	3.3	3.1	3.0	2.9	3.0	3.0	2.8

Source: Varoufakis et al. (2011: 59)

increased, peaking in the EMU period. The same could be said for the relationship between change in indebtedness and GDP, with the exception of the years 1993 to 2003, due to the very high growth rates in GDP at that time. The causes of this large increase in debt in the early years of the new century, above and beyond the easy lending we have mentioned, could have to do with the increase in public spending in 2007–2009 for reasons that will be explained below. In summary, the key point was not the increase in indebtedness in absolute figures but its disproportionate increase in relation to growth in GDP, resulting in a high percentage of GDP going towards the repayment of debt (Table 2.12).

The conclusion is that there is a clear difference between the interest paid by Greece and that paid by both the EU and EMU countries. This not only reflects Greece's fiscal difficulties but also a distancing that will then be able to function as a trigger for confronting the crisis of confidence that will subsequently beset the Greek economy (see below). Only Italy and Belgium present a picture comparable to that of Greece but both these countries, unlike Greece, have a primary surplus, from which they are able to finance a part of the costs of paying interest.

The Question of the Public Deficit and the Role of Taxation

Before we move onto presentation of the public deficit and the contribution it has made to this taxation system that was being implemented in Greece, it is important to recapitulate what we have argued so far. According to the publicists of the dominant ideology, the whole problem is centred, on the one hand, on the "over-inflated" public sector that generates deficits and, on the other, on the low productivity of the Greek economy owing to increases in real wages, resulting in an increase in the current account deficit. At the same time, the existence of a significant public deficit led to a failure to cover the current account deficit, and things would have been different if there had been a primary surplus. These two deficits led to a rise in indebtedness, a prelude to bankruptcy. Without challenging some aspects of this argumentation, the position maintained here is entirely different. The real problem of Greece's capitalist economy cannot be centred either on the limited rise in salaries (which have remained the lowest after Portugal's in the EU15) or on the productivity of labour, which does not appear to have fallen in the period between 1995 and 2009, by comparison with the other 34 countries with which Greece has transactions. GDP fell due to the effects of the global crisis and mostly due to the intensity with which the low-productivity Greek economy experienced these effects.

The main problem has been that the lack of competitiveness of Greek capitalism due to the lack of technological modernization, in conjunction with the impact of the crisis in the monetary union, only served to exacerbate the inherent contradictions of the previously dominant strategy. Neither the borrowing nor the government deficit would have been a problem if GDP had not fallen so much in 2008 and 2009 and if there

Table 2.13 Evolution of the public deficit 2001–2009

Year	2001	2002	2003	2004	2005	2006	2007	2008	2009
Public revenue	40.9	40.3	39.0	38.1	39.0	39.2	40.8	40.7	38.2
Public expenditure	45.3	45.1	44.7	45.5	44.6	45.2	47.6	50.6	53.9
Public deficit	4.4	4.8	5.7	7.4	5.6	6.0	6.8	9.9	15.6
Public expenditure EU15	46.3	46.7	47.3	47.0	47.1	46.5	45.9	47.6	51.5
Primary public expenditure	38.8	39.5	39.8	40.7	39.9	40.5	42.8	45.6	48.7
Primary public expenditure EU15	42.8	43.5	44.3	44.1	44.3	43.9	43.2	44.7	48.8

Source: Melas (2013: 178) and Argeitis et al. (2011: 20)

had not been such an obvious prospect of continued decline in 2010 and 2011. The GDP fell because of the effects of the global crisis and above all because of the intensity with which it was experienced in the Greek economy, plagued as it was by an exceptionally low level of productivity.

So now let us see how the public deficit took shape between 2001 and 2009 (Table 2.13).

The first interpretation that could be offered is that there was indeed an increase in public spending between 2007 and 2009, while public revenue remained static, sending the public deficit off the rails. But this is only one aspect of the reality. There are a number of other parameters that need to be taken into account if we are to understand what is going on. The first parameter concerns the comparison between primary public expenditure and the corresponding EU15 public expenditure. Here it is observed that throughout the period, with the exception of 2008, Greek primary public expenditure fell short of the European figure. So the problem in relation to overall public expenditure has to do with the increased interest rates as a percentage of GDP paid by the Greek side and not some particular oversizing of the Greek state. In any case, it is only in the 2007–2009 period that Greek public spending is higher than the EU15 average. That said, the fact remains that the composition of public spending is important. The Argeitis, Dafermos and Nikolaidi study shows that between 1995 and 2009, primary public expenditures, on average, were in the vicinity of two to three units lower than those of the EU15. General expenditure was at 46.1%, as against the EU15 figure of 47.7%. At the same time, the proportion of socially related transfers in Greece came to only 35.4% of GDP, compared to 42.1% for the EU15. The reason for this is that Greece lags behind the EU15 in a number of areas: environment (0.5% vs 0.7%), housing infrastructure (0.4% compared with 1.0%), health (4.6% instead of 6.4%), culture and recreation (0.4% as against 1.1%) and social protection (16.5% vs 18.9%). In contrast, Greece clearly spends more on defence (2.9% rather than 1.6%) and on general public expenditure (11.0% as against 7.1%), but these figures also include the interest on the public debt (Argeitis et al. 2011: 22). These findings lead us to the conclusion that the main problem in the composition of public spending is not the overly large public sector, nor the excessive social expenditure, but the cost of borrowing and of armaments.

Having clarified that, there is another dimension to be highlighted, which has to do with the dimensions, structure and social identity of public revenue (Table 2.14).

The conclusion that can readily be drawn is that in Greece public revenue is clearly deficient if compared with the norm for the EU15, making them a contributory factor to the public deficit. But it is not enough just to say this. One must necessarily also examine the tax burden on the capital derived from income (interest, business profits, profits of freelance professionals) and on wealth. The existing data for the period between 2000 and 2005 indicate that the average for the EU15 is between 27.6% and 30.2%, with Greece lagging between 16.3% and 19.9% (Argeitis et al. 2011: 18). At the same time, the tax burden on large enterprises in Greece fell from 29.9% in 2000 to 18.6% in 2006, whereas the same year (2006) the corresponding tax rate in Spain was 53.3%, in France 31.4%, in Italy 27.1%, in England 27.7% and in the EU25 28.7%. The real tax on labour in 2000 was 34.5%; in 2006, it had reached 35.1%, whereas the same year in England, it was 25.8%, in France 41.9%, in Italy 42.5% and in Portugal 28.6%, with the EU25 average at 36.4%. The result is that real taxation on labour in Greece corresponds to the EU25 average, whereas real taxation on large enterprises is one-third less than in the EU25 (Institute of Labour—Greek General Confederation of Labour 2009: 93).[17] The result of the reduction in corporate income tax was that

[17] It is characteristic that the most powerful faction of Greek capital, the ship-owners, enjoy 60 tax breaks, with the result that they pay to the State just €12 million in taxes at a time when migrants pay a fee amounting to €50 million (Milios 2011). Specifically, under Law 27/1975 "on the taxation of ships", ship-owners' capital is exempt from any income tax in relation to the profits resulting from the

Table 2.14 Public revenue as a percentage of GNP 1995–2009

Year	1995	1996	1997	1998	1999	2000	2001	2002	2003	2004	2005	2006	2007	2008	2009
Greece	41.1	41.9	43.6	45.3	46.3	43.0	40.9	40.3	39.0	38.1	39.0	39.2	40.7	40.7	38.3
EU15	45.0	45.6	45.6	45.5	45.9	45.5	44.9	44.2	44.2	44.1	44.6	45.1	45.0	45.1	44.7

Source: Eurostat

taxes on profits accounted for only 28.7% of total revenue from income tax in 2010, down from 46% in 2004. In the 2004–2008 period, in particular, while profits increased by 35.2%, corporate tax revenue decreased by 1.3% (Ioannidis 2013: 62). In total, confirmed taxation as a percentage of the taxable income of all companies operating in Greece shows a decrease from 32.2% in 2002 to 21.2% in 2008. What is interesting is that this tendency is characteristic of all categories of company: SA companies decreased from 33.9% to 21.6%, limited liability companies from 34.8% to 23.8%, and partnerships and limited partnerships from 22.2% to 17.6% (Pelagidis and Mitsopoulos 2012: 298–299).

That said, there is the question of the relationship between direct and indirect taxes: throughout the period under consideration direct taxes in the EU15 remain between 12.6% and 14.1% and in Greece between 6.4% and 9.7% (Argeitis et al. 2011: 15). This is attributable to the clear difference in the ratio between direct and indirect taxes, which in the EU15 ranges from 0.98 to 1.08, whereas in Greece, the range is more limited: between 0.51 and 0.73 (Argeitis et al. 2011: 16).[18]

Above and beyond the institutional provisions aimed at lightening the burden on capital and transferring it onto the shoulders of workers, there is also an added dimension in the form of a problem that has to do with the operations of the State mechanism itself and its "inability" to collect taxes.

The figures in Table 2.15 show that between 2004 and 2009, there were wide divergences in all forms of taxation compared to the previous

---

operation of ships, from any taxation or surplus due to the sale of a ship, from the income tax on profits made by ship-owners engaged enterprises other than shipping. But the problem is not confined to ship-owners. Greek technical companies whose profit comes from overseas projects, foreign technical companies with profits in Greece, companies listed on the stock exchange that draw profit from the sale of shares and all NGOs are all fully exempt from paying taxes. Also, nearly zero taxes are paid by offshore companies: of the 16,580 active companies listed in Finance Ministry records, only 383 submitted tax returns in 2003, paying a total tax of €4.8 million. In 2009, there were 201 tax declarations and the tax they were called upon to pay was €3.4 million. Finally, companies using the so-called transfer pricing system are also included in the general under-taxation framework. A product is produced by a multinational subsidiary in a country with cheap labour costs and then resold in Greece, and not only in Greece, by the same multinational with offices in Greece, and at a price corresponding to Greek production costs. Thus a product that costs €5 is priced at €90 and sold for €100 and the company is taxed on the virtual profit of €10 and not on the actual profit of €95 (Charalambopoulos 2013).

[18] It is characteristic that in 2009 the proportion of indirect taxes in total taxation was 56.9%, with direct taxes comprising only 43.1% (Institute of Labour—Greek General Confederation of Labour 2009: 93).

Table 2.15 Divergence between actual figures and targeted figures in the budgets of the years 2000–2009 (millions of euros)

	2000–2003	2004–2009	2000–2003	2004–2009
	Average annual deviation	Average annual deviation	Overall deviation for the period	Overall deviation for the period
Direct taxes	550	−959	−202	−5751
Property taxes	7.6	−329	30	−1971
Taxes on legal persons	116	−524	464	−3143
Indirect taxes	−165[a]	−1711	−661	−10,267

Source: Zografakis and Spathis (2010: 24)
[a]The negative sign means less revenue than was budgeted

period (2000–2003). In our opinion, this is not a technical problem but an example of political vested interests seeking to create social alliances through tax evasion. It *also* involves petty bourgeois strata if we factor in the amount of indirect taxation that is not being collected.

Essentially it is a political stance towards tax evasion in accordance with which in 2009, 83% of self-employed/non-retired individuals (entrepreneurs, self-employed farmers) reported income below the tax-free ceiling of €10,500 and 47% declared zero income. In contrast, only 53% of employees and pensioners (who cannot evade tax because their income is taxed at source) declared an income below the tax-free ceiling and only 0.2% declared zero income.

We reach corresponding conclusions if we take also into account the VAT collection figures. It can be seen that in 2006, 7.70% of confirmed VAT was collected, 7.01% in 2007, 7.32% in 2008 and 7.58% in 2009 (Zisimopoulos and Economakis 2013: 30).

The social alliance can also be seen from the fact that although the self-employed comprised a larger proportion of the economically active population in Greece than in the EU15 (18.5% as against 11.3% in 2009), they paid around the same percentage of GDP for insurance contributions (1.8%) as the percentage paid by the self-employed in the EU17 (1.9%) (Giannitsis 2013: 79).

We can thus understand not only why there is a very large grey economy in Greece but also why it showed an upward trend in the early years of the new century (Table 2.16).

Table 2.16 Shadow economy as a percentage of GNP

	1996	1998	2000	2002	2003	2004	2005	2006
Greece	28.1	27.7	28.7	29.8	30.2	29.2	31.4	30.8
OECD	16.8	17.3	17.4	17.8	17.8	17.9	18.6	18.7

Source: Schneider et al. (2010: 25)

The first observation that might be made is that the shadow economy is a reality in the OECD countries *also*. If we examined the most detailed data, we could see that there is a shadow economy even in Switzerland and the United States (making up an average of 8.4% and 8.7%, respectively, of the overall economy in the period under examination). But the differences from country to country are significant, because the two lowest percentages are in the countries just mentioned, with the highest in Greece and Mexico (29.5% and 31.4%). So, and this is the second observation, Greece is very far from the average: It includes—over time—a very pronounced shadow economy. But most interesting of all is the fact that this percentage has risen even further in recent years, as a consequence, we may suppose, of the policies of "relaxation" of the tax collection mechanisms that have been pursued.

The general conclusion to be drawn from this section is that harsh class-motivated policies have unfolded around the public deficit and taxation in the first decade of the twenty-first century. One parameter of the situation is the attempt to "resolve" the problem of the competitiveness and profitability of Greek capitalism at the international level through the reduction in taxation on business profits, the perpetuation of high proportions of indirect taxation and the dysfunctionality of tax collection mechanisms. Correspondingly, the other dimension has been tolerance of tax evasion and tax avoidance by small entrepreneurial strata, resulting in reproduction of a social alliance, within the specific framework of the country's low competitiveness and the pressures generated by the EMU.

Of course this has brought in its train significant problems, because the creation of deficits through low revenue will lead to an increase in borrowing. Another factor has been high public spending due to interest on loan servicing, not to mention high military spending.

The Banking System

The Greek banking system expanded in the first decade of the twenty-first century. One of the factors contributing to this was the high Greek debt and the need for its management, the international trend for creating new banking products and also the particular Greek conditions that had paved the way for this expansion: low interest rates on lending by the European Central Bank (ECB), increased household and business needs for recourse to lending, but also the growth of the economy, which led to a more than doubling of deposits and repurchase agreements (repos) in financial institutions from €135 billion in 2001 to €280 billion in 2008. Household participation, despite its increase in absolute terms from €103 billion to €105 billion, fell from 76.3% of total deposits to 66.1%. Business participation increased from €23 billion to €42 billion but in relative terms decreased from 16.9% to 15%. The participation of the general government remained stable at around 2.9% and participation by euro area residents at 0.7%. On the other hand, a significant increase was recorded in participation by non-euro-area residents: from 3.7% to 15.4% (Institute of Labour—Greek General Confederation of Labour 2011: 93).

So, to conclude, there has been a shift by households and businesses in the direction of consumption, and on the other hand, a significant flow of money from abroad, either in the form of deposits or in the form of repos.

This is confirmed when we also take into account the funding of residents of Greece by monetary financial institutions in the same 2001–2008 period, when there was more than a doubling in absolute funding, from €120 billion to €286 billion. In 2001, the government generally received 38.3% of the funding but in 2008 this declined to 13%, falling even in absolute terms (from €46 billion to €37 billion). In 2001, firms received 42.5% of the total and by 2008, this rose to 46.3%. Private individuals and private non-profit institutions went from 19.4% to 40.9% (Institute of Labour—Greek General Confederation of Labour 2011: 110). Interestingly, while deposits and repos increased by 107% between 2001 and 2008, the level of funding increased by 138%, which helped increase the ratio of loans to deposits from 0.64 in 2002 to 1.07 in 2008. This is a development that in the medium term was very likely to cause significant problems, as indeed it did in the Greek banking system because deposits are included in the category of short-term demand, unlike grants that are medium or long term in character. In any case, in order for a banking system with such high indices to be sustainable, there must be steady growth in the economy, especially since the Tier1 index, which reflects availability of funds for grants, was very low between 2002 and 2008[19] (Drybetas and Kalogeridis 2014: 78–80; 85).

This enormous increase in funding was due to the country's entry into the EMU and the liberalization of the banking system, which has led to significant interest rate cuts due to intense competition. The single monetary policy was objectively more relaxed for Greece because of the difference in the rate of inflation, leading to lower real interest rates (Economou 2010: 8). Inflation in Greece in fact between 2000 and 2008 went from 2.9% to 4.2%, compared to 1.9% to 3.7% in the EU and 2.1% to 3.3% in the Eurozone (Varoufakis et al. 2011: 78). While short-term real interest rates in the 1990s had been around 5.4%, after 2000, they were close to 0%, recording even negative values at some points (Milios 2011).[20]

Greek banks, therefore, began borrowing at a low rate from abroad to fuel domestic consumption: Loans from credit institutions went from 19 billion in 2002 to 112 billion in 2009. Having borrowed at a low interest rate, Greek banks began to lend lavishly. The result was an explosive growth in lending to people in Greece (average for the 2001–2008 period was 25.6% of GDP for households) (Institute of Labour—Greek General Confederation of Labour 2011: 112). One important parameter was mortgage loans, which more than doubled between 2001 and 2008, starting at €15.5 billion and reaching €77.4 billion.[21] There was a similar

[19] Although it is assumed that this specific indicator should be higher than 10%, in 2002, the National Bank had a Tier1 index of 10.40, Alpha 9.90, Piraeus 11.00 and Eurobank 7.99, and in 2008, National Bank had 14.50, Alpha 7.80, Piraeus 8.00 and Eurobank 4.19.

[20] It is characteristic that in 2003 interest rates in Greece were at a level of 6.73%, as against the Eurozone average of 5.49% and the 2009 figure of 5.81% for Greece and 4.06% for the Eurozone.

[21] On the one hand, seeing the financial liquidity they had at their disposal as a result both of the increase in deposits and repos and of the reduction in ECB interest rates, banks began to hand out housing loans left, right and centre. As a result, real estate prices rose; banks provided yet more

more than quadrupling of consumer loans from €7.9 billion in 2001 to €36.4 billion in 2008 (Institute of Labour—Greek General Confederation of Labour 2011: 113). In 1998, mortgage loans in Greece amounted to 5.8% of GDP and in the Eurozone 24.2%. By 2009, they had reached the figure of 33.9% and in the Eurozone 39.5%. Correspondingly, consumer loans in Greece rose from 2.5% of GDP in 1998 to 16.5% in 2009 and in the Eurozone went from 6.6% to 15.6%. Loans to non-financial corporations went from 32.3% of GDP to 51.3% in 2008 (Toussaint 2017: 125). As a result, bank assets rose from €168 billion in 2002 to €402 billion in 2009 (Drybetas and Kalogeridis 2014: 74) and the ratio of bank assets to GDP went up from the 2002 figure of 1.12 to 2.00 in 2010, whereas in 1998, bank deposits were approximately twice as high as loans (Toussaint 2017: 125).

Initially this frenzy had a very positive impact on the profitability of Greek commercial banks and commercial banking groups, to the extent that they had profits higher, as a percentage of their assets, than those of the banks in the EU14 countries (excluding Luxembourg)[22]: The corresponding figures for 1998 are 0.8% for the Greek banks and 0.6% for the banks of the EU14, for 2001, 1% for Greece and 0.8% for the EU14 and for 2005, 0.9% for Greece and 0.7% for the EU14 (Pelagidis and Mitsopoulos 2010: 239). Return on equity in 2005 stood at 26%, as against the EU average of 17.4% (Toussaint 2017: 127) In absolute terms, the post-tax profits for Greek commercial banks rose from €1932 million in 2005 to €2028 million in 2006 and €2999 million in 2007 but after that started to fall: €662 million in 2008 and a loss of €354 million in 2009. Correspondingly, Greek commercial banking

loans on overpriced homes, with the house price index rising by 87.5% between 2000 and 2008 (Giannitsis and Zografakis 2018: 138) and the bubble expanded, as shown in Table 11.1 of the Appendix in Chap. 11. Interestingly, the dynamic generated around the ability to buy a home led to credit expansion greatly outpacing the rise in real estate prices. In Athens, in 2000, there was a 31.2% growth in mortgage loans, with real estate prices rising by only 11%; in 2003, the corresponding figures were 25% and 7%, in 2008, 12% and 3% (Pelagidis and Mitsopoulos 2010: 312). Regarding the real estate situation in non-Athens properties in 2000, the annual change in mortgage loans was 31.2% and real estate prices increased by 11%; in 2003, the corresponding figures were 25% and 7%, and for 2008, 12% and 3% (Pelagidis and Mitsopoulos 2010: 312).

[22] The task of strengthening the role of banks in increasing banking profitability was undertaken through the political decision to strengthen banking capital given the Greek government's agreement to have the public sector borrow from Greek banks at an interest rate of 5% at a time when those banks were borrowing from the ECB at 1% interest rate (Bogiopoulos 2011: 323).

groups showed profits after tax of €2480 million in 2005 and €2880 million in 2006, declining to €2590 in 2008, €700 million in 2009 and a loss of €897 million in the first nine months of 2010 (Institute of Labour—Greek General Confederation of Labour 2011: 124–125). Bank assets similarly fell, for the first time, from €402 billion in 2009 to €392 billion in 2010 (Drybetas and Kalogeridis 2014: 74).

An important role in the negative trajectory of Greek banks was played by the mushrooming of outstanding loan payments for first home purchases, which in 2008 reached a figure of €41.5 billion and involved 450,000 households (Giannitsis and Zografakis 2018: 140), with the percentage of non-performing loans rising from 5.6% in 2001 to 10.4% in 2010 (Drybetas and Kalogeridis 2014: 74). The heedless extravagance of the banks' lending policy is reflected in the fact that households' debt as a percentage of their disposable income jumped from 6.6% in 1995 to 70.6% in 2009, with mortgage loans going from 5.1% to 47.2% and consumer loans from 5.1% to 21.7% (Marselou and Basiakos 2013: 16). To all this, there should be added the parameter of the limited equity ratio, which in March 2009 came to just 6.2% of the bank's budget, as a result of the high level of distribution of profits to shareholders that had prevailed between 2005 and 2008 (Toussaint 2017: 131).

Even before being drawn into the maelstrom of the crisis, the Greek state in 2008 attempted to help the banks in three ways: (a) capital strengthening by banks by issuing preference shares in favour of the Greek government against bonds of equal value of up to €5 billion, (b) guarantees by the Greek state for lending to, or refinancing of, the banks to issue new medium- and long-term loans to be concluded and securities to be financed to a total amount of up to €85 billion, and (c) their disposal to banking institutions, against provision of adequate insurance (Tsakloglou et al. 2016: 108).

The Coming of the Crisis

What we have said about the competitiveness problem of the Greece's capitalist economy has been aggravated by the emergence of the crisis globally and in Europe. Specifically this means that from as early as 2005, numerous indicators began to deteriorate (tourism, shipping revenue, community subsidies) and, shortly afterwards, banking profitability started to decline. This would come as a result of the reduction in profits as a proportion of the loans granted, interruption of the flow of private external financing, increase in the number of non-performing loans, a fall in the value of real estate (Toussaint 2017: 131–132), parameters that would lead to a contraction in loan advances: The annual change in bank financing for local businesses would be as follows—2007 (December) 25.7%, 2008 (December) 21.4%, 2009: 5.1% and 2010: 1.1%—and the corresponding bank financing for housing was 2007 (December): 21.9%, 2008 (December): 11.5%, 2009: 3.7%, 2010: −0.3%—resulting in a drop in private consumption (2007: 3.6%, 2008: 4.0%, 2009: −1.3%, 2010: −3.6%) and a consequent significant reduction in corporate profitability (return on capital fell from 115% in 2007 to 92% in 2009) (Institute of Labour—Greek General Confederation of Labour 2011: 146). Against this background and on the basis of what was said about the attempt to restore financial profitability through a shift to risk premiums (country default spreads, CDS), in the autumn of 2009, Greece appeared to be the country in the greatest danger of bankruptcy. This was because the government deficit and government debt rose as a percentage of GDP due to a decline in the latter as a result of a combination of domestic and external crises. It is worth noting that in addition to the structural problems already mentioned as important but not decisive, a role was also played by the poor schedule, which within a short time required repayment of a large part of the Greek debt: In 2009, total debt had an average remaining life of 7.74 years, which means sooner than what in 2008 was 8.42 years. Of this debt, 12.2% was short term and 39.7% medium term (one to five years), with the result that the whole 2010–2014 period appears particularly difficult, because the overall debt burden for 2010 alone came to €53,200 million (Kotios and Koutoulakis 2014: 399). One important factor in this scenario was the continuing deterioration in the banking sector. At the end of 2009, Greek banks had to repay €78 billion in short-term debt to foreign banks, and if we include other foreign financial institutions lending to Greece, the arrears amounted to €112 billion. Greek banks were able, exceptionally, to continue to repay external creditors thanks to a credit facility from the ECB and the Central Bank of

Greece. The loans to Greek banks from the ECB ranged between 40 billion and 55 billion. This was equivalent to between 6% and 8% of this ECB credit facility, whereas Greek banks accounted for only about 2% of Eurozone banking assets. In the autumn of 2009, ECB executives implied that they were planning to terminate this credit facility. This caused very serious concerns on the part of the foreign creditors of Greek banks and also of the Greek bankers themselves. If Greek banks were unable to continue to repay their debts to foreign banks, there was a risk of a serious crisis (Toussaint 2017: 136–137).

In this context, the yield of Greek bonds started to rise rapidly after November 2009. Whereas in October of the same year, Greek credit default swaps stood at 130 basis points (i.e. a holder of a Greek five-year bond valued at €1 million had to pay an annual premium of €130,000 for those five years), in the first half of 2010, they averaged 800 basis points, with some exceeding 1000 basis points (Varoufakis et al. 2011: 42). For ten-year bonds, the yield rose rapidly from 4.84% in November 2009 to 7.97% in May 2010. This was because investors were reluctant to have Greek bonds in their portfolios: They were regarded as being at high risk of default. This stance was encouraged by the downgrading of the country's credit rating by rating agencies after October 2009 (Arghitis et al. 2011: 42–43). The conclusion is that there was a dialectical relationship between a weak competitive model of accumulation that intensified the contradictions due to the country's participation in the EMU and the exploitation of the need for part of the international capital that was required for rapid profitability and recovery from the preceding situation.

Under other conditions, it is likely that the contradictions would have unfolded at a slower pace. Yet this does not mean that they could have been indefinitely suspended. To put it somewhat differently, the banks' problem was not the decisive factor in the Greek crisis, as some writers like to argue (Toussaint 2017: 137), but a consequence of the weak competitiveness of Greek capitalism. Under the threat of bankruptcy, it is likely that the Papandreou government artificially inflated the public deficit[23] so as to justify foreign financial assistance and the introduction

[23] According to the Truth Committee on Public Debt, which was established and operated by the SYRIZA-ANEL government from January 2015 to August 2015, there was an explosion in public

of monetary controls aimed at creating a framework for support of the most powerful capitalist interests in the country, with the assistance of the banks.

The European elites, on their part, did not want to have a Western capitalist country on the brink of bankruptcy for the following reasons: (a) Eurozone banking institutions in Greece were significantly exposed, to the amount of €186.5 billion, of which €37.6 billion involved German banks and €82.2 billion involved French banks (Katsikas 2017: 254);[24] (b) Foreign investors also held 72.5% of Greek government bonds and Treasury bills, to a value of about €201 billion (Katsikas 2017: 261); (c) There was significant penetration of the Greek banking system by French banks, as a result of the frantic growth recently experienced by the former. In 2004, Société Générale purchased the bulk of the capital of Greece's General Bank, and in 2006, Crédit Agricole bought out Emporiki Bank (Toussaint 2017: 127); (d) The Greek banks largely controlled the banking system of two other European countries: Romania and Bulgaria;[25] (e) The bankruptcy of a country in the euro area would lead to great turmoil in the financial markets, depressing the value of the common cur-

---

deficit in 2009, with the inclusion of a range of unapproved hospital expenditures, resulting in a 2.3% increase in public indebtedness. Through similar practices (conversion of public sector expenditures into public debt), public debt was raised by 7.8% (Truth Committee on Public Debt 2015: 18). These differences cannot justify the fall in all the aforementioned economic indicators. They merely highlight the determination of the government of the time to implement the Memorandum measures.

[24] By December 2010, the initial amount had already been reduced by 42% (French banks €56.7 billion, German banks €34 billion, American banks €7.3 billion) (Bogiopoulos 2011: 253–254). This happened because through the measures for the first Memorandum, they were given time to rid themselves of a high proportion of the Greek debt, something that subsequently intensified even further when in December 2011 foreign banks' exposure to Greek debt had been reduced to €35 billion. The final result was that by the 2012 elections, they had been almost totally relieved of the Greek debt.

[25] In total, in the period between 2000 and 2009, the National Bank of Greece had foreign investments in the order of $6.8 billion (in Bulgaria, Romania, Turkey, Serbia and Montenegro, and Egypt), and Eurobank €1.4 billion (in Bulgaria, Romania, Turkey, Serbia and Montenegro, Cyprus and the Netherlands), Bank of Piraeus €524 million (Bulgaria, Romania, Serbia and Montenegro, Egypt, Ukraine, the United States) and Alpha €385 (Romania, and Serbia and Montenegro) (Bitzenis and Vlachos 2011: 16). The problem seemed very short term and so Moody's downgraded nine Greek banks in May 2010; the Bulgarian affiliate of the National Bank of Greece (NBG), United Bulgarian Bank, had its credit rating cut by S&P in April 2010, and Fitch downgraded the affiliates of the National Bank of Greece (NBG) and EFG Eurobank in Romania and Bulgaria in late February 2010 (United Nations 2010: 54).

rency and also propagating elements of crisis in an international economy that had been attempting to recover from the effects of the property bubble.[26] This, in any case, is why the International Monetary Fund (IMF) agreed to participate despite the objections being raised inside the organization[27] about the sustainability of the Greek debt; (f) It was an opportunity to experiment with a new model of capitalist accumulation, whose generalized implementation would be conducive to a recovery in overall profit rates.

In this sense, before we embark on a presentation of the contents of the Memorandum packages, it may be worthwhile to focus on the strategic content of these choices. The packages of economic measures adopted will have a threefold function: to release segments of European capital, to prevent the crisis from recurring at the European level and to serve as a compass for the new form that capitalism "will have to" take, and in this the Greek social formation will comprise a field of social experimentation.

The aim is to achieve a massive reduction of the large mass of the population, a contraction of the non-monopoly sectors of capital, a reduction of the recently emerged petty-bourgeois strata to the status of wage labour and a form of acute state authoritarianism that would drastically shrink any margins for social resistance. The dominated strata will live in an atmosphere of "lowered expectations". The desideratum will be

[26] In the event that Greece fails to serve its loan instalments, it would be very likely that the various investors would stop lending to Portugal, Spain and Italy, so the governments of these countries could not refinance their debts, which cumulatively came to €1.76 trillion, with the result that the three largest French banks, which were the main lenders, were facing the risk of losing 19% of their assets, when a loss in the order of 3% would be enough to render them insolvent. The sequel would have been for the French State to have borrowed six times its incoming revenue from taxes in order to cover the shortfall of these three banks. But then interest rates on the French public debt (€1.29 trillion) would have gone through the roof, rendering the debt unserviceable and rapidly spreading the contagion to the rest of the Eurozone economy (Varoufakis 2017: 30–31).

[27] As illustrated by the minutes of the IMF board meeting of 9/5/2010, the main concern of the powerful Western States was to disengage German and French banks from the Greek debt. The United States was thinking about its own exposure, to the tune of $3 trillion in European banks. Serious objections had been expressed at that time by representatives of Brazil, India, Argentina, Canada, Russia, even Switzerland (!), who could not comprehend why the question of rescheduling the debt was not tabled for discussion, while they considered it impossible for such a heavy programme to be successful, see the relevant article by Thomas Catan in the *Wall Street Journal* of 7/10/2013.

not for a person to have permanent employment with a respectable income but simply to have work, irrespective of how many hours he/she works and for what payment.

At the level of a power coalition, changing the pattern of accumulation means expelling or downgrading the non-monopoly factions as part of the clearing operations of the crisis. There is a corresponding aspiration to reinforce the surviving monopoly sectors. Extraneous capital (foreign but also shipping capital)[28] which will arrive to establish itself in the country is also implicated. Given that large volumes of foreign capital are expected to be invested because of the "opportunities" that will be created, it can be predicted that the relationship between endogenous and exogenous capital will be overturned. At the same time, the petty bourgeois classes will reduce their role as class supports of the dominant social bloc. This is because the traditional petty bourgeoisie will undergo contraction owing to the strengthening of the monopolies. The new petty bourgeoisie will polarize towards the working class given that it will have been largely transformed into a wage-earning stratum, its income will have been reduced and its role in a monopolized enterprise will have become ever more menial in character. This will be of momentous significance for Greek society, which traditionally has been characterized by a greater presence of petty bourgeois strata than other Western societies (see Chap. 6). This Greek peculiarity is due to the existence of a large farming population, the small property/family character of many light industrial and commercial enterprises (resulting from the need of the defeated side in the civil war to find a livelihood)[29] and the resort to real estate ownership as a secure form of investment in a country with a stormy political life.

Following Greece's accession to the EEC, the Common Agricultural Policy (CAP) led to a dramatic contraction of Greek agriculture. And still, the remaining factions of the "middle classes", which had been inflated in the 1980s, had to face further cutbacks. This was only partially

[28] Greek ship-owners to a significant extent either have their headquarters in London or are, for tax reasons, registered elsewhere rather than in Greece.

[29] Citizens who were not regarded as belonging to the winning conservative side were banned from appointment to the public sector and faced many difficulties in finding a job in the private sector as well. This prompted many of them to turn to self-employment.

achieved through the neo-liberal policies of the last 20 years. More drastic policies were required, and so the politics of Memoranda was implemented.

All the above encourage regroupment both in the form of social alliances and in the content of bourgeois hegemony and the degree of social consensus secured. The new social alliance embraces primarily bourgeois strata and, in order to be able to lead, needs a new project, whose orientation will not necessarily be positive. One basic structural component underlying the social consensus supporting capitalism was belief in change for the better and the expectation of upward social mobility. All of this now changes to limit itself to the horizon of minimal expectations.

This should not lead us to postulate conspiracies by the elites. Some time will be required for them to perceive that the situation represents both danger and opportunity for them: danger that the crisis will be unmanageable, with uncontrolled consequences portending an uncertain future; opportunity for a great amount of wealth to be appropriated from the popular strata, a conservative restructuring of labour relations, along with liquidation of non-competitive capital. On the other hand, foreign capital and the imperialist centres, apart from their short-term risk of losing the capital invested in Greek bonds, saw the capacity to effect further strategic transformations, namely the utilization of an advanced capitalist formation as an "experimental" terrain for structural transformation of the social relation of forces with a view to implementing a new model in addition to purchasing Greek public property (airports, harbours, public enterprises) at bargain basement prices coupled with FDI in the near future of a very lucrative regulatory framework.

References

Argeitis G. and M. Nikolaidi, 2014, *Economic crisis and productive restructuring in Greece: the role of manufacturing industry*, Athens: Institute of Labour—Greek General Confederation of Labour (in Greek).

Argeitis G., G. Dafermos and M. Nikolaidi, 2011, *The public debt crisis in Greece. Causes and prospects*, Athens: Institute of Labour—Greek General Confederation of Labour (in Greek).

Asimakopoulos I, A. Karapappas, S. Brisimis, F. Symigiannis and N. Tsaveas, 2010, "Funding the current account balance: structure, developments and policy", in Economou G., I. Sambethai and G. Symigiannis (eds.) in *Greece's Current Account Balance: Causes of imbalance and policy proposals*, Athens: Bank of Greece, pp. 427–442 (in Greek).

Athanasoglou P., E. Georgiou and K. Bakinezou, 2010, "The Greek economy's export performance: the effect of competitiveness and of merchandises' composition", in Economou G., I. Sambethai and G. Symigiannis (eds.) *Greece's current account balance: causes of imbalance and policy proposals*, Athens: Bank of Greece, pp. 163–204 (in Greek).

Bilias F., 2014, *Seeking an alternative productive model for Greek agricultural production*, mimeo (in Greek).

Bitzenis A. and V. Vlachos, 2011, "Outward FDI from Greece and its policy context", *Columbia FDI Profiles*, pp. 1–20.

Bogiopoulos N., 2011, *'It's capitalism, stupid.' The culprits for the crisis and the 'debt' that will bring them down. A polite answer to the praetorians of the MEMORANDA*, Athens: Livanis (in Greek).

Charalambopoulos L., 2013, "Tax robbery and tax exemption: the fleecing of the weak and the 'I won't pay' of the strong", *Unfollow* vol. 13, http://unfollow.com.gr/print-edition/forolehlasia/, accessed on 31/1/18 (in Greek).

Dafermos G. and C. Papatheodorou, 2011, *The paradox of social policy in Greece: why has the increased expenditure on social protection not reduced poverty?*, Institute of Labour—Greek General Confederation of Labour, pp. 1–6 (in Greek).

Drybetas E. and N. Kalogeridis, 2014, "The dynamics and the role of the banking system", in Roukounas S. and P. Sklias (eds.) *Greek political economy 2000–2010: from the EMU to the support mechanism*, Athens: Livanis, pp. 66–95 (in Greek).

Economakis G., M. Markaki and G. Androulakis, 2014, "Extraversion and crisis of the Greek economy: a study", *Bulletin of Political Economy* vol. 8 no 2, pp. 175–204.

Economakis G., M. Markaki and A. Anastasiadis, 2015, "Structural analysis of the Greek economy", *Review of the Radical Political Economics* vol. 47 no 3, pp. 424–445.

Economou G., 2010, "Current account balance: conclusions from the analysis and policy proposals", in Economou G., I. Sambethai and G. Symigiannis (eds.) *Greece's current account balance: causes of imbalance and policy proposals*, Athens: Bank of Greece, pp. 3–74 (in Greek).

Fotopoulos T., 2010, *Greece as protectorate of the supranational elite. The need for immediate exit from the EU and a self-sufficient economy*, Athens: Gordios (in Greek).

Giannitsis T., S. Zografakis, I. Kastelli and D. Mavri, 2009, *Competitiveness and technology in Greece*, Athens: Papazisis (in Greek).

Giannitsis T. and S. Zografakis, 2018, *Crisis management in Greece*, IMK Studies 58-2018, IMK at the Hans Boeckler Foundation, Macroeconomic Policy Institute.

Giannitsis T., 2013, *Greece in crisis*, Athens: Polis (in Greek).

Hardouvelis G., 2008, "Macroeconomic management and the need for structural reforms following entry into the monetary union", in Giannitsis T. (ed.) *Greek economy: crucial questions of economic policy*, Athens: Alpha Bank Historical Archive, pp. 77–116 (in Greek).

Iliou I., 1962, *The truth about the common market*, Athens (in Greek).

Institute of Labour—Greek General Confederation of Labour, 2009, *The Greek economy and employment. Annual report 2009*, Athens: Institute of Labour—Greek General Confederation of Labour (in Greek).

Institute of Labour—Greek General Confederation of Labour, 2010, *The Greek economy and employment. Annual report 2010*, Athens: Institute of Labour—Greek General Confederation of Labour (in Greek).

Institute of Labour—Greek General Confederation of Labour, 2011, *The Greek economy and employment. Annual report 2011*, Athens: Institute of Labour—Greek General Confederation of Labour (in Greek).

Institute of Labour—Greek General Confederation of Labour, 2013, *The Greek economy and employment. Annual report 2013*, Athens: Institute of Labour—Greek General Confederation of Labour (in Greek).

Institute of Labour—Greek General Confederation of Labour, 2014, *The Greek economy and employment. Annual report 2014*, Athens: Institute of Labour—Greek General Confederation of Labour (in Greek).

Institute of Labour—Greek General Confederation of Labour, 2016, *The Greek economy and employment. Annual report 2016*, Athens: Institute of Labour—Greek General Confederation of Labour (in Greek).

Ioakeimoglou I., 2011, *Labour cost, profit margins and competitiveness in Greece 1995–2009*, Athens: Institute of Labour—Greek General Confederation of Labour (in Greek).

Ioannidis G., 2013, "The peculiar distributional character of the Greek taxation system (1995–2008) and the necessary reform which never happened", *Synchrona Themata* vol. 10, pp. 61–68 (in Greek).

Kapaktsis A., 2012, *The 'Greek problem', origin, development, outcome*, Thessaloniki: iWrite (in Greek).

Katsikas D., 2017, "Is it true that that way of handling the Greek crisis was dictated by the need for saving European banks?", in Katsikas D., K. Filinis and M. Anastasatou (eds.) *Understanding the Greek crisis. Answers to crucial questions on the state, the economy and Europe*, Athens: Papazisis, pp. 249–272 (in Greek).

Klouri A. and A. Karapappas, 2010, "The tourist industry", in Economou G., I. Sambethai and G. Symigiannis (eds.) *Greece's current account balance: causes of imbalance and policy proposals*, Athens: Bank of Greece, pp. 205–220 (in Greek).

Kotios A. and E. Koutoulakis, 2014, "Economic policy and the consequences for access to international borrowing", in Roukounas S. and P. Sklias (eds.) *Greek political economy 2000–2010: from the EMU to the support mechanism*, Athens: Livanis, pp. 384–414 (in Greek).

Labrianidis L. and N. Vogiatzis, 2013, "The mutually reinforcing relation between international migration of highly educated labour force and economic crisis: the case of Greece", *Southeast European and Black Sea Studies* vol. 13, no 4, pp. 525–551.

Laskos C. and E. Tsakalotos, 2012, *22 Things they tell us about the Greek crisis that are not true*, Athens: kapsimi (in Greek).

Lykos M., 2012, "Research and technology in the Greek regions", in Maraveyas N. (ed.) *Exit from the crisis*, Athens: Themelio, pp. 146–185 (in Greek).

Manassaki A. and E. Koltsida, 2010, "The contribution of transfers from the EU to the balance of payments and economic development", in Economou G., I. Sambethai and G. Symigiannis (eds.) *Greece's current account balance: causes of imbalance and policy proposals*, Athens: Bank of Greece, pp. 235–260 (in Greek).

Manassaki A., C. Kaiforis and M. Vassardanis, 2010, "The international competitiveness and the Current Account Balance of Greece", in G. Economou, I. Sambethai and G. Symigiannis (eds.) *Greece's Current Account Balance: Causes of Imbalance and Policy Proposals*, Athens: Bank of Greece, pp. 77–130 (in Greek).

Maniatis T., 2011, "The fiscal crisis and the social wage in Greece", in Vlahou A., N. Theocharakis and D. Mylonakis (eds.) *Economic crisis and Greece*, Athens: Gutenberg, pp. 206–226 (in Greek).

Marselou A. and G. Basiakos, 2013, *Over-indebted households and Greek economy*, Athens: Institute of Labour—Greek General Confederation of Labour (in Greek).

McKinsey and Company, 2011, Greece 10 years ahead. Defining the new growth model for Greece, http://www.sev.org.gr/Uploads/pdf/Greece_10_Years_Ahead_Executive_summary_Greek_version_small.pdf, accessed on 29/1/13 (in Greek).

Melas K., 2009, *Befuddled Europe*, Athens: Exantas (in Greek).

Melas K., 2013, *Small lessons in Greek economy. Peculiarities. The road to the memorandum. Hubris and nemesis*, Athens: Patakis (in Greek).

Milios, 2011, "The Greek crisis as a version of the global economic crisis and the crisis of the European Monetary System" http://www.rednotebook.gr/details.php?id=2075, accessed on 7/2/2014 (in Greek).

Nikolaidis E., 2005, "The agricultural sector in Greece. A contribution to highlighting its true dimensions", in Argeitis G. (ed.) *Economic changes and social conflicts in Greece. The challenges at the beginning of the 21st century*, Athens: Gutenberg, pp. 87–125 (in Greek).

OECD, 2011, "Government at a glance 2011" http://www.oecd-ilibrary.org/docserver/download/4211011ec027.pdf?expires=1391032406&id=id&accname=guest&checksum=754DE0EB3673B1F2D74C139C1D4CE150, accessed on 29/1/2014.

OECD, 2014, "Social expenditure update" https://www.oecd.org/els/soc/OECD2014-SocialExpenditure_Update19Nov_Rev.pdf, accessed on 18/2/2018.

Panagiotou S. and Z. Bragoudakis, 2010, "Marine transport—seagoing shipping", in Economou G., I. Sambethai and G. Symigiannis (eds.) *Greece's current account balance: causes of imbalance and policy proposals*, Athens: Bank of Greece, pp. 221–234 (in Greek).

Pelagidis T. and M. Mitsopoulos, 2010, *The moment of the turn for the Greek economy. How progressive pragmatism can place it once more on a developmental course*, Athens: Papazisis (in Greek).

Pelagidis T. and M. Mitsopoulos, 2012, *Understanding the crisis in Greece*, Athens: Psychogios (in Greek).

Petropoulos D., D. Fatouros, G. Kyriazopoulos and D. Paschalidis, 2010, "Long-term development of the dimensions of external trade in agricultural products in Greece in the 1994–2008 period", in *Proceedings of the Hellenic conference on administration and economy*, Kavalla 4–6 June, pp. 320–332 (in Greek).

Sakellaropoulos S., 2013, "Organization of state power in the Post-Junta period. A benign break in the capitalist continuity", *Ektos Grammis* vol. 34, pp. 39–43 (in Greek).

Schneider F., A. Buehn and C. Montenegro, 2010, "Shadow economies all over the world: new estimates for 162 Countries from 1999 to 2007" http://www.econ.jku.at/members/Schneider/files/publications/LatestResearch2010/SHADOWECONOMIES_June8_2010_FinalVersion.pdf, accessed on 8/2/2014.

Stasinopoulos G., 2005, "Entrepreneurship: the deficient developmental parameter in the Greek economy", in Argeitis G. (ed.) *Economic changes and social conflicts in Greece. The challenges at the beginning of the 21st century*, Athens: Gutenberg, pp. 127–168 (in Greek).

Toussaint E., 2017, *The public debt. Its history and importance in today's crisis*, Athens: Red Marks (in Greek).

Truth Committee on Public Debt, 2015, *Preliminary report*, Athens: Greek Parliament.

Tsakloglou et al., 2016, *Map for exit from the crisis. A new productive model for Greece*, Athens: Dianeosis (in Greek).

Tsiboukakis I., 2012, "The development of agricultural production in Greece", *Kommounistiki Epitheorisi* no. 6, http://www.komep.gr/2012-teyxos-6/h-ekseliksh-ths-agrotikhs-paragoghs-sthn-ellada, accessed on 17/2/2019 (in Greek).

United Nations, 2010, *World investment report. Investing a low carbon economy*, New York and Geneva.

Varoufakis Y., T. Patokos, L. Tserkezis and C. Koutsopetros, 2011, *The economic crisis in Greece and Europe in 2011*, Athens: Institute of Labour—Greek General Confederation of Labour (in Greek).

Varoufakis Y., 2017, *Adults in the room. My battle with Europe's deep establishment*, ebook: Farrar Straus and Giroux.

Vlahou A. and G. Lambrinidis, 2011, "Crisis and uneven development in the context of the EMU: The External Trade Balance and the international competitiveness of the Greek Economy", in Vlahou A., N. Theocharakis and D. Mylonakis (eds.) *Economic crisis and Greece*, Athens: Gutenberg, pp. 229–255 (in Greek).

Zisimopoulos G. and G. Economakis, 2013, "Labour relations in Greece. The impact of restructuring of the public sector", *Theseis* vol. 122, pp. 13–36 (in Greek).

Zografakis S. and P. Spathis, 2010, "Economic crisis and Greek economy: the end of budget gaps and the consequences", in Bank of Greece (ed.) *The Greek labour market: characteristics, developments and challenges*, Athens, pp. 13–42 (in Greek).

3

Addressing the Crisis Through Support Packages and Memoranda

As mentioned in the previous chapter, since autumn 2009 it has gradually become clear that Greece is entering a financially difficult period, resulting in the emergence of speculative practices against the possibility of Greek bankruptcy. This trend became more pronounced after Greece's successive downgrades—on December 8, 2009 by Fitch, on December 16, 2009 by Standard and Poor and on December 23, 2009 by Moody. From early 2010 onwards, there was a continually growing trend towards the development of spreads, with the result that ten-year bonds from 300 points had gone to more than 1000 by the beginning of April.

Attempting to deal with the situation, on February 9, 2010 the Papandreou government[1] announced measures for the public sector that included wage freezes, 10% cuts to allowances and overtime, and travel cuts. These were obviously measures of limited scope which affected only the public sector.

But the spreads continued to widen, which in conjunction with the gradual consolidation of the idea that opportunities for profoundly con-

[1] The PASOK government under the prime ministership of George Papandreou came to office after winning the 2009 elections with key slogan that "the money is there" for implementation of a more progressive social state.

S. Sakellaropoulos, *Greece's (un) Competitive Capitalism and the Economic Crisis*,
https://doi.org/10.1007/978-3-030-14319-0_3

servative changes had been created in Greek society, motivated the adoption of a new package of measures. Such measures commenced on March 3, 2010 consisting in a 30% reduction in Christmas, Easter and Holiday bonuses for public sector workers combined with a 12% reduction in all allowances for civil servants. At the same time salaries in the public enterprises (DEKO) and the broader public sector declined by 7%, public employment having been suspended in 2010 and the principle of one recruitment for five departures for retirement established, excepting in the sectors of health, education and security. A 30% reduction was announced in staff recruitment, on indefinite and fixed-term contracts, in the public sector. Beyond that, value-added tax (VAT) on various product categories was increased from 4.5% to 5%, from 9% to 10% and from 19% to 21%. So, what we have is intensification of austerity measures in the public sector, in both the narrower and wider sense, and an increase in indirect taxation and cost of living indicators.

Notwithstanding these measures, spreads continued to widen, and it was at this time that the government resorted to the European Union, the European Central Bank and the International Monetary Fund, requesting a loan totalling 110 billion euros, basically in order to service the public debt but also to save the banks (see below). Of course, for the request to be approved, Greece was required to accept a number of painful economic measures. The application was announced on April 23, 2010 and some of the measures that had been agreed with the lenders were made public on May 2, with others programmed to be adopted through legislation in 2010. These measures as a whole were to comprise the framework for the first Memorandum, marking a conspicuous break from the two previous packages of measures. The 13th and 14th salaries of civil servants were replaced by a single allowance totalling 1000 euros, and the allowance was abolished for those who earned more than 3000 euros per month. The 13th and 14th pensions were also replaced by a total allowance of 800 euros payable only to those with a pension of up to 2500 euros per month. Public servants' allowances were further reduced by 8%. A 3% reduction was imposed on people working for public enterprises (DEKO) and not receiving allowances. VAT increased in all three product categories: in the first from 5% to 6.5%, in the second from 10% to 11% and starting from January 1, 2011 to 13%, and in the third from 21% to 23%.

In terms of labour relations, there was a provision for a reduction of up to 75% in the warning time for regular termination of contracts, which led to reduction of up to 18 salaries in compensation for long-term workers. At the same time, an unlimited increase in instalments for compensation payments was introduced, along with a reduction in the amount of each instalment. Additionally, the ceiling for layoffs was raised by 50% for businesses employing up to 150 employees and by 150% for larger businesses (Kouzis 2011a: 38–39). The possibility was established of recruiting newcomers into the 18–24 labour market, with payment of up to 84% of the minimum wage plus coverage of insurance contributions by the Hellenic Manpower Employment Organization (OAED). A special apprenticeship contract for young people aged 15–18 was set up, entitling them to 70% of the minimum wage. The remit of arbitration decisions was limited to the issue of basic salary. As regards social insurance policy, the provision was to increase the women's retirement age to 65 years in the public sector.

So, what we observe is on the one hand a deterioration in the wages situation for employees in public sector and workers in public enterprises and organizations (DEKO), an increase in indirect taxation, and on the other hand targeting of private sector workers through raising the ceiling on limits to redundancies, reduction of the minimum wage, changes to the pension system and abrogation of a range of arbitration functions. This favours employers, who can opt for regulation of labour issues at the individual level (bonuses, institutional framework of labour relations), because once there is no mandatory framework the arbitration mechanism will not ensure regulation at a collective level (Kazakos 2011: 28). In addition abolishing surcharges for overtime and perpetuating low pay for part-time work contributes to further growth of part-time employment (Kouzis 2011a: 39).

The impasse of the implemented economic policy (to be discussed in the next chapter) would lead to a new package of measures, the fourth in a row, voted on June 29, 2011, and called the "Mid-term Financial Strategy Framework 2012–2015". In the public sector exemptions to the 1:5 ratio between recruitment and retirement were abolished; a 15% reduction on the levels of 2010 in public sector recruitment, on fixed-term work contracts, was announced; a 10% pay cut was imposed on employees of companies and public bodies who were being paid more than 1800 euros per month. In addition, working hours in the public sector were increased from 37.5 to 40 hours per week. Taxation measures included adoption of a change in the tax scale, with additional burdens for those reporting an income over 8000 euros. VAT was increased on products and catering services. As regards direct taxation, a graduated residential tax employing objective criteria was introduced, an annual fee for self-employed professionals and a special solidarity levy for all taxpayers, amounting to between 1% and 4% of their total income. For pensioners the level of tax withheld from pensions was increased from 4%–10% to 6%–14% for pensions over 1450 euros, and a special contribution imposed for beneficiaries from supplementary insurance. As for labour relations, a labour reserve measure was adopted for workers in public entities that were to be abolished, for new appointees without professional experience provision was made for remuneration 20% less than that stipulated by the National Collective agreement, waiving any limitations on the use of subcontracted labour. The maximum time for making an employee available on loan was extended from 18 to 36 months and this form of employment was introduced into the public sector. The permissible time for utilization of alternate labour (four-day working week, three-day working week) was extended from six months to nine months per year. Extra pay for part-time labour in case of overtime and in case of employment at less than 20 hours per week was abolished and the duration of fixed-term contracts increased from two to three years.

From all this it emerges that on this occasion the objective was to increase overall taxation, place a burden on freelancers and institute significant changes in labour relations in the private sector. This meant that the attack from capital was becoming generalized, targeting not only civil servants, pensioners and private sector employees but also the self-employed.

But very soon it was concluded that even these measures were not sufficient and by the end of the summer it had become clear that the Greek economy was not meeting the targets set in the agreements with the lenders. Thus, in early September 2011, a new package of measures was announced, the fifth, including the introduction of a labour reserve scheme in the public sector, paying 60% of the basic salary for redundant staff, extending the 1:5 ratio for recruitment and retirement in the public sector until 2015 (and 1:10 especially for 2011), limiting recruitment on fixed-term contracts to 50% of appointments for 2011 and to 10% for the period 2012–2015. Above and beyond that, an extraordinary tax was imposed on houses with electricity; there were new reductions in primary and supplementary pensions, significant cuts in lump sum payments and further cuts in wages of public employees. These changes were voted on October 20.

Shortly afterwards, on December 9, 2011, the government introduced a bill on private sector labour relations and wage issues in State enterprises and organizations (DEKO). On the subject of labour relations, there were provisions for business contracts to be predominant in sectoral collective agreements, the only restriction being that relating to the level of the basic salary in the National Collective agreement. A 12-month probationary period was instituted that could be terminated without notice and without compensation. On the other hand, the extension of sectoral agreements was suspended.

In these measures too, we see a strengthening of the aggression against public and private sector employees, retirees and the self-employed, while at the same time the burden of taxation on home ownership continued to increase. Changes in labour relations were particularly important. The transition from collective agreements, firstly to company union organizations, and if they did not exist, to the first level sectoral organizations, was to have catalytic effects. Until then trade union intervention at the company level had been based on sectoral agreements and from there further claims could be formulated. Now this safety net had been abolished (Kazakos 2011: 22–23). Not only was this happening but extension of collective sectoral agreements was also suspended, with the result that each company in a sector could withdraw recognition from sectoral trade unions and then negotiate the employment terms individually (individual employment contracts) (Kazakos 2011: 26).

But because these measures too were regarded as insufficient, a sixth package of measures was given the name "second Memorandum" and adopted by the parliament on February 12, 2012. Now it provided for repeal of the National General Collective Labour Agreement for the years 2010–2012, a 22% cut in the minimum wage (from 751 euros to 586 euros) and a 32% cut for new entrants up to 25 years of age, so abolishing the role of the National Collective agreement as a policy tool for determining the lowering of wages, and replacing it with a ministerial decree (Kouzis 2018: 91). Permanency of appointment was abolished for positions in the public organizations and enterprises (DEKO) and in State-controlled banks. The afteractivity[2] time for collective agreements was reduced from six to three months, retaining only the basic salary and certain allowances and abolishing the right of unilateral recourse to arbitration in case of rejection of the mediator's proposal and institution of arbitration following a joint application. There were also provisions for further cuts in pensions and allowances. State spending was cut on operating costs, defence and health. Tax exemptions were abolished and a single property tax was instituted.

The most basic point about these measures was the total overturn of labour relations in the private sector, where labour costs were sharply decreasing both because of the lowering of the minimum wage and because of the reduction in afteractivity time. Since the heart of a capitalist economy is the private sector, these changes amount to a radical break, a "paradigm shift" for adoption of a new framework of overexploitation of the working class which in a second phase could be "exported" to other social formations, contributing to the exit from the profitability crisis.

The seventh package of measures came together with adoption of the so-called Medium-Term Fiscal Strategy Framework 2013–2016, which was voted by the parliament on November 7, 2012. In accordance with this framework, the 13th and 14th salaries were definitively abolished in the public sector, new cuts were introduced to special pay scales and availability for a year with payment of 75% of salary was introduced in response to abolition of jobs, with the possibility of definitive dismissal in the event of case of non-appointment to another post in the public sector. Provision was also made for abolition of private-law positions of indefinite duration. Last but not least, recruitment of contract and casual employees was reduced by 20% against the level for 2012 (Mitropoulos 2013: 20). As far as the retirement pension is concerned, from January 1,

[2] The term afteractivity means continuing the validity of the regulatory terms of an expired or terminated Collective Labor Agreement.

2013, the pension of State employees and workers in public enterprises and organizations would be calculated on the basis of the average earnings of the last five years.[3] There were pension reductions of 5 to 15% for pensions of 1000 euros or more and a reduction of up to 83% on the amount of the lump sum.

In the private sector, the period for notice of dismissal for contracts of indefinite duration was reduced to a maximum of four months from the previous six months. The overall minimum wage was to be determined by State law, given the abolition of the related competences of the General National Collective Labour Convention, but its application to payment conditions was now generally enforced only for companies that were members of employers' organizations subscribing to the contract. With regard to allowances, there was provision for suspension of increases in allowances every three years until such time as the unemployment rate is reduced to 10%. Bonuses were abolished for the lowest wage levels. Compensation in case of dismissal was limited to 12 salaries for 16 years of service, with an additional salary, subject to certain conditions, for each additional year of service, and with a maximum of 2000 euros per month. Last but not least, there was a change in the five-day eight-hour-a-day working week—a Collective Labour Agreement made it possible for there to be a working week of six days and up to 48 hours, when this was deemed necessary.

As regards social security, the changes provided for insured persons in all funds who until then could be retired at age 65 now to retire at age 67. Men who had completed 10,000 salary-days at IKA (the Hellenic Social Insurance Institute) in order to qualify for a reduced pension would need to have reached the age of 62, and for a full pension to have reached the age of 67. Men who were civil servants or worked in the extended public sector would no longer be entitled to retirement after completing 25 years of insurance payments and could only get a reduced pension when they

[3] This development obviously leads to a conspicuous reduction when it came to calculation of new pensions. This is because, for the years before 2008, the pension was calculated on the basis of 80% of the last salary whereas for the period 2008–2012 it was calculated on the basis of the accumulated years or months. This did not cause any particular problems since most of the work time was calculated under the old system and the pay cuts were for a short period of time (Mitropoulos 2013: 24).

reached the age of 62 and a full pension at the age of 67. Women working in the public sector and the broader public sector would also have to have reached the age of 62 to be entitled to a reduced pension and 67 for a full pension. The retirement age for farmers went from 65 to 67 years.

There were also new changes in public sector wages and in labour relations in both the private and public sectors. Additionally, there was a profound change in the social security system. Until recently, when a worker had completed a certain number of years of employment, he or she could retire regardless of age. It was considered that he had fulfilled his debt to the community as a whole and could now be permitted to rest. Now the exact opposite applied—no matter how many years he had worked, he could not get a full pension until he was at least 67 years old. In our view this did not have to do just with trying to raise money for the funds, whose reserves were illegally appropriated by the State through their mandatory deposit in the Bank of Greece at a low interest rate.[4] It was the first step in a broader effort to link retirement age to life expectancy (see below).

Subsequently, after the backdown by SYRIZA in the summer of 2015 (see below), the third Memorandum would be concluded, introducing the eighth package of measures.

The first concern was the creation of a 50 billion euros Property Development Fund, which would have its headquarters in Greece and to which the assets of the Greek state would be transferred, and then be sold to individuals. Priority was accorded to the sale of the Piraeus Port, the Port Authority and the regional airports. Beyond this, these included an increase in VAT from 13% to 24% on a large number of products, abolition of numerous tax breaks, doubling of the tax to be prepaid for the following year and lowering of the taxation floor from 8660 euros to 5000 euros from January 1, 2020. In terms of labour relations, Sunday work was allowed for six months a year in large areas of the country considered to be of tourist interest, collective redundancies were facilitated

[4] For exactly 40 years (1951–1990) governments obliged insurance companies to deposit employees' social security contributions at a negative rate of interest in banks, which have made significant profits from this practice. In 1950, the employees' social security contributions were deposited at a negative rate of -7.6%, in 1954 at -11.1%, in 1974 at -21.8%, in 1981 at -13%, in 1986 at -8.0% and in 1990 at -2.4% (Bogiopoulos 2011: 329–330).

by the abolition of the veto of the Ministry of Labour. It was decided that claims by banks have precedence over those of workers for settlement of accrued debts and severance pay in the case of liquidation of companies that have been declared bankrupt. New pension cuts were provided for in the pension scheme starting from January 1, 2019. At the level of State administration, the General Secretariat of Public Revenue was now fully independent of the elected government. Decrees issued by the Secretariat were of equal validity to decisions of the Cabinet. Then there was the Council for Fiscal Discipline, with five members, operating along the same lines and able to impose cuts on any expenditure given a suspicion that there might be a deviation from fiscal targets, which demand a 3.5% surplus from 2018.

Globally, by 2016, Greece had through this process borrowed 227 billion euros. 23 billion came from the IMF, 59 billion from Germany, 44 from France, 39 from Italy, 26 from Spain, 12 from the Netherlands and 24 from other European countries. It should be noted that 43% of this funding went to repayment of amortization, 23% to interest payments, 19% to rescuing the banking system and 15% to wages and pensions.

Should we wish to evaluate the policy orientations that these eight packages of measures introduce, we could infer the following:

1. High priority is given to reducing wage costs in the public sector. This policy also exerts downward pressure on private sector salaries.
2. The reduction of public operating costs (public expenditures) coupled with the reduction in staff numbers on the one hand increases the reserve labour force by forcing the wage level in the private sector even further down, and on the other hand assigns a number of formerly public functions to private capital through subcontracting.
3. Reducing public investment strengthens competition among the strongest factions of capital, contributing in this way to the liquidating functions of the crisis.
4. The change in labour relations in the public sector serves as "a paradigm" for the private sector and in conjunction with the reduction of

staff numbers (which is an indirect way of securing redundancies) and the increase in working hours, intensifies workplace pressures.

5. The sharp decline in wages in the private sector contributes to a rapid increase in profitability, for those companies that manage to cope with the crisis conditions.
6. Deterioration in the tax regime for the self-employed, especially in crisis conditions, disrupts one kind of social alliance, contributing to a shift towards polarization towards wage labour.
7. The focus on geometric increase in the rate of property tax is aimed at expropriating a core asset of the working class for the benefit of business groups, which will acquire the property either through auctions or through hedge funds they have purchased, including through "red" housing loans.
8. Changes in labour relations in the private sector impose a regime of facilitating redundancies, reinforcing flexible and precarious forms of employment, dismantling and essentially abolishing the system of collective bargaining (Kouzis 2011b: 8–10) with a view to individualizing labour relations, restricting the protection of workers from dismissal and reducing classical forms of employment as typified by the indefinite duration work contract and full-time employment (INE-GSEE 2012: 335).
9. Viewed globally, all these developments reflect the creation of a new accumulation model, a paradigm shift in which the social gains of decades are nullified and an attempt is made to return to the earliest forms of capitalist exploitation so that the balance of power can be radically changed and the most dynamic parts of capital succeed in overcoming the crisis. In other words, the environment that will emerge after the end of the crisis will be characterized by very low labour costs and a significant number of privatized formerly public bodies. In the same vein, the drastic reduction in the number of public sector employees, who will exert pressure as a reserve army of labour, will constitute a factor for business profitability. Moreover, there will be further contraction of the already shrinking private sector wages and further continuation of the changes in labour relations (INE-GSEE 2012: 336).

10. In a second phase, such a change, also taking into account the relevant specificities, may serve as a model for other national formations.

References

Bogiopoulos N., 2011, *'It's capitalism, stupid.' The culprits for the crisis and the 'debt' that will bring them down. A polite answer to the praetorians of the MEMORANDA*, Athens: Livanis (in Greek).

Institute of Labour—Greek General Confederation of Labour (INE-GSEE), 2012, *The Greek economy and employment. Annual report 2012.* Athens: Institute of Labour—Greek General Confederation of Labour (in Greek).

Kazakos A., 2011, "From collective labor agreements to violence of individual employment contracts", in *Crisis and Labour*, Athens: ESIEA Cultural Foundation, pp. 20–32 (in Greek).

Kouzis G., 2011a, "The labour landscape in Greece following the Memorandum" in *Crisis and Labour*, Athens: ESIEA Cultural Foundation, pp. 34–43 (in Greek).

Kouzis G., 2011b, "Labour in the vortex of the economic crisis and the memorandum: ten points", *Outopia* no 97, pp. 7–12 (in Greek).

Kouzis G., 2018, "Labour under attack during the period of crisis and austerity", in Sotiris P. (ed.) *Crisis, movement, strategy: the Greek experience*, London: Brill, pp. 88–95.

Mitropoulos A., 2013, *Society in the gunpoint. The violent internal devaluation,* Athens: Livanis (in Greek).

4

Changes in the Economy

Introduction

This chapter will examine the changes brought about in the Greek economy by the eight packages of measures. We will start with an examination of the overall changes in macroeconomic aggregates and go on to present the situation in each sector separately, and then in each subsector. The leading sectors and subsectors in Greek capitalism will be highlighted, together with a presentation of the tendency for some of the most oligopolistic segments of Greek capital to be reinforced, concluding with a reference to the most recent positive developments for a great number of companies that have managed to survive the crisis.

The Evolution of Key Elements in the Greek Economy

The evolution of key elements in the Greek economy is outlined in Table 4.1.

A study of the Greek economy in the crisis years brings to light a number of different aspects of the situation. Undoubtedly in the field of

S. Sakellaropoulos, *Greece's (un) Competitive Capitalism and the Economic Crisis*,
https://doi.org/10.1007/978-3-030-14319-0_4

Table 4.1 Evolution of key elements of the Greek economy (billion euro)

	2009	2012	2016	2009/2016 (%)
Private consumption	164,646	128,866	116,821	−29.1
Public consumption	47,349	41,564	35,239	−26.6
Gross capital formation	43,042	26,339	18,842	−56.2
Gross domestic product	237,494	193,749	174,200	−26.7
Imports	46,078	41,681	41,068	−10.9
Exports	15,319	21,717	24,487	+59.8
Exports as % of GDP	6.45	11.36	14.05	+117.8
Imports as % of GDP	19.40	21.64	23.58	+21.5
Goods balance	−30,760.3	−19,651.2	−16,581.9	−46.1
Travel receipts	10,403.3	10,442.5	13,220.0	+27.8
Service balance	12,640.2	14,630.8	15,320.2	+21.2
Foreign balance	−23,057	−9744	−1261.6	−1111.8
Current account balance	−24,613.5	−4615.0	−1103.9	−2229.7
GDP per capita	21,091	17,161	16,154	−23.4
Gross value added	209,610	168,979	151,818	−27.6
Unemployment rate %	9.6	24.4	23.5	+144.8
Deposits	237.5	161.4	121.4	−48.9
Assets	353	309	277[a]	−21.5
Net fixed assets	204	190	170[a]	−16.7
Equities	131	120	107[a]	−18.3
Turnover	201	173	159[a]	−20.9
EBITDA profits	17.2	10.6	11.7[a]	−32.0
Pre-tax profits	3.7	−6.1	−1.5[a]	–
Primary balance as % of GDP	−10.6	−3.8	3.7	–
Primary balance as % of GDP (including interests)	−15.8	−8.9	0.4	–
Central government debt	301	305	312	+2.4
Central government debt as % of GDP	126.7	159.6	180.3	+42.3
Primary outlays: government budget	86.3	55.3	49.0	−43.2
Salaries and pensions: government budget	25.8	20.5	18.1	−29.8
Revenue from taxes	49.6	47	47.5	−4.2
Income tax of individuals	10.8	–	8.1	−25.0
Real estate price index (1997 = 100)	249.8	199.2	151.8	−39.3
Athens stock exchange index	2196	908	643	−70.7
Non-performing loans as % to gross loans	7.0	23.3	45.9	+555.8
FDI inflows	3835	2004	3438	−10.3

(continued)

Table 4.1 (continued)

	2009	2012	2016	2009/2016 (%)
FDI outward stock	29,763	34,062	25,122[c]	−15.6
Corporations (exclusive of banking, insurance and finance)	25,168	19,621	15,771	−37.3
Small enterprises	849.389[b]		692.286[a]	−18.5

The EBITDA Index (earnings before interest, tax, depreciation and amortization) shows the company's earnings from operational before the impact of financial and extraordinary income and expenses, together with depreciation on fixed assets

Source: ICAP (2011, 2016, 2017); Bank of Greece; National Statistical Service

[a]2014

[b]2008

[c]2015

production the results have been catastrophic. Gross domestic product (GDP) has fallen by 26.7%, GDP per capita by 23.4%, gross capital formation by 56.2%, gross value added by 27.6%, turnover by 20.9%, assets by 21.5%, equities by 18.3%, net fixed assets by 16.7%, corporations by 37.3%, small enterprises by 18.5%, the Athens Stock Exchange index by 70.7% and the unemployment rate has risen by 144.8%. Outward foreign direct investment (FDI) stock has fallen by 15.6%, private consumption by 29.1%, public consumption by 26.6%, the real estate price index by 39.3% and deposits by 48.9%. This is the longest-lasting peacetime recession of a national economy, even by comparison with 1930 in the United States. At that time the US economy recovered and within four years had regained the lost ground. The causes of this unprecedented destruction of capital were mentioned in a previous chapter. Among its consequences have been as follows: 10.3% reduction in FDI inflows, 4.2% reduction in revenue from taxes and 25% in income tax of individuals (despite the imposition of a plethora of new taxes and of increases in older taxes) and a 555.8% increase in non-performing loans as a percentage of gross loans (!). Even the Central Government Debt, whose reduction was supposed to have been dealt with through the eight packages of measures, rose in absolute terms by 2.4% and in relative terms by 42.3%.

This is one aspect of the crisis, but there is another dimension to it that should not be ignored. A fall in imports has been detected in absolute terms and not in relative, but most importantly exports have skyrocketed by 59.8% in absolute terms, with their ratio to GDP more than doubling. This has resulted in a 46.1% reduction in the trade balance on goods. This, combined with a 21.2% increase in the trade balance on services (due to a 27.8% increase in traffic receipts) will mean the almost total disappearance of the foreign balance and current account balance deficits. At the same time, the 43.2% reduction in primary outlays from the government budget (with a 29.8% drop in salaries and pensions) would help to change the sign on primary balance and primary balance (including interest). This would generate an image of gradual improvement of the Greek economy in some fiscal indices. To this should be added the fact that a decrease in the negative sign is observable in pre-tax profits and an improvement in EBITDA profits. Does this mean that the country is moving into a trajectory of recovery? For those who believe that the crisis was a question of the public deficit and public debt being too high, the answer would appear to be positive, even if the expectation is that a long transition period will intervene and it will be necessary to continue implementing the directives contained in the eight packages of measures. But for those who argue that the crisis has to do with the low competitiveness of Greek capitalism, the problem is more complex.

For it to be answered an interpretation must be offered of this increase in exports. In the period between 2009 and 2016 world exports grew by 29.2%—only half of the figure for Greek exports. The main recipient countries for Greek exports in 2009 were the OECD countries with a 52.9% share, the EU25 with 47.6%, the EU15 with 37.1%,[1] the Balkans with 17.2%, North Africa and Middle East with 8.9%, Cyprus with 6.5% and North America with 5.7%. So, there was a clear export preference for the countries of the developed capitalist West (EU15 + North America) and, on the other hand, to a lesser extent, the neighbouring countries (Balkans + North Africa and Middle East + Cyprus). In 2017 Greek exports were directed to the OECD countries with a 54.5% share,

[1] Obviously there are multiple overlaps as a country can be included in more than one of these categorizations.

the EU28 with 53.4%, the Eurozone countries with 37.2%, the G-7 countries with 29.4%, the Balkans with 21, Middle East and North Africa with 15.1%, Cyprus with 6.1% and North America with 5.1%. The issue that emerges is that the exports to neighbouring countries have gone from 32.6% in 2009 to 42.6% in 2017.[2] They thus exceed the share of exports to the European Monetary Union countries, continuing and intensifying the process of reorientation of Greek exports that has begun and has to do with the preference for less capitalistically developed areas, to which relatively low-tech Greek products can more easily acquire access.

The conclusion that emerges from the above is that, despite the extensive destruction of capital described, austerity policies and major changes in labour relations, the overall picture of the character of Greek capitalism has not changed. Perhaps through the eight packages of measures public spending has been reduced and imbalances in current accounts have almost been eliminated, but this has been due to internal devaluation, which has contributed to a significant extent to the reduction in labour costs and resurgence in tourism. So, there is no qualitative change placing Greek capitalism on a new basis in the international division of labour.

In this sense, the reduction in imports in absolute but not relative terms corresponds to nothing more than a fall in the standard of living and not, of course, to a successful import substitution policy, given the simultaneous collapse of the industrial sector and of trade (see Table 4.3), not to mention the decline in labour productivity (GDP/per working hour). Between 2010 and 2016 productivity in European Monetary Union countries increased by 5.8%, whereas in Greece it decreased by 6.7%. In other words, the gap is widening and the competitiveness problem of Greek capitalism remains despite its strengthening due to the fall in labour costs which has, however, reached its limits. Greece is therefore far from having achieved structural overcoming of the causes of the crisis.

[2] All the data is taken from the web page of the Exports Research Centre (KEEM) http://www.pse.gr.

The Situation in Individual Sectors and Subsectors

The Table 4.2 depicts the situation in the various sectors of the Greek economy for the period 2009–2015.

Although the five (four for the financial sector) aggregates presented differ in significance, they nevertheless help to convey a first impression of the developments. The most significant change has to do with banks and shows the magnitude of the damage they suffered as a result of the crisis. Specifically, the crisis entering into the Greek formation leads to a revaluation of the credit risk, which in turn will halt the transfer of funds from the international financial system to the Greek economy (Milios 2011). But the crisis on its own would not suffice to bring the banks to the brink of bankruptcy if there had not also been the damage from the haircuts of Greek bonds, participation in the programme for repurchasing bonds and the explosion of the so-called non-performing loans. The increase in non-performing loans has already been mentioned, so it is important also to refer to the haircut issue. In 2012, in an attempt to reduce Greek debt, the government, in agreement with the lenders decided to proceed with a haircut of Greek bonds to the sum of €139.7 billion,[3] the so-called Private Sector Involvement (PSI). Greek banks lost about €27 billion from that haircut due to a decrease in the value of the securities they held. Following the PSI the first recapitalization of the banks took place in 2013 due both to the losses caused by the PSI and to the remaining liquidity problems that the crisis had inflicted. In the course of the first recapitalization, the Greek Financial Stability Fund provided €24.4 billion, in exchange for shares, to the four systemic banks (the National Bank, Bank of Piraeus, Eurobank and AlphaBank) and another €17.6 billion for the reorganization—liquidation—of non-systemic banks. A total of €42 billion, which came from State borrowing,

[3] It should be noted that apart from on the banks, the effects of bond haircuts were very serious on the insurance funds, where the initial nominal amount was around 15 billion, which was deposited in the Bank of Greece's Common Fund and was found in July 2012 not to exceed 8.1 billion. It should be borne in mind that the insurance funds also lost a large amount of interest and revenue deriving from the initial sum (Labour Institute of the Greek General Confederation of Labour 2012: 287).

Table 4.2 Evolution of the various aggregates in sectors of the Greek economy 2009–2015

	Assets			Equity			Liabilities			Turnover			Gross profits		
Corporate sector (exclusive of banking, insurance and finance)															
Sector	2009	2012	2015	2009	2012	2015	2009	2012	2015	2009	2012	2015	2009	2012	2015
Agriculture-fishing	1.3	1.0	0.9	1.0	0.7	0.5	1.6	1.2	1.2	1.0	1.0	1.2	0.7	07	0.7
Mining-quarrying	0.3	0.3	0.7	0.3	0.3	0.4	0.3	0.3	0.9	0.3	0.2	0.2	0.3	0.3	0.1
Manufacturing	25.6	23.2	23.2	27.1	23.2	20.9	24.6	23.2	24.8	27.3	32.3	30.3	26.9	26.3	27.3
Electricity, gas and water supply	9.6	12.2	14.3	11.9	13.2	16.0	8.0	11.3	13.0	5.0	10.0	8.7	4.9	4.3	6.5
Construction	7.7	7.5	6.9	8.8	9.3	6.7	7.2	6.6	7.1	4.2	2.3	3.5	2.6	1.7	1.7
Trade	21.1	17.0	15.2	13.9	12.8	12.5	25.6	19.7	16.8	41.2	35.6	35.5	39.9	40.1	32.7
Hotels and restaurants	5.3	5.1	4.1	6.8	6.9	6.0	4.5	4.2	3.0	2.1	1.7	1.7	2.8	2.3	3.1
Transport and communications	12.2	18.0	18.8	9.1	13.3	14.7	13.9	20.6	21.0	7.6	7.8	9.2	10.0	13.5	16.4
Other services	16.8	15.6	15.9	20.9	20.2	22.4	14.5	13.0	12.2	11.4	9.0	9.7	12.1	10.8	11.5
Total	100	100	100	100	100	100	100	100	100	100	100	100	100	100	100
Banking, insurance and finance															
Banking	91.8	88.1	90.0	65.5	−57.5	74.7	4.5	95.3	96.1	76.4	69.4	67.1			
Insurance	2.7	4.3	4.9	3.2	20.1	7.0	13.9	0.6	0.8	16.7	25.4	24.7			
Other financial services	5.5	8.7	5.1	31.3	137.6	18.3	14.5	4.1	3.2	4.1	5.1	8.2			
Total	100	100	100	100	100	100	100	100	100	100	100	100	100	100	100

Source: ICAP (2011, 2014, 2017)

was added to the country's debt. But because the banks were unable to recover, two more recapitalizations took place. The second (2014) was conducted exclusively with private capital (€8.3 billion) and in 2015 the third recapitalization took place, again with private capital, except for two banks (the National Bank and the Bank of Piraeus) which received a total of approximately €5.4 billion from public funds because they had not succeeded in securing a sufficient supply of private capital.

Bearing all this in mind, we may return to the figures in Table 4.2, where we see that whereas in 2009 banks held 65.5% of total assets in the financial sector, by 2012 this had fallen to −57.5% in 2012, due to the disastrous consequences of the banking crisis, with at the same time a decline observable in two other sectors. Thus, "*other financial services*", from the €16,806 billion in assets they held in 2009, by 2012 were down to €12,719 billion in 2012, which is a 24.3% decrease. But this is "negligible" compared to what happened to banks, which from €35,154 billion in assets fell to €-5,335,868 billion![4] For it to become comprehensible what has happened, we might mention that of the total assets of all companies (both in the financial and not financial sector), which in 2009 came to €154,951 billion (€101,247 financial sector and €53,704 non-financial sector) *banks* held 22.7%, *other financial services* 10.8% and all the financial sector together 34.66% of the total. Three years later assets in the economy as a whole came to €100,048 billion (€90,805 billion for companies outside the financial sector and €9243 billion for companies within the financial sector), with *banks* appearing under a negative sign whereas *other financial services* accounted for 12.7% of the total and all the financial sectors together 9.2% of the total. The conclusion that emerges is, given that assets are the point of departure for the operations of banking, that assets were in a state of bankruptcy and the broader financial sector was undergoing a rapid downgrading. Recapitalization of banking would be needed to bring about the radical changes in the landscape that became visible in the 2015 data. *Banking* would find itself with assets in the order of €33.4 billion euros, barely less than the figures for 2009. But for *other financial services* the same would not apply as they would have only €8.2 billion of their own capital, that is, half the sum of

[4] The figures in absolute terms are derived from the ICAP reports (ICAP 2011, 2014).

six years before. But the magnitude of the bank's losses also is reflected in the decline in assets from €467 billion in 2009 to €295 billion in 2015 (−36.8%). This is even truer of the bank's turnover, which has fallen from €22 billion to €9.8 billion (−55.5%).

That said, there is an evident strengthening in the sector of *electricity, gas and water supply* (the reasons for which are to be sought in the extensive domestic use of natural gas and the increase in the use of alternative forms of energy [photovoltaic, wind energy]). *Construction, Hotels and Restaurants* and *Agriculture and Fishing* are in decline, while the situation in *Other Services* and *Manufacturing* is more ambiguous. *Trade* and *Construction* saw a decline due to the sharp drop in income but also the banking crisis that led to a cut-off in housing loans and drastic curtailment in public spending on construction projects. We judge that the decline in incomes can also be traced to contraction in the Hotels and Restaurants sector.

Above and beyond the fall in private consumption, the contraction in *Agriculture-Fishing* must linked to the continuing impact of the Common Agricultural Policy (see the section on the changes in the farming strata in Chap. 6 of this study). The issue of *Other Services* demands more specialized knowledge, and further investigation is required of what is taking place in the individual subsectors as well as in *Manufacturing*.

But before presenting the developments in the subsectors, it is important to highlight the dynamic in each sector in crisis conditions. Table 4.3 is based on the business cycle of one sector in the economy as a whole. The data is in absolute magnitudes so as to examine not the evolution of its share in the economy as a whole, but its dynamic in the crisis, whether—in other words—in absolute terms it is growing or shrinking.

The conclusions that emerge from a survey of the seven-year trajectory of the business cycle by economic sector are that the seven-year period between 2008 and 2015 is a catastrophic period for the Greek economy. This is clearly demonstrated by the fact that turnover falls from 224 billion to 142 billion, that is, by 37.4%, with only sectors showing an absolute increase—*electricity, gas and water supply* and *Other financial services*, notwithstanding the small scale of turnover for the latter and the slight downturn in *Transport and Communications, Insurance* and *Agriculture-Fishing* (that too limited in scale and with some inelastic boundaries at

Table 4.3 The evolution of turnover between 2008 and 2015, by sector

	2008 (billion euros)	2010 (billion euros)	2012 (billion euros)	2015 (billion euros)	2008 (%)	2010 (%)	2012 (%)	2015 (%)
Sector								
Agriculture-fishing	1684	1457	1511	1516	0.8	0.8	0.9	1.1
Mining-quarrying	511	487	369	298	0.2	0.3	0.2	0.2
Manufacturing	57,580	48,658	50,075	38,754	25.7	25.1	28.7	27.2
Electricity, gas and water supply	8913	12,855	15,482	11,167	4.0	6.6	8.9	7.8
Construction	8155	5529	3634	4430	3.6	2.9	2.1	3.1
Trade	77,271	65,606	55,316	45,457	34.4	33.8	31.7	31.9
Hotels and restaurants	3858	3219	2706	2181	1.7	1.7	1.6	1.5
Transport and communications	12,243	13,691	12,125	11,796	5.4	7.1	6.9	8.2
Other services	20,759	18,025	14,050	12,368	9.3	9.3	8.1	8.7
Banking	27,248	18,228	13,363	9845	12.2	9.4	7.7	6.9
Insurance	4147	4600	4913	3627	1.8	2.4	2.8	2.5
Other financial services	1181	1464	984	1209	0.5	0.8	0.6	0.8
Total	224,249	193,818	174,529	142,648	100.0	100.0	100.0	100.0

Source: ICAP (2009, 2011, 2013, 2017)

the lower end of its portion). That said, examining the share of each sector separately, we see that electricity, gas and water supply present a special dynamic, with its turnover more than doubling in the period between 2008 and 2012 but declining subsequently. The causes must be related to what we mentioned earlier (the use of natural gas, alternative forms of energy) but also to the fact that these activities reached a certain point and then arrived at a limit. By contrast, *banks* and *trade* show a steady decline in consequence of the magnitude of the crisis. It is interesting to note the fact that in *construction* there was an initial decrease in turnover, something to be expected given the real estate crisis, but more recent years have seen a recovery, which must be attributable to the spread of Airbnb-style practices on the one hand and on the other to the fact of the social strata that have withstood the crisis were taking advantage of the fall in building costs and proceeding either to purchase a home or carry out renovations. Questions arise from the volatile situation in *manufacturing*, which confirms the need for research to be extended to the relevant economic subsectors. Something similar should be done for the very important *Transport and Communications* sector. Finally, Insurance presents a dynamism that is attributable to a reduction in pensions and cutbacks in the expenditure of the Greek welfare state.

Having concluded this presentation, we may now move on to investigation of the dynamics of the subsectors on the basis of the data in Table 4.4.

More detailed data helps us to draw more secure conclusions about what has happened. As far as *Manufacturing* is concerned, the basic subsector is *Oil refining*, where turnover has almost doubled (and risen by around 19% in absolute terms: from €10,233 billion in 2009 to €12,188 billion in 2015).[5] *Food-Beverages* also record a relative rise. If, however, we look at it in absolute terms, we see that there was a drop in the order of 10.9% from a turnover of 11,517 billion in 2009 to 10,381 billion in 2015. This may be attributed to the relatively inelastic character of consumer expenditure on products of this type. Above and

[5] It is also characteristic that in terms of industrial production this particular sector has a very significant momentum: with 2010 as its base year its production figure for 2017 is 134, at a time when the figure for the processing sector generally is 71.9 and for industry 97.

Table 4.4 Evolution of the 2009–2015 business cycle by sector and subsector

	Billions euro	Billions euro	%	%
Sector	2009	2015	2009	2015
1. Agriculture-fishing	1713	1516	0.8	1–1
1.1 Agriculture	1005	929	0.5	0.6
1.2 Aquaculture	708	587	0.3	0.4
2. Mining-quarrying	498	298	0.2	0.2
3. Manufacturing	47,215	38,754	22.5	27.2
3.1 Food-beverages	11,517	10,381	5.5	7.3
3.2 Tobacco-products	520	733	0.2	0.5
3.3 Textile	624	377	0.3	0.3
3.4 Clothing	1045	442	0.5	0.3
3.5 Leather	121	43	–	–
3.6 Wood	409	141	0.2	–
3.7 Paper	930	922	0.4	0.6
3.8 Publishing	2168	747	1.0	0.5
3.9 Oil refining	10,233	12,188	4.9	8.5
3.10 Chemicals	2321	1657	1.1	1.2
3.11 Pharmaceuticals	3189	2068	1.5	1.4
3.12 Plastic products	1565	1377	0.7	1.0
3.13 Non-metallic products	2915	1403	1.4	1.0
3.14 Basic metals	3110	2376	1.5	1.7
3.15 Metal products	2441	1614	1.2	1.1
3.16 Machinery equipment	523	329	0.2	0.2
3.17 Computers et al. optical prod.	535	320	0.3	0.2
3.18 Electrical machinery	1285	742	0.6	0.5
3.19 Vehicles	337	234	0.2	0.2
3.20 Other transport equipment	427	28	0.2	–
3.21 Furniture	455	115	0.2	–
3.22 Other manufacturing	543	518	0.3	0.4
4. Electricity, gas and water supply	8562	11,167	4.3	7.8
5. Construction	7196	4431	3.4	3.1
6. Trade	71,224	45,457	33.9	31.9
6.1 Sale of motor vehicles	9358	2171	4.5	1.5
6.2 Wholesale trade	45,377	29,685	21.6	20.8
6.3 Retail trade	16,489	13,602	7.8	9.5
7. Hotels and restaurants	3616	2181	1.7	1.5
8. Transport and communications	13,141	11,796	6.3	8.2
8.1 Land transport	1168	1013	0.6	0.7
8.2 Water transport	849	726	0.4	0.5
8.3 Air transport	742	1104	0.4	0.8
8.4 Auxiliary transport activities	3164	3526	1.5	2.5
8.5 Post	824	547	0.4	0.4

(*continued*)

Table 4.4 (continued)

Sector	Billions euro 2009	Billions euro 2015	% 2009	% 2015
8.6 Telecommunications	6395	4481	3.0	3.1
9. Other services	19,741	12,368	9.4	8.7
9.1 Real estate	861	566	0.4	0.4
9.2 Operational leasing	720	558	0.3	0.4
9.3 IT services	1409	825	0.7	0.6
9.4 Research and development	2	4	–	–
9.5 Other business activities	6363	3802	3.0	2.7
9.6 Education	414	225	0.2	0.2
9.7 Health	2075	1269	1.0	0.9
9.8 Environmental protection	248	259	0.1	0.2
9.9 Recreation, culture and sporting	7552	4810	3.6	3.4
9.10 Other services	99	51	–	–
10. Banking	22,065	9845	10.5	6.9
11. Insurance	4702	3627	2.2	2.5
12. Other financial services	1384	1209	0.7	0.8
Σύνολο	201,059	142,648	100.0	100.0

Source: ICAP (2011, 2017)

beyond that, a significant fall is to be noted in *publishing*, a familiar phenomenon in times of crisis, and in *Non-metallic products*. As far as Trade is concerned, which also suffers a downturn, this is due basically to the steep fall in the *Sale of motor vehicles* (similarly to be expected in a period of crisis). In the sector of *Transport and Communication* the subsector *Auxiliary Transport Activities* stands out, having increased turnover not only in relative, but also in absolute, terms, a phenomenon which must have to do with the more general growth in transport as a side effect of the upturn in Greek tourism. *Other services* record a decline that is related to the falloff in activity in the subsector of *Recreation, culture and sport* owing to the effects of the crisis, but also in the subsector *Other business activities*. The latter has a twofold explanation: on the one hand, in 2015 there were 1518 enterprises in this category, a number indicating that most of them were small in size and had difficulty competing with companies of higher productivity; on the other hand, many of the most important enterprises were associated with public investment, which was also in decline because of the crisis.

The Survival and Growth of the Most Competitive Oligopolistic Enterprises

Apart from the sectors and subsectors, we have mentioned that there has been another protagonist that has emerged strengthened from the process of crisis. The reference is to the most powerful monopolized/oligopolistic sectors which, despite the problems they have faced as a result of the recession and the sharp decline in domestic demand, have managed to take advantage of the liquidating functions of the crisis and from a certain point onwards to display not only elements of growth but also indications of increased profitability.

In a first analysis, this is evident from fact that in 2008 in the economy as a whole business which employed up to ten people comprised 62.2% of total employment, whereas in 2017 this figure had dropped to 56.5%. On the other hand, the share of larger companies rose from 37.8% to 43.5%. Above and beyond that, the trend becomes particularly apparent if we take into account developments in the 500 most profitable businesses between 2009 and 2015. In 2009 the 500 largest companies accounted for 85% of EBITDA profits and 51% of the total turnover of the 29,852 companies that had been included in the ICAP database. For 2015 they would come to 65% of the total turnover of their 9962 businesses, whereas EBITDA profits will be 10.8 billion euros at a time when EBITDA earnings from all businesses would be negative. Interestingly, in 2009, 106 companies (21.2%) of the corresponding 2008 classification are not included in the new classification. Of these, 30 had suffered losses and the other low EBITDA takings. Similarly, in 2015 there were 136 businesses (27.2%) which were not included in the new classification. It is worth noting that there are 112 companies ranking continuously from 2007 to 2015 among the 500 most profitable businesses, making them the "hard core" of the most profitable companies in the country.

With regard to sectorial distribution of profits, in 2009 the six most profitable businesses in the industry accounted for 36% of EBITDA profits for the corresponding 150 industrial companies, while the three companies marketing oil and coal products accounted for 38.6% of the industry's turnover. In Trade the five top companies took 21% of the

EBITDA profits and 13 supermarkets covered 26% of the turnover of the trade. In Other services the six most profitable companies accounted for 62% of the total corresponding profits of the 159 companies in the sector. In Banks-Factoring Companies the five most profitable businesses covered 81.2% of EBITDA's total earnings before depreciation, with six banks among the twenty most profitable businesses. In 2015 the five most profitable industrial companies secured 41.5% of the EBITDA earnings in the sector, and the petroleum and coal industries accounted for 43.5% of the industry's turnover. In trade, the five largest companies made 38.5% of EBITDA's total profits, and supermarkets–hypermarkets account for 28.5% of total turnover. In other services, the five largest enterprises accounted for 41.4% of EBITDA's total profits in the sector.

In conclusion, the evolution of the most profitable Greek businesses between 2009 and 2015 shows that the crisis has had a strong impact since within a space of six years the number of companies in the ICAP register fell from 29,852 to 9962 (a decrease of 66.6%). Existing evidence suggests that the crisis was already having a significant impact on Greek businesses from 2008 to 2009 onwards. Over the next six years the liquidating operations of the crisis would unfold, resulting in the closing of thousands of businesses and an overall decrease in profitability. By the end of 2015 the 500 most profitable operations would have increased their share in overall turnover but also their overall profits to a degree clearly superior to the rest of the companies. It has also become obvious that the banking sector was under very great pressure for reasons already indicated, while on the other hand oligopolistic entities have managed not only to survive but to show considerable dynamism—the five most profitable industrial enterprises, the five most powerful companies in commerce and the five largest companies in other services.

Attempting a more comprehensive, and more strategic, evaluation, we might venture to suggest that the advent of the crisis came as a surprise to the Greek enterprises that were not prepared for something of such duration and depth. One segment of primarily monopolistic companies derived significant benefits and strengthened its position. Another segment tried to stabilize its presence, judging that after the crisis the new purged landscape would be more favourable for them, but there were also oligopolistic entities that found themselves in a difficult position and were even forced to close. At the same time such small and medium-sized enterprises as survived had to deal with many more problems. Focusing on specific sectors and subsectors, *Banking* was on the margins of survival and if it succeeded in staying in the game this was due to the banks being recapitalized. Also, in a difficult position were *Construction, Non-metallic Products, Sale of Motor Vehicles, Publishing*, the subsector of *Recreation, Culture and Sport* and the *Other Business Activities* in the *Other Services* sector. On the other hand, *Electricity, Gas and Water Supply, Insurance*, the subsectors *Oil Refining* and *Auxiliary Transport Activities* all possessed a remarkable momentum. *Food-Beverages* and *Plastics* also maintained their previously satisfactory performance. Above and beyond that, oligopolistic status played an important role in overall economic concentration and centralization.

But apart from the question of who is deriving special benefit from this period, the most recent data shows that from a more comprehensive perspective, the profitability of Greek capitalism, that is to say the segment of companies that have survived, is showing signs of recovery. In 2015 although the turnover of 16,168 enterprises (out of a total of 23,000) decreased by 3% from €131.6 billion in 2014 to €127.9 billion, there was nevertheless an increase in capitalist profitability, mainly due to the decrease of the sales costs (i.e. labour costs). Total gross profits increased by 9% to € 27 billion. As a result, a significant return to profitability was recorded, with before tax earnings before tax of €2.1 billion as against €196 million in 2014 and with 62% of companies recording profits. Taking into account the entire corporate sector of the economy (23 thousand businesses), and focusing exclusively on those making a profit, a net profit of €6.7 billion in 2015 emerges, as compared to €5.7 billion in 2014 (the 38% of companies that were recording losses reported losses of €4.4 billion and €5.4 billion, respectively).

To conclude, during the crisis there were sectors, subsectors and oligopolistic enclaves that managed not only to survive but also to expand their profit margins. There were also sectors and enterprises which, after being harshly tested, managed to survive and have recently experienced a return to profitability.

References

ICAP, 2009, *Greek financial guide 2013/Greece in figures/5*, Athens, http://dir.icap.gr/mailimages/e-books/GrFigures2013/index.html, accessed on 1/6/2014 (in Greek).

ICAP, 2011, *Greek financial guide 2011/Greece in figures/5*, Athens (in Greek).

ICAP, 2013, *Greek financial guide 2013*, Athens (in Greek).

ICAP, 2014, *Greek financial guide 2014*, Athens, http://dir.icap.gr/mailimages/e-books/GrFigures2014/index.html, accessed on 1/6/2014 (in Greek).

ICAP, 2016, *The six years of crisis 2008–2016*, Athens (in Greek).

ICAP, 2017, *Greece in figures 2017*, Athens (in Greek).

Institute of Labour—Greek General Confederation of Labour, 2012, *The Greek economy and employment. Annual report 2012*, Athens: Institute of Labour—Greek General Confederation of Labour (in Greek).

Milios, 2011, "The Greek crisis as a version of the global economic crisis and the crisis of the European Monetary System" http://www.rednotebook.gr/details.php?id=2075, accessed on 7/2/2014 (in Greek).

5

The Social Impact of the Crisis

Introduction

The points already mentioned in the previous sections of this book about the strategy of the policy applied, the content of the eight packages of measures, and the consequences for the functioning of the economy had a very profound impact on the country's social situation. In this chapter, there will be a presentation of the impact on income, labour relations, the distribution of wealth, the generation of poverty and the effects of the crisis on health care for the people of Greece.

Impact on Income

The first major change has to do with wages. The major contractions that will be discussed below are the effect of severe wage cuts in the public sector and the reduction of salaries in the private sector. These are linked to the dismantling of collective bargaining, the personalization of pay, and the conversion of full employment into forms of flexible and undeclared work (see below). A common feature for all tax payers is the explosion in

S. Sakellaropoulos, *Greece's (un) Competitive Capitalism and the Economic Crisis*,
https://doi.org/10.1007/978-3-030-14319-0_5

income tax, which of course has a significant impact on employees and pensioners, who are the majority of the population (Institute of Labour—Greek General Confederation of Labour 2012: 334).[1]

To be more specific, as measured by the European Commission's Ameco database, the reduction in average real earnings per employee is cumulative for the period 2010–2015 at −20.1% at a time when the European Union (EU) average is +2.0%, with the result that of all EU countries Greece comes last in the index of change in average real earnings (Institute of Labour—Greek General Confederation of Labour 2016: 142). It is characteristic that while in the second quarter of 2009 only 7.4% of public sector employees received €800 per month or less, by the second quarter of 2016 this figure had risen to 11%. The 11.6% who in 2009 were receiving between €800 and €1000 would rise to 23.6%, and only 13% would be receiving between €1300 and €1800, compared with 25.3% in 2009 (Institute of Labour—Greek General Confederation of Labour 2017: 112). At the same time for people working in the private sector, whereas in the second quarter of 2009 27.9% of such employees were being paid a net salary of €800 per month or less, by the second quarter of 2016 this had risen to 51.6%. The 25.6% of employees who in 2009 were receiving €800 to €1000 will be reduced to 17.3% and only 4.4% will receive between €1300 and €1800 as opposed to 6.7% in 2009 (Institute of Labour—Greek General Confederation of Labour 2017: 110).

As for the minimum wage, before the advent of the Memoranda it came to €751, reduced to €586 in the second Memorandum (an annual reduction of 22%) and for young people under 25 it fell to €510 (an annual reduction of 32%). In terms of units of purchasing power, Greece fell from the seventh place that it occupied in the first half of 2010 to the eleventh place among the countries of the EEC in the first half of 2016, having significantly narrowed the distance from Poland and Portugal (Institute of Labour—Greek General Confederation of Labour 2017: 106).

[1] Taxation of income has grown as a percentage of GDP from 8.4% in 2009 to 10.3% in 2016 and total tax revenue risen from 32.5% to 41.2%. This is attributable to the abolition of many exemptions and concessions that were previously part of the taxation process for natural persons, to the increase in taxes on property ownership and the increase in the coefficients for indirect taxation. The result of all this would be that in 2014 the total tax burden as a proportion of gross income for a couple with two children where only one parent works would be at 28.7% (compared to 22.2% for EU21, 20.1% for the OECD) (Kaplanoglu 2017: 71).

On the subject of pensions, following the successive reductions, in December 2017 21.5% of retired pensioners (422,711 pensioners) received a pension of less than €500, 19% (374,188 pensioners) received between €500 and €700, 6% (325,725 pensioners) between €700 and €1000 and only 42.9% (845,352 pensioners) over €1000, euro resulting in an average pension of €980.

Overall, according to a relevant Credit Suisse Survey, average assets of Greek households have decreased from EUR 158,315 in 2009 to EUR 103,569 in 2016 (−52.9%).

The Changes in Labour Relations

On the subject of labour relations, significant changes have taken place in accordance with the provisions in the various packages of measures. These changes were implemented along the following five axes: (a) downgrading of the role of full and stable employment in favour of flexible forms of work; (b) dismantling of collective agreements: deregulation of the way remuneration is calculated; (c) flexibilization of working time, adapting it to the needs of the enterprise; (d) weakening the terms of protection from dismissal and (e) convergence of the status of labour in the private and public sectors within a context of overall deterioration (Kouzis 2016: 9).

A first basic dimension of implementing the programme involves changes in labour relations in the public sector, an approach assigning special priority to reducing the number of employees on the basis of one recruitment to every five retirements (initially the measure was 1/10), shrinkage of the number of temporary employment posts which largely covering permanent needs, obligatory transfers, extension of the working week from 37.5 hours to 40 hours, burdening workers with additional tasks and intensification of the pace of work in consequence of the staff shortages caused by the policy of reducing public sector employment and adoption of an employee loan regime (Kouzis 2016: 11).

The second dimension has to do with facilitating redundancies by reducing their costs, shortening from 24 to 4 months the maximum required period of notice for termination of contracts and 50% reduction in redundancy payments for workers with long years of service, with employers able to dispense redundancy pay in more, and smaller, instalments. At the same time, the minimum working time required for obligatory payment of compensation was lengthened from 2 to 12 months, the limit for collective redundancies was raised from four to six employees for enterprises employing between 20 and 150 employees and from 2% to 5% for larger enterprises, with abolition of the prerequisite for ministerial approval of a redundancy rate exceeding these limits.

The third dimension is linked to the promotion of flexible and precarious forms of employment. It includes lifting restrictions on the practice of lending employees, raising the maximum permitted time for lending workers, increasing the maximum period for renewal of temporary contracts, extension of the duration of rotating work timetables, abolition of pay increases for part-time work in the case of overtime and working schedules of less than twenty hours per week.

The fourth dimension concerns the dismantling of the system of collective bargaining and collective employment contracts, constituting an intermediate stage in the individualization of labour relations and the establishment of the wage levels. So there has been legislative recognition of the ability of companies to sign collective bargaining agreements with unfavourable content. In this way the sectoral equivalent is overriding, reducing the general minimum wage through legislative intervention that has abolished the role of the overall National Collective agreement. This has been replaced by a ministerial decision which abolishes seniority allowances for the long-term unemployed, who are then paid the minimum wage. It enforces the suspension of collective increases in basic salaries and the suspension of extending the application of sectoral and affiliated professional agreements to all workers in the industry and the profession, which encourages firms to withdraw from the employers' organizations that sign relevant collective agreements, binding for them. At the same time, other companies do not implement collective agreements but rather sign individual contracts which commit them to conformity only with the overall minimum wage levels. This allows the reduction in the time given for expiration of collective agreements, in the event that they run out or are terminated. Thus, the after activities on individual employment terms only cover just basic salary and child, education, long-service and hazardous employment allowances. This is a development that obliges trade unions to accelerate the acceptance of collective agreements before the end of the quarter (the institutionally underwritten negotiation period) under the pressure of the conditions laid down by employers, so as to avoid individual negotiation of salaries (Kouzis 2016: 13).

The fifth dimension has to do with the weakening of the role of collective agreements by transferring negotiation to the individual firm, in this way enhancing the employer's bargaining power, for the ultimate purpose of fully personalizing the terms of employment (Kouzis 2016: 16).

At the empirical level the result was that in 2016 only 10 sectoral affiliated professional agreements and 318 company collective agreements (constituting the later 95.21% of the total) were signed. By way of contrast, in 2010 65 sectoral affiliated professional agreements and 227 company collective agreements (constituting the later 74.18% of the total) were signed. It is interesting that in absolute figures, company contracts skyrocketed from 227 in 2010 to 976 in 2012, falling to 318 in 2016. The reason for this must be that after 2012 Law 4024/11 came into general application, providing for legislative intervention against the generality of commitment to the National Collective Labour Convention. In consequence, there was no need to conclude company contracts because the employer's obligation now was to pay employees on the basis of the minimum national wage (Institute of Labour—Greek General Confederation of Labour 2016: 130). Finally, it is worth noting that sectoral agreements that have been signed in recent years are for people working in tourism, tourist offices, shipping companies, banks, whereas sectoral agreements are absent from wide sectors of the economy such as trade and the food industry (Institute of Labour—Greek General Confederation of Labour 2017: 114).

As with what is occurring with flexible working relationships, there is a snowballing tendency for appointments to be made on the basis of relationships such as individual part-time employment or rotational contracts. Specifically, whereas in 2009, 21% of new recruits were on flexible work schedules (16.8% part-time and 4.2% rotational), by 2017 this would have risen to 54.9% (40.9% part-time and 14.9% rotational work). Against this background, there is another negative dimension to the conversion of full-time contracts into flexible forms of work. Whereas in 2009 there were 16,977 relevant cases, in 2016 the figure would reach

51,262 (+201.95%). Conversions at the unilateral instigation of an employer opinion rose from 612 in 2009 to 5541 in 2016 (+790.69%) (Institute of Labour—Greek General Confederation of Labour 2017: 118). These changes also have a significant impact on working hours—the percentage of workers working on Saturdays has risen from 24.6% in 2008 to 31.2% in 2014 and those working on Sundays from 5.8% in 2008 to 12.7% % in 2014. The figure for those working at night increased from 3.7% in 2008 to 6.3% in 2014 (Institute of Labour—Greek General Confederation of Labour 2016: 111). Finally, the cutback on full employment and the general context of austerity explain why almost half (44.5%) of the new jobs on offer are remunerated at €400 euros per month or less. Certain others (43.9%) are paid between €400 and €800, 9.9% pay between €800 and €1000 and just 1.7% pay more than €1000.

The Rise in Unemployment

A third, very important consequence, mentioned briefly in the previous chapter, has been the steep rise in the level of unemployment from 7.9% in November 2008 to 20.9% in November 2017 (EU-27 average 7.3%, Eurozone average 8.7%), with Greece having the highest rate of unemployment both in the Eurozone and in the EU-28. It is indeed characteristic that between 2008 and 2014 the number of households with one unemployed member rose from 286,000 to 788,000, the number with two unemployed members from 31,000 to 168,000 and with three or more unemployed members from 3000 to 36,000. The number of unemployed heads of households as a percentage of total unemployed rose from 19.8% to 31.3% and in absolute terms from 98,000 to 245,000 (Giannitsis and Zografakis 2018: 241–212). That said, it should be emphasized that the majority of unemployed people (75.7% of the total) are long-term unemployed and the rate of unemployment among those aged under 25 increased from 22.4% in the third quarter of 2008 to 43.7% in the third quarter of 2017. As regards the correlation between educational level and unemployment, it is noted that higher education graduates have an unemployment rate (second quarter of 2017) of 16.2%, post-secondary education (25.3%) and secondary education

(23.3%). This leads us to the conclusion that the possession of a degree of relatively little significance, a finding that must be related to the traditional and not particularly innovative character of Greek capitalism. Beyond that, even these very high unemployment figures are regarded as an underestimate. That is because they do not include people who have become disillusioned and are no longer trying to find work, or unemployed immigrants who do not have a residence permit, or disabled people who want to work, but cannot because of lack of infrastructure (Ioannidis and Pieros 2015: 41). To these must be added those who work, like it or not, in positions that offer underemployment. If this methodology is followed, according to estimates by the Institute of Labour—Greek General Confederation of Labour, then real unemployment is over 27% in the second quarter of 2017. And we will have to wait until 2030 for it to fall below 10%.

Apart from the question of how unemployment is calculated, it is undeniable that the unemployment benefit in Greece is low, both in value and in duration, given that it does not correspond to a percentage of the lost salary but is 57% of the general minimum wage, for a maximum of twelve months, but also with numerous constraints. The result is that the allowance was paid only to 86,773 unemployed people in January 2018, of the 903,303 registered with Organization for the Occupation of Labour Force (OAED), that is, 9.6% of the registered unemployed. In March 2010 296,245 people were paid the allowance, of the 734,059 registered. This amounted to 40% of the total.

The Distribution of Wealth and the Growth of Social Inequalities

These developments have made a decisive contribution to the redistribution of wealth, among both the poorest and the wealthiest strata as well as within the richest strata.

The first interesting point is that the number of very wealthy people in Greece increased between 2011 and 2014. Specifically, in 2014 there were eleven multi-billionaires, as against the nine that were counted in 2013. Their total wealth increased from $16 billion to $18 billion. In 2011 there were 445 people who each had over $30 million in assets, with a total fortune coming to $50 billion or 24% of gross domestic product (GDP). By 2014 their number had risen to 565, and their total property was estimated at $70 billion, or about 39.5% of GDP (Wealth 2014). At the same time, the 576 richest Greeks owned a fortune worth $88 billion, equivalent to 50% of the country's total GDP in 2014. According to the banks' "Private Banking", it is estimated that just on the Athens Stock Exchange 2500 people have shares exceeding €1 million in value. The Greeks, on the other hand, who are simply millionaires, have been calculated by Julius Baer to number 34,723, or 0.8% of the country's population and accounting for around 20% of GDP. All this was mentioned to show that there have also been winners in the crisis, whose share of total wealth is rising. But it does not mean that there is not simultaneous destruction of capital, as already indicated in Chap. 4. Some may, either in absolute or in relative terms, have strengthened their presence, but there has also been that part of the economic elite that saw its position weakened. The number of millionaires in Greece between 2006 and 2016 fell from 54,800 to 40,000; the number owning more than 10 million fell from 2050 to 1500; the number with more than 100 million fell from 85 to 62 (The wealth report 2017: 67). This data reveals the contradictory character of the clearing functions of the crisis, which for some may be an opportunity but for others is a disaster.

To return to the big picture, it should be noted that whatever the losses to the more affluent strata, the clear class content of crisis management will have the effect of increasing social inequalities, since the main issue is not regrouping within the bourgeoisie but developments within society as a whole.

Thus, according to the most recent data from the National Statistical Service of Greece, the 2016 survey, citing information on income from the year 2015, revealed that inequality between the richest 20% and the poorest 20% increase in the period 2009–2015—in 2009 the richest fifth of households had an income 5.8 times higher than the poorest fifth, in 2011 6.0 and in 2015 6.6. Similarly, the Gini inequality ratio rose from 33.1 in 2008 to 34.3 in 2015, with the result that Greece is ranked third among EU-15 members in terms of income inequality already in 2014 while also showing the third highest change for the period 2009–2014

(Institute of Labour—Greek General Confederation of Labour 2017: 134). At the same time, the most prosperous tenth saw its 25% share of income remaining steady throughout the period between 2008 and 2016 while the poorest tenth fell from 2.5 to 2.0, that is to say the ratio between the poorest tenth and the richest fell from 1/10 to 1/12.5 (Giannitsis and Zografakis 2018: 199). Other calculations, made by Leventi and Matsaganis, indicate that the ratio between the poorest and the richest fifth went from 1/5.4 in 2009 to 1/6.5 in 2014, and the ratio between the poorest and the richest 10% went from 8.9 in 2009 to 14.3 in 2014 (Leventi and Matsaganis 2016: 9). This development should not be thought surprising if we bear in mind that the rate of income tax and social security contributions rose by 2.95% for the poorest households as against 1.63% for the richest. It is a situation that becomes even worse if one bears in mind that property tax for poor households increased from 0.14% of their gross income (2010) to 6.04% (2015) and for wealthier households from 0.12% to 2.46% (Institute of Labour—Greek General Confederation of Labour 2017: 134).

The Growth of Poverty

Increasing inequalities also led to a corresponding increase in poverty, albeit to a differing extent depending on how it is calculated. Relative poverty showed a very small increase from 20.1% in 2010 to 21.2% in 2016. This was, however, significantly higher than in other EU countries (EU-28: 17.3%). The limited dimensions of the increase is attributable to the fact that the relative poverty rate shows the proportion of the population with income below a floating threshold, which is conventionally defined in relation to the median income for the whole population.

Given that the relative poverty threshold by definition varies with the average disposable income, the relative poverty index may not change much, or may remain stationary. In Greece, in the latest survey, the monetary threshold of relative poverty for a single-person household was €4500 per year (compared to €7178 in the 2010 survey). For a four-person household with two adults and two children it was €9450 (In 2010: €15,073).[2] The average annual disposable income of all the country's households rose to €14,932 in the 2016 survey and proceeded to show a continuous decline throughout the crisis (in 2010: €24,224). In contrast, taking into account the relative poverty gap, which measures the difference between the poverty line (for the whole population) and the median income equivalent for people below the poverty line (as a percentage of the latter), the gap amounts to 31.9% according to the 2016 survey (2010: 23.4% Mitrakos 2018: 15). Correspondingly, a very high percentage of the population of Greece is at risk of poverty or social exclusion (i.e. people living in material deprivation and/or performing low-intensity labour), according to the 2016 survey amounting to 35.7% of the population (EU-28: 23.7%), whereas in 2010 reached 27.7%.[3] Another important indicator compares the standard of living of each family to what it was in the recent past, measuring the percentage of the population with an income below the poverty line of some previous year, at real prices. On this basis, while the poverty rate for the survey year 2010, calculated on the basis of the 2005 poverty line (60% of 2005 median income expressed in 2010 prices based on the Harmonized Index of Consumer Prices) was 16.3%, the corresponding figure for 2016 was as high as 43.0%. According to EU-SILC (Statistics on Income and Living Conditions) data, in Greece 48.9% of the population would be classified as poor on the basis of the conditions of 2008, whereas in 2010 the corresponding percentage was much lower (24.9% of the population). It is worth noting that for the EU as a whole, the poverty rate set for a fixed poverty line increased between 2010 and 2014 from 13% to 15% on the basis of the conditions of 2005 (from 17% to 19% on the basis of the conditions of 2008) (Mitrakos 2018: 17–18). Finally, it should be noted that the various social transfers reduce poverty in Greece by only 4.1% (EU-28: 8.7%, Eurozone: 8.5%), placing it second last in the EU-28 in this connection.

[2] Which means that these people have to live from less than 12.63 EUR per day (if living alone) or survive on less than 6.62 EUR per day and person (for a household composed of 2 adults and 2 children below 14 years of age).

[3] In other words, they have to survive on less than 8.42 EUR per day (for a single household) or on less than 4.42 EUR per day and person for a family household with 2 adults and 2 children.

That said, enlisting the data on households from the Greek National Statistical Service, the material deprivation indicator,[4] that is, the percentage of households unable to meet at least four of the nine basic needs reached 22.4% in 2016, compared to 11.0% in 2009 (Greek National Statistical Service 2016). More specifically, the percentage of the population living in a house where conditions are cramped comes to 28.7% (up from 25.5% in 2010). The percentage of households stating that they do not have the financial means to secure adequate heating in the winter is 29.2% (up from 15.4% in 2010),[5] whereas in the EU in 2015 it was 9.4% (as in 2010). The proportion of households unable to pay their regular bills was 39.2%,[6] while 54.1% of households that have taken a consumer loan for the purchase of goods and services claim that they are facing great difficulties repaying it or keeping up with the installments (up from only 12.4% in 2010). A total of 54.7% could not deal with unexpected expenses in the order of €384[7] whereas in the EU the figure was 37.3% in 2015 (and 36.7% in 2010). A total of 12.1% cannot afford to have chicken, meat or fish in their diet every other day (up from 7.9% in 2010) whereas in the EU the figure for 2015 was 8.5% (compared to 8.8% in 2010). In addition, 52.5% declare themselves unable to afford a week's holiday (up from 46.5% in 2010), and the minimum net monthly income required to meet the needs of Greek households is €1716 (down from €2464 in 2010). Overall the average of goods and services of which individuals are deprived comes to 4.0 (up from 3.7 in 2010) (Hellenic Statistical Authority 2010; Hellenic Statistical Authority 2016; Institute

[4] Material deprivation—proportion of people facing serious economic difficulties with the result that they lack least four basic items from the total of nine: (a) difficulties in meeting regular expenses such as rent or instalments on loan repayments, regular bills (electricity, water, natural gas, credit card payments or instalments on household appliance, and so on; (b) financial inability to pay for one week's holiday; (c) financial inability to purchase food including chicken, meat, fish or vegetables of equivalent nutritive value every other day; (d) financial inability to face unexpected but necessary expenses to the sum of around €384; (e) financial inability to afford a telephone (including a mobile phone); (f) financial inability to afford a colour television; (g) financial inability to afford a washing machine; (h) financial inability to afford a private car and (i) financial inability to afford adequate heating.

[5] Resulting in a 62.5% reduction in monthly consumption of heating oil in the 2008–2013.

[6] It is largely attributable to this that Greece has currently the highest rate of housing cost overburden in the European Union with increased steeply from 18.1% (2010) to 40.7% (2014).

[7] The 2010 figure was 28.2% but for the figure of €584.

of Labour–Greek General Confederation of Labour 2017: 132.) In terms of expenditure, between 2008 and 2016 Greek households reduced their monthly expenditure by 21.2% for food, 24.4% for alcohol and tobacco, 26.6% for education, 30.6% for housing and 33.8% for health (Greek Statistical Authority 2017). The proportion of households with spending lower than income fell from 21.9% in 2009 to 13.5% in 2014 (Charalambakis 2017: 50). It should be added to this that the number of children classified as deprived more than doubled between 2007 and 2015, when the percentage rose from 20% of the total to 45% (Papatheodorou et al. 2017: 27–28).

The result is that, from being ninth in 2009 among the European countries in the percentage of population suffering from material deprivation, by 2016 Greece had by 2016 risen to third place, as shown in Table 5.1. More importantly, during the period under review, material deprivation in Greece doubled (+11.2%), whereas in the EU it declined slightly (−0.6%) and in the Eurozone increased only slightly (+0.8%).

The Crisis in Health Care

In the health sector too, the crisis affects the possibilities of access. There are three reasons for this as follows: (a) Memorandum policies have led to public expenditure on health being reduced from 6.8% of GDP in 2010 to 5.4% in 2016, to numerous public hospitals being closed, and too the insured persons are forced to pay 40% of the total price every time they are buying pharmaceutical drugs in 2015, whereas in 2011 it was only 9% (Burgi 2017: 82; 90); (b) the increase in unemployment has contributed to expansion in the numbers of uninsured people and (c) austerity policies have reduced possibilities for access through extra-institutional channels ("fakelaki"[8] but also the entry ticket to hospitals that was in force for a time). Eurostat estimates that the overall percentage of those who, for economic reasons, did not make use of health services, was 9.7%

[8] The "fakelaki" is a particularly widespread practice in Greece, and involves the patient giving an extra sum (in a small envelope—fakelaki in Greek) to a doctor in a public hospital to ensure that treatment is made available more promptly.

Table 5.1 Distribution of population facing serious material deprivation in Europe: 2009–2016

Countries	2009	2016
Bulgaria	41.9	31.9
Rumania	32.1	23.8
Latvia	22.1	12.8
Hungary	20.3	16.2
Lithuania	−15.6	13.5
Greece	11.0	22.4
Croatia	14.3[a]	12.5
Cyprus	9.5	15.4
Italy	7.3	11.9
Poland	15.0	6.7
Slovakia	11.1	9.0
Estonia	6.2	4.8
Portugal	9.1	8.4
Malta	5.0	4.4
G. Britain	3.3	5.2
Czech	6.1	4.8
Slovenia	6.1	5.2
Belgium	5.2	5.5
Spain	4.5	5.8
France	5.6	4.4
Germany	5.4	3.9
Austria	4.3	3.0
Finland	2.8	2.2
Denmark	2.3	3.7
Holland	1.4	2.7
Norway	2.2	2.0
Luxembourg	1.1	2.0
Sweden	1.6	0.7
Eurozone-19	6.0	6.8
European Union	8.4[a]	7.8

Source: National Statistical Authority
[a]2010

in 2014, as against 4% in 2009. As a result, the percentage of people with a chronic health problem has risen from 39.7% in 2009 to 49.7% in 2014, and those who feel that they have been obliged for health reasons to limit their activity has increased from 22.8% to 29.7%. 2.1% of the population aged 15 years or over have had a stroke or experiences the chronic effects of a past stroke whereas in 2009 the figure was 1.7%. 9.2% of the population suffers from diabetes, compared to 7.9% in 2009.

4.7% of the population is plagued by depression, a percentage also higher than in 2009 (2.6%).

In this context it becomes understandable how between 2008 and 2016 the number of births in Greece declined from 188,302 to 92,898 (−27.3%) while in 2008–2015 in the EU-28 the number of births declined by 6.7%. Overall, between 2008 and 2016, the population decreased by 326,000 (−3%). Greece has the fifth lowest birth rate in the EU and is ranked 192nd of 203 countries worldwide. Infant mortality (deaths of infants under one year of age) increased between 2009 and 2016 from 2.65 deaths per 1000 live births to 4.17 deaths (+57.4%). The number of deaths rose from 108,316 in 2009 to 118,785 in 2016 (+9.7%), with the ratio per 1000 inhabitants rising from 9.60 to 11.02. Last but not least, in a country where suicide rates until recently had been the lowest on a global scale, they increased from 391 cases in 2009 to 521 in 2015 (+35.1%).

In conclusion, at the level of social practices all the above helps to explain why there has been a significant increase in the provision of food aid by various bodies (church, municipalities), and the number of people who are supplied with food and medicine by social supermarkets and pharmacies has proliferated, with a significant sector of poverty-stricken strata becoming largely dependent on the solidarity of its kinship network and social environment (Giannitsis and Zografakis 2018: 175, 223).

They also explain how it is that after several decades there has been a re-emergence of the phenomenon of emigration, and indeed this time with people of a high educational level. Specifically, it is estimated that between 2010 and 2015 203,000 emigrated, of whom 174,000 remain abroad. Of these, 135,000 are university graduates, and the proportion of graduates among the emigrants rose from the 25% that it was in the 1980s to 80% in the period of the crisis (Labrianidis 2015).

References

Burgi N., 2017, "Le démantèlement méthodique et tragique des institutions grecques de santé publique", *La Revue De l' IRES* vol. 91–92, pp. 77–110.

Charalambakis E., 2017, "How much has the crisis affected the situation of Greek households?", *Financial Bulletin of the Bank of Greece* vol. 45, pp. 37–54 (in Greek).

Giannitsis T. and S. Zografakis, 2018, *Crisis management in Greece*, IMK Studies 58-2018, IMK at the Hans Boeckler Foundation, Macroeconomic Policy Institute.

Hellenic Statistical Authority, 2010, *Research study on income and living conditions in households for the year 2010*, Athens (in Greek).

Hellenic Statistical Authority, 2016, *Research study on income and living conditions in households for the year 2016*, Athens (in Greek).

Institute of Labour—Greek General Confederation of Labour, 2012, *The Greek economy and employment. Annual report 2012*, Athens: Institute of Labour—Greek General Confederation of Labour (in Greek).

Institute of Labour—Greek General Confederation of Labour, 2016, *The Greek economy and employment. Annual report 2016*, Athens: Institute of Labour—Greek General Confederation of Labour (in Greek).

Institute of Labour—Greek General Confederation of Labour, 2017, *The Greek economy and employment. Annual report 2017*, Athens: Institute of Labour—Greek General Confederation of Labour (in Greek).

Ioannidis G. and C. Pierros, 2015, *A proposal for 10% reduction in the rate of unemployment within three years*, Athens: Institute of Labour—Greek General Confederation of Labour (in Greek).

Kaplanoglu G., 2017, "Is it true that Greeks are overtaxed?", in Katsikas D., K. Filinis and M. Anastasatou (eds.) *Understanding the Greek crisis. Answers to crucial questions on the state, the economy and Europe*, Athens: Papazisis, pp. 59–78 (in Greek).

Kouzis G., 2016, "The crisis and the memoranda flatten labour", *Social Policy* vol. 6, pp. 7–20 (in Greek).

Labrianidis L., 2015, *Outward migration from Greece during the crisis*. Final report, http://www.lse.ac.uk/europeanInstitute/research/hellenicObservatory/CMS%20pdf/Research/NBG_2014_-Research_Call/LOIS%20LAMBRANIIDIS_Outward%20migration%20from%20Greece%20during%20the%20crisis%20.pdf, accessed on 7/3/2018.

Leventi C. and M. Matsaganis, 2016, *Estimating the distributional impact of the Greek crisis (2009–2014)*, OECD Economics Department Working Papers, no. 1312, OECD Publishing, Paris.

Mitrakos T., 2018, "Economic inequalities, poverty and social exclusion: international experience and the case of Greece in the recent crisis", *Social Policy* vol. 9, pp. 7–24 (in Greek).

Papatheodorou C. and S. Papanastasiou/Unicef, 2017, *The situation of children in Greece 2017: children of the crisis*, Athens: Unicef (in Greek).
The Wealth Report, 2017, "*The global perspective on prime property and investment*", KnightFrank.com/WealthReport, accessed on 25/2/2018.
Wealth X., 2014, *World ultra wealth report 2013–2014*, http://www.worldwealthreport.com, accessed on 10/4/2018.

6

Change in Social Stratification in the Greece of Crisis (2009–2017)

Introduction

In this chapter, I deal with the registration and interpretation of changes in social stratification in the country during the crisis period of 2009 to 2017. This period has been chosen to enable us to study how far the economic crisis has influenced the changes in presentation of social classes in the country and how far it is conducive to investigation of its specific causes. But before I move on to describing and interpreting developments, it is important that there should be a preceding theoretical reference to the issue of social classes.

The Theoretical Framework

Within the framework of a chapter focused on the changes which have been made in the morphology of Greek society during the crisis, it is not possible to make an extensive reference to theoretical issues of social class theory, something with which have been analysed in detail in other work (Sakellaropoulos 2014). For this reason, I will just mention certain of my

S. Sakellaropoulos, *Greece's (un) Competitive Capitalism and the Economic Crisis*,
https://doi.org/10.1007/978-3-030-14319-0_6

theoretical findings, avoiding embarking on any more exhaustive discussion, whether inside or outside the Marxist schema.

In my opinion Lenin's celebrated definition is as pertinent as ever, assisting with clarification of the multi-faceted problem of defining social classes: "Classes are large groups of people which differ from each other by the place they occupy in a historically determined system of social production, by their relation (in most cases fixed and formulated in law) to the means of production, by their role in the social organization of labour, and, consequently, by the mode of acquisition and the dimension of the share of social wealth of which they dispose" (Lenin 1977: 13).

It may be noted that in Lenin's definition there is a co-articulation of three criteria: (1) position in relation to the means of production, (2) position in the social division of labour, (3) means of acquisition of—and level of—income (Bensaid 1995: 203).

The common denominator that traverses these three criteria in Lenin's definition is the phenomenon of exploitation. The possessor of the means of production exploits the person who possesses only his labour power, because he pays him less than the value of his labour. However, in order for this social relation derived from the possession of capital to be reproduced (after all this is why Marx claimed that capital is primarily a social relation) some structural characteristics must be shaped in the production process that will facilitate circulation of capital and create the hierarchical structures necessary for working discipline to become attainable.

In this way what is elaborated is an internally intricate but at the same time externally pyramidal organization of production wherein, for the relations of exploitation to be implemented, relations of domination are also absolutely essential.

In this sense exploitation, and on a second plane relation of domination, but above all the way they are articulated into a social structure (Croix 1984: 94), are the agents in formation and reproduction of social classes.

The conclusion is thus that, on the one hand, the foundations of prevailing social arrangements are to be situated in the existence of relations of exploitation and domination, and on the other hand that membership in a particular class depends firstly on ownership of the means of production and secondly on position in the division of labour and the amount of social wealth that each person extracts.

Nevertheless, it must be made clear that the economic element (relation to the means of production, level of income etc.) is the most important, in the final analysis the decisive, but not the only, element. The "position occupied by individuals" may be determined by reference to both the political and the ideological elements that contribute to shaping the relations of domination. Thus, the top echelon of the State bureaucracy, members of government, high-ranking military personnel and so on, belong, by virtue of their position in the machinery of power, to the bourgeois class.

The intervention of capital and the State in maintenance and reproduction of relations of exploitation is continuous and embraces all levels of social activity. The reason for this is that capital does not only exploit the worker economically but also exercises power over his functioning in the workplace, from the moment that it determines what he will produce, and how. At the same time, through the Ideological Apparatus of the State[1] it integrates him ideologically, for the worker accepts the terms of his political and economic exploitation as the "natural" result of the exchange of the equivalents "wage" and "labour power". To put it differently, the framework of the relations of exploitation is reproduced by the functioning of the political and ideological mechanisms within which capitalist power is also reproduced not through the realization of surplus value but through reproduction of managerial and executive labour.

With these general definitions as our starting point, I proceed to some conclusions about the most significant characteristics of the bourgeois class: it is the class that directs the capitalist productive process, the class that, always with a view to its own interests, defines the context and the hierarchies of the social praxis dominated by capital (Bihr 1989: 88–89). Its position is based on the ownership of the means of production and on subjection of society to its power. At a level of high abstraction its members are defined as non-productive exploiters/possessors/extractors of surplus labour-cum-organizers of the mechanisms of domination (Johnson 1977: 203).

The working class is deprived of possession of the means of production and performs all those practices that are aimed at furthering reproduction of capital and reinforcement of social power. It neither possesses control

[1] For the importance of the role of the Ideological State Apparatus, see Althusser (2001).

of nor is able to influence the context of its labour. It simply plays an executive role within the social division of labour (Bihr 1989: 90). In a more abstract away the working class could be defined as consisting of exploited/non-possessors/producers/wage earners enduring the constraints imposed by the mechanism of domination (Johnson 1977: 202–203).

Nevertheless, the existence of the two basic classes of the capitalist mode of production does not mean that there are not also other social classes in a society. Only at a high level of abstraction, that of the mode of production, is it possible to speak of two, and only two, classes. At the level of national social formations the number of classes is greater, precisely because the different historical development of each formation includes more modes of production and also "(a) because there are more modes of production, that is to say forms of organization of the productive process, which are not based on the appropriation of surplus labour, on exploitation, and (b) because some of the class functions of the dominant class are normally delegated to social groups that are not part of the dominant class (are not owners of the means of production)" (Milios 2002: 64).

This social class, which occupies, in the active sense of the term, a position between the two basic classes of the capitalist mode of production, the working class and the bourgeoisie, is named the petty bourgeoisie.

The basic characteristic that is common to members of the petty bourgeoisie is that their income is greater than what is necessary for reproduction of their labour power, irrespective of how this is achieved. Sometimes it is realized through the appropriation of surplus value and sometimes through earnings that exceed the cost of reproduction of their labour power. Above and beyond that a second characteristic is that they are not exclusively subjected to domination by other classes. The traditional petty bourgeoisie exerts power over the workers it employs, the new salaried petty bourgeoisie is subject to the power of capital but *also* exerts power over the working class, whereas the self-employed (who are also to be included in the new petty bourgeoisie) neither exert power nor are subjected to it.

Further refining this line of thought it could be argued that the petty bourgeoisie is divisible into two factions: the traditional petty bourgeoisie and the new petty bourgeoisie. The traditional petty bourgeoisie includes owners of small manufacturing companies, small family businesses and small commercial enterprises that are not involved with extended reproduction of capital (that is to say employing up to nine workers).[2] The new petty bourgeoisie is comprised of all those who work either as self-employed professionals or as salaried employees engaged in supervision and organization of the work system, realization of surplus value, oversight of the cohesiveness of capitalist operations or, finally, legitimation of the terms of reproduction of existing social relations.

Nevertheless, if the theoretical approach of social stratification is to be comprehensive it will be necessary, above and beyond reference to the basic class divisions and to the petty bourgeoisie, for there to be an approach to cross-class social categories such as farmers, civil servants and intellectuals.

As regards the *agricultural strata* and small landowners, that is, those who, in Greece, are proprietors of up to 50 acres, they are the less affluent layers of rural society and do not employ wage labour. Correspondingly, proprietors who make limited use of wage labour in cultivation of their land, those who in Greece own between 50 and 200 acres and are engaged in simple reproduction of their capital (Panitsidis 1992) belong to the intermediate rural strata, whereas those who employ a wide range of salaried employees, those who in Greece are proprietors of more than 200 acres, which enables them to proceed with extended reproduction of capital, belong to the wealthy rural strata.

Another stratum that is distinctive for its cross-class characteristics is that of the civil servants. This is attributable to the fact that a civil servant may be employed in very different sectors. A significant sector employed in public enterprises such as processing, energy and water supply, communications, transport and banks are productive working people (Meiksins 1986: 17), because they are paid for less than the value of their work when they exchange their labour power for capital. In that sense individuals in this category are *both* productive workers and people exploited by the collective capitalist and to be included in the working class.

---

[2] For why more than nine workers are needed for there to be extended reproduction of capital, see Sakellaropoulos 2001: 170.

On the other hand people working in the educational apparatus, in cases where education is provided free, and administrative personnel in the various public bodies and ministries, are not productive workers but, with the exception of senior and middle-ranking officials in the ministries, the armed forces, university professors and civil servants who are members of the new petty bourgeoisie (engineers, lawyers and doctors) and work in the public sector, belong to the working class for the following reasons:

1. They do not own their means of production.
2. Their surplus labour is subject to extraction.
3. They perform the function of the collective worker (Carchedi 1977: 134).
4. They are remunerated with a salary which is determined by State income policy (Lytras 1993: 98), which is equal to the value of their labour power, because it correlates directly with salaries in the private sector (Bouvier-Ajam and Mury 1963: 73) which tend not to rise above the level of reproducing their labour power.

On the basis of this reasoning, civil servants as a collectivity, united essentially by the institution of permanent tenure, are a cross-class entity, the great majority of whose personnel are to be classified as working class, the middle-ranking officials in the ministries and public enterprises, university teachers and military personnel, apart from the top echelon of the officer corps, belong to the petty bourgeoisie, and the heads of administration (political, military and academic) and the managers of State-owned companies belong to the bourgeoisie by virtue of the dominant position they occupy within the collective capitalist known as the State.

Another category of individuals not belonging to a specific social class is that of intellectuals. Of course, this is not a professional category but a social layer, a large number of whom are salary earners. Gramsci, who involved himself assiduously with the question, regarded the action of intellectuals as confined to the realm of the superstructure and pertaining to both the "private sphere" and "political society". The former are concerned primarily with the functioning of their hegemony, the latter with the management of their direct domination (Gramsci 1972: 62). There is obviously an internal graduation to their activity. The highest rung is occupied by individuals who have undertaken the formulation, organization and systematization of the dominant ideology (Gramsci 1972: 63) and who belong to the bourgeoisie. The lower levels include executive officers whose concern is the generation and promotion of consent and discipline and who are to be included in the petty bourgeoisie.

Workers who contribute intellectual labour constitute a separate category. They produce surplus labour/surplus value for their employers (as, e.g. educators in the private sector). These strata of "intellectual workers" from whom surplus labour/surplus value is extracted belong to the working class. They do not count as "intellectuals" because they are charged not with planning and organizing consent but rather with implementing the terms of its realization.

Changes in Social Stratification

On the basis of the theoretical framework that has just been presented, we can proceed to an assessment of social classes in the Greek social formation between 2009 and 2017.

Above and beyond the preceding theoretical inferences, we propose to utilize existing data from the Labour Force Quarterly Data on the mode of employment of the workforce (occupation *and* position in the workplace) in addition to the methodology has been adopted in a preceding study (Sakellaropoulos 2014) which we cannot present in detail here. The final result for 2009 can be seen in Table 6.1.

Employers (7.4%) of the economically active population (EAP) are divided into those belonging to the bourgeoisie, those belonging to the traditional petty bourgeoisie and those belonging to the wealthy agrarian strata. The bourgeoisie class comprises 0.5% employers with enterprises of more than nine employees and 1% senior managers (they have been calculated at two on average per business) as well as 0.5% senior public sector executives, so the bourgeoisie overall accounts for 2% of the EAP. A total of 0.7% of employers in the farming sector belong to the wealthy agrarian strata, corresponding to those owning over 20 hectares (according to the 2010 data that is closest to the period under review—see

Table 6.1 Groups of individual professions and positions in the profession 2009

	Occupation status	Employers	Own account workers	Workers in a family business	Salaried employees	Unemployed
Profession						
(1)	9.2	3.4	4.2	0.1	1.2	
(2)	13.4	0.8	2.5	–	10.1	
(3)	7.7	0.2	0.9	0.1	6.5	
(4)	9.4	–[b]	0.1	0.3	9.0	
(5)	13.1	0.3	0.9	1.9	10.1	
(6)	10.3	0.9	6.9	2.2	0.4	
(7)	12.0	1.4	2.2	0.5	7.9	
(8)	6.6	0.2	1.3	0.1	4.8	
(9)	6.8	–	0.4	–	6.2	
(10)	1.2	–	–	–	1.2	–
Unemployed	10.3					
% EAP[a]	100.0	7.4	19.5	5.3	57.5	10.3

(1) Managers (2) Professionals (3) Technicians and associate professionals (4) Clerical support workers (5) Service and sales workers (6) Skilled agricultural, forestry and fishery workers (7) Craft and related trade workers (8) Plant and machine operators and assemblers (9) Elementary occupations (10) Other unclassified persons

Source: Hellenic Statistical Authority, Labour Force Survey 4th Quarter 2009

[a]Marginal deviations due to rounding off

[b]Negligible percentage

National Statistical Service of Greece [ESYE] 2010) and 0.2% to the middle agrarian strata, whereas those who do not carry out expanded capital reproduction and belong to the traditional petty bourgeoisie account for 4.5% of the EAP.

The self-employers comprise 19.5% of the EAP and can be divided into the following three categories:

The first category includes people employed in agriculture (6.9% of the EAP). They are farmers who do not employ a salaried workforce. Either they extract their surplus from their own employment or else they simply manage to subsist. In order to further distinguish them, the data on the distribution of arable land must be utilized as a basis. So, given that in 2009 about 75% of the farmers owned up to 5 hectares (ESYE 2010) and only 20% owned 10 to 20 hectares it could be concluded, respectively, that 5.2% of the EAP in the self-employed category are poor farmers and the remaining 1.7% are in the middle agrarian strata.

The second category includes members of the new petty bourgeoisie, that is to say all branches of the liberal professions who do not experience exploitation or domination and who together comprise 11.6% of the EAP. The third group consists of small entrepreneurs (small traders and small sellers) who do not exceed 0.9% of the EAP and are to be included in the traditional petty bourgeoisie.

The category of *Salaried Employees*, which is also the most populous statistical category (57.7% of the EAP), consists primarily of members of the working class and also the members of the bourgeoisie (1.2% of the profession of "managers") and the new petty bourgeoisie (10.1% of the category "professionals" and 6.5% of the category "technicians and associate professionals", not counting the teachers belonging to the working class, who account for 3.5% of the EAP (Kappos 2004: 158) and adding 1.5% for security forces (Iordanoglou 2013: 130). From that point on, the remaining 39.9% + 3.5% of teachers −1.5% of the security forces = 40.9% are members of the modern working class, with the new petty bourgeoisie class coming to 14.6% (10.1% + 6.5% – 3.5% + 1.5%).

Workers in a family business account for 5.3% of the EAP, primarily consisting of agricultural workers (2.2% of the EAP) and secondarily those performing ancillary tasks in trade (1.9% of the EAP). They are individuals involved in family-run economic activities. Therefore, this 2.2% should be included among the poor agricultural strata, and 1.9% among the members of the traditional petty bourgeoisie who are not engaged in expanded capital accumulation, and there are also 1.2% who are self-employed professionals belonging to the new petty bourgeoisie.

What needs to be emphasized, above and beyond what has been already mentioned, is that there is also an indeterminate number of members of the working class who are unemployed. Undoubtedly 10.3% of the unemployed are not part of the working class, as sections of the new petty bourgeoisie are affected by the problem of unemployment, as are small entrepreneurs who close their businesses. However, taking into account that 2.1% of the EAP were unemployed people with higher education degrees (ESYE 2009), it could be concluded that 10.3% of the unemployed are divided into 8.2% working class and 2.1% members of the new petty bourgeoisie class.[3]

It may be concluded, in brief, that the bourgeois class comprises 3.2% of the EAP, the wealthy agrarian strata 0.7%, the class of the traditional petty bourgeoisie, 7.3%, the new petty bourgeoisie class, 29.5%, the intermediate agrarian strata, 1.9%, the poor agrarian strata 7.4% and the working class 49.1%.

Table 6.2 is based on data for 2017:

As mentioned earlier, employers (5.7% of the EAP) can be divided into three main social groups: those belonging to the middle class, those belonging to the traditional petty bourgeoisie and those who are part of the wealthy agrarian strata. To estimate the size of the bourgeoisie, it could be posited 26,000 employers (i.e. 0.5% of the EAP), with more than nine employees[4] and pursuing expanded reproduction of capital as

[3] It should be noted that this calculation is performed to highlight general tendencies, global trends. It could not be considered that every graduate of higher education is to be included in the new petty bourgeoisie class, since there are graduates who perform executive tasks, but clearly the majority belong to this class, due to their intermediate role in production.

[4] According to the ERGANI information system, in autumn 2016 there were 233,151 companies, of which 26,121 employed more than nine people.

Table 6.2 Groups of individual professions and positions in the profession 2017

	Occupation status	Employers	Self-employers	Workers in a family business	Salaried employees	Unemployed
Profession						
(1)	1.8	0.8	0.3	–	0.7	
(2)	15.3	1.0	3.1	–	11.2	
(3)	6.3	0.3	0.7	–	5.2[a]	
(4)	8.4	0.2	0.2	0.2	7.8	
(5)	18.7	1.8	3.7	1.2	12.0	
(6)	8.8	0.7	6.5	1.3	0.3	
(7)	7.5	0.7	2.1	0.2	4.5	
(8)	4.8	0.2	1.1	–	3.5	
(9)	5.9	–[b]	0.2	0.1	5.6	
(10)	1.4	–	–	–	1.4	
Unemployed	21.1					21.1
% EAP	100.0	5.7	17.9[a]	3.2[a]	52.1	21.1

(1) Managers (2) Professionals (3) Technicians and associate professionals (4) Clerical support workers (5) Service and sales workers (6) Skilled agricultural, forestry and fishery workers (7) Craft and related trade workers (8) Plant and machine operators and assemblers (9) Elementary occupations (10) Other unclassified persons

Source: Hellenic Statistical Authority, Labour Force Survey 2d Quarter 2017

[a]Marginal deviations due to rounding off

[b]Negligible percentage

belonging to the bourgeoisie. Also to be included in the bourgeois class are the category senior managers, working in large Greek companies which, due to their size, have a vertical structure and a staff with clear managerial responsibilities: this covers about 52,000 people (with two directors on average for each major unit of production), or about 1.1% of the EAP. In addition to these there are State officials and employees of the broader public sector, who could be estimated to number about 25,000,[5] that is, 0.5% of the EAP. Correspondingly, 0.6% of agrarian employers who in 2010 owned more than 20 hectares (Pan-Hellenic Confederation of Agricultural Co-operatives 2013), belong to the wealthy agrarian strata. At the same time there are employers who have their own small businesses, usually family businesses, employing up to nine workers, and amount to 3.0% of the EAP. They are assigned to the class of the traditional petty bourgeoisie (small traders, small craftsmen etc.).

The self-employed come to 17.9% of the EAP and can be divided into three broad categories: the first includes those employed in agriculture (6.5% of the EAP). They are farmers who do not employ a salaried workforce or who extract a surplus from their own employment or simply pursue subsistence farming. It could be subjected to further subdivision based on data concerning the distribution of arable land. So, given that the most recent data (Pan-Hellenic Confederation of Agricultural Co-operatives 2013) for 2010 shows that about 76.6% of land belongs to those owning up to 5 hectares and only 18.8% to those owning 5 to 20 hectares, it may be concluded that 5.0% of the EAP are poor farmers and that the remaining 1.5% belong to the medium agrarian strata.

The second category consists of members of the new petty bourgeoisie, that is, self-employed workers of all kinds who are neither exploited nor dominated and who together make up 7.7% of the EAP. Finally, the third category includes small entrepreneurs (petty traders and sellers) who amount to 3.7% of the EAP and belong to the traditional petty bourgeoisie.

[5] This figure emerges if it is considered that, according to the October 2013 civil service census; there were 48,608 civil servants in positions of responsibility (Head of Service—Director). From the previous analysis could be concluded that the directors belong to the bourgeoisie and the heads of services to the new petty bourgeoisie. As there is one director for three heads of service, there are approximately 12,000 directors in total, to which should be added senior judges, ministerial advisers, high-level academics and national and local government civil cadres.

The most populous category, *wage earners* (52.1% of the EAP), is comprised primarily of members of the working class and also members of the bourgeoisie (0.7% of the EAP are in the "managers" category) and the new petty bourgeoisie, a total of 7.6% (4.5% in the category of "Technicians and Associate Professionals" and about 3.1% (150,000 people) comprising all categories of military and police personnel (83,000 from the Ministry of Defence, 60,000 from the Ministry of Public Order and 7500 from the Ministry of Shipping) (Petropoulos 2013: 55). The remaining 43.8% are members of the contemporary working class.

The category of family workers, which comprises 3.2% of the EAP, consists primarily of workers in agriculture (1.3% of the EAP) and ancillary personnel in trade and services and other branches of the secondary and tertiary sector (1.2% of the EAP). They are essentially people engaged in family-related economic activities. A total of 1.3% of them should, therefore, be classed with the poor rural strata, 1.2% as members of the traditional petty bourgeoisie who do not carry out extended capital accumulation, not to mention 0.7% self-employed professionals to be categorized belonging to the new petty bourgeoisie.

What must be emphasized, also, for the Table 6.2, is that there is an indeterminate number of working class members who are unemployed. Without that 21.1% is not to be included in the working class as a whole, because sections of the new petty bourgeois class are also affected by the problem of unemployment, as are small entrepreneurs who are unemployed because of the crisis. However, if taking into account that 5.4% of the EAP in 2014 were unemployed graduates with higher education (ESYE 2017), it may be concluded that 21.1% of the unemployed are to be divided into 15.7% belonging to the working class and 5.4% belonging to the new petty bourgeoisie.

In summary, it may be concluded that the bourgeoisie accounts for 2.8% of the EAP, the wealthy agrarian strata 0.6%, the traditional petty bourgeoisie 7.9%, the new petty bourgeois class 21.4%, the medium agrarian strata 1.5%, the rural poor 6.3% and the working class 59.5%.

Table 6.3 is based on the data for 2009 and 2017:

The figures in Table 6.3 relate to the transformations of social stratification from December 2009 to June 2017. The first conclusion that emerges is a contraction of the bourgeoisie. The reasons for this are to be

Table 6.3 Change in the social structure 2009 (4th quarter) and 2017 (2nd quarter) (%)

Class	2009	2017	Change 2009–2017
Bourgeois class	3.2	2.8	−0.4
Wealthy agrarian strata	0.7	0.6	−0.1
Traditional petty bourgeois class	7.3	7.9	+0.6
Medium agrarian strata	1.9	1.5	−0.4
New petty bourgeois class	29.5	21.4	−8.1
Working class	49.1	59.5	+10.4
Poor rural strata	7.4	6.3	−1.1
Not classified	0.9	–	−0.9

sought in the liquidating functions of the crisis, which has brought numerous companies to bankruptcy, but also in the reduction in the numbers of high-level staff in the public sector, where many executives have preferred retirement and monetary compensation to remaining in employment in very uncertain conditions.

It is interesting to note the small but real rise of the traditional petty bourgeoisie. The reasons for this have to do with the fact that because of the crisis, companies formerly of medium size in their capital holdings, have now reduced their turnover and have been transformed into small units. But there are also signs of a slow recovery getting under way from the summer of 2016.

Some changes are to be observed in the agrarian strata, and what emerges from this is an unequal decrease in the presence of the three categories of the rural strata. The explanation has been given, first and foremost, is that the global impact of the Greek crisis has affected the agrarian strata, even if not to the same degree, similarly to how it has affected the purely capitalist economy. In addition, the 2003 revision of the CAP, where subsidies were disconnected from the volume of production and the emphasis was placed on the area of cultivated land, led to further losses, particularly for middle-income landowners engaged exclusively in agriculture, whereas smallholders have of necessity turned to various forms of off-farm employment. It is likely that this is also the case for companies in the secondary and tertiary sectors: a significant proportion of medium-sized farmers have sold a part of their property and are now in the category of small farmers and this may also be the case of those who until recently were small farmers and who have remained without any property, thus becoming unemployed or wage earners. At the same time, a small proportion of the wealthiest farmers seem to be losing their fortunes. This development must be linked to the inability of certain well-off segments to cope with the conditions of competition vis-à-vis other wealthy rural strata. The estimate is therefore that the average area available to farmers who continue to own more than 20 hectares must be larger than in the past.

There is a significant growth of the working class, which must be due to the downward mobility created by the dismissals caused by the crisis, when highly qualified people who were in other positions have found themselves at a lower level in the division of labour. If this is combined with the contraction in the agrarian strata and the increasing turnover in large monopolistic enterprises, we arrive at a convincing interpretation for the expansion of the working class. However, it should be clarified here that the size of the working class is considered to have been underestimated. The reason for this is that even if a large proportion of foreign workers are registered in the surveys whether or not they possess a residence permit, there must certainly be others who are not registered, but obviously belong to the working class because they are employed mainly in construction, for manual labour, in trade and services, as agricultural workers and so on.

References

Althusser L., 2001, "Ideology and Ideological State Apparatuses" in L. Althusser, Lenin and Philosophy and other essays, London and New York: Monthly Review Press, pp. 127–186.

Bensaid D., 1995, *Marx l'intempestif*, Fayard: Paris.

Bihr A., 1989, *Entre Bourgeoisie et Prolétariat*, Paris: L' Harmattan.

Bouvier-Ajam M. and G. Mury. 1963, *Les classes sociales en France*, Paris: Editions Sociales.

Carchedi G., 1977, *On the Economic Identification of Social Classes*, London: Routledge.

Croix de ste G., 1984, "Class in Marx's Conception of History, Ancient and Modern", *New Left Review* no 146, pp. 94–111.

Gramsci A., 1972, The intellectuals. Athens: Stochastis (in Greek).

Hellenic Statistical Authority (ESYE), 2009, Concise Statistical Yearbook, Athens (in Greek).
Hellenic Statistical Authority (ESYE), 2010, Census of Agricultural and Livestock Holdings, Athens (in Greek).
Hellenic Statistical Authority (ESYE), Labour Force Survey 2nd Quarter 2017, Athens (in Greek).
Iordanoglou C., 2013, *State and interest groups*, Athens: Polis.
Johnson T., 1977, "What is to be known?". *Economy and Society*, vol 6 no 2, pp. 194–233.
Kappos T., 2004, *The social structure of the Greek modern society*, Athens: Alitheia.
Lenin V. I., 1977, *A Great Beginning*, Peking: Foreign Languages Press.
Lytras A., 1993, *Introduction to the Theory of Greek social structure*, Athens: Livanis (in Greek).
Meiksins P., 1986, "Beyond the boundary question", *New Left Review* no 154, pp. 101–120.
Milios G., 2002, "The question of the petty bourgeoisie. A single class or two discrete class aggregations?" *Theseis* no 81, pp. 59–80. [in Greek.]
Pan-Hellenic Confederation of Agricultural Co-operatives, 2013, *Recent developments in the Greek rural economy.*
Panitsidis G., 1992, *Approaches to the class structure of our farm economy*, Athens: Synchroni Epochi (In Greek).
Petropoulos D., 2013, "The public servants: victims of the memoranda policy", *Aristeri Syspeirosi* no 26, pp. 47–56.
Sakellaropoulos S., 2001, *Greece in the post-junta period 1974–1988*, Athens: Livanis (in Greek).
Sakellaropoulos S., 2014, *Crisis and social stratification in the Greece of the 21st century*, Athens: Topos (in Greek).

7

Transformations in the State

Introduction

In the third and fourth chapters we saw the content and the economic implications of the Memoranda and the packages of measures and in the fifth, we saw the social implications of this policy. But in order for this to become a reality what was needed was a profound transformation of the State, a transformation that would begin from all the authoritarian changes that have been made in these Western states in recent years (the phenomenon of authoritarian statism), with the focus on the Greek state so that conclusions can be drawn and directions elaborated for more general use.

The International Context

The Issue of Authoritarian Statism

The course towards authoritarian statism at the international level got under way essentially in the 1970s, as a result of both the need to manage

S. Sakellaropoulos, *Greece's (un) Competitive Capitalism and the Economic Crisis*,
https://doi.org/10.1007/978-3-030-14319-0_7

the international economic crisis of 1973 and of the ruling classes' fear of the dynamic of the 1968 global explosion. This orientation was consolidated at the time, but it assumed more intense forms, starting with the war "against terrorism" at the beginning of the twenty-first century when the attack on the Twin Towers was used as a trigger for introducing legislation that—from a human-rights viewpoint—would have been unthinkable under other circumstances (detention of suspects without charge, legalization of electronic surveillance through Bush's Patriot Act, declaration of martial law in France in the autumn of 2005 in response to mobilizations in the Paris suburbs, introduction of special anti-terrorist legislation which not only criminalizes ideas but makes it possible for there to be detention without trial, testimonies from anonymous witnesses etc.; Belantis 2012c). Today the need to manage the current international economic crisis is accelerating this development even further.

Authoritarian statism is that form of the State whose predominant tendency is monopolistic management of all sectors of social and economic life, which is articulated through degradation of representative institutions and formal restriction of traditional civil liberties (Poulantzas 1984: 292). This development constitutes a twofold reality: on the one hand, there is a process of weakening certain sectors of State activity, which, on the other hand, engenders a strengthening of the State in other sectors, resulting in the uneven development and functioning of the whole mechanism.

The implications of the above are the contemporary state as a latter-day Janus: a formally democratic schema surviving as a relic of earlier popular struggles that had imposed institutions of representative democracy and the presence of demands by the dominated classes within the bourgeois state, together with simultaneous emergence of a prophylactic institutional system aimed at forestalling aggravation of the class struggle created by the proliferating effects of economic crisis. The State is obliged to block all the channels that might permit intrusion by popular struggles and at the same time resolve the crisis in favour of the most powerful sectors of monopoly capital.

This development also represents an innovation compared to what was happening in the past: we no longer have to do with a power bloc uniting different sections of capital underwritten by supporting classes and hegemonic vis-à-vis the dominated classes. The failure to resolve the crisis has created a whole new reality. Within this reality, the State will have the task of achieving hybrid implementation of a plan in which the predominant elements will be extraction of surplus value and/or unpaid labour, effected through the imposition of protocapitalist political mechanisms. At the level of a class coalition, this implies a thorough reorganization of social alliances. The intensity of the crisis and its corresponding management by the State entail a liquidation of non-competitive capital, leading to the gradual disappearance not only of non-monopoly capital but also of important sectors of monopoly capital. It is a situation that is clearly worse at the level of the petty bourgeois strata that are threatened with total extinction, ceasing to be part of a class alliance. This is because the traditional petty bourgeoisie is constantly contracting due to the activation of monopolies, whereas the new petty bourgeoisie is polarizing towards the working class as its status becomes that of the employee, its income falls and its role in a monopolized business is confined to executive tasks.

In conclusion, the steady trajectory towards authoritarian statism is intensified by the acuteness of the international economic crisis. The State, in today's conjuncture, is not called upon simply to limit the dynamics of popular struggles, if necessary by autocratic means. It is required to seal off the entry points for social mobilizations within it and manage capitalist power (i.e. to replicate the capital/labour polarity institutionally) without exercising hegemony, at least in its old sense. We are thus led to a reorganization both in the form of social alliances and in the content of bourgeois hegemony and extortion of social consensus. The new social alliance, since it mainly includes bourgeois strata—if it is to lead—needs a new imperative whose outlook will not necessarily appear positive. But one should not forget that a basic, structural element constituting the social consensus that favoured capitalism was the belief in change for better and the presumption of upward social mobility. This is now changing and is set at the level of minimum expectations. The dominated classes will no longer hope for improvement in their lives, but will agree on whatever plan promises non-worsening, or even a not-so-rapid worsening.

In order to face the legitimation deficit, the State intervenes directly in favour of the narrow interests of the most powerful monopolies. In this way, the former social compromises are subverted, both between the ruling and subordinate classes and between the different sectors of the ruling class. This is because there has been a change in the Carl Schmitt concept of "domination". What is "dominant" is no longer the sum of class wills of the coalition of power, under the hegemony of capital, and in particular its monopoly sector. It is almost exclusively the class will of monopoly capital. The result is that important aspects of pre-existing constitutional legitimacy are starting to be circumvented: regulations protecting the aspirations of the most powerful monopolies are shielded and expanded, being the state's absolute priority, whereas those concerning social rights are curtailed due to the "state of exception" (Belantis 2012d).

In this way, however, the State is led to the following reality: On the one hand, a form of State crisis emerges, as the latter ceases to be the organizer of overall bourgeois hegemony but merely the hegemony of its strongest sector, and on the other hand the State transforms the economic crisis into a process of liquidating non-competitive capital.

At this point, and before moving on to the report on the special characteristics of authoritarian statism, it is necessary to make a clarification. Contrary to the belief that universal suffrage and parliamentary democracy go hand-in-hand with the market economy, the truth is completely different. The biggest political problem for the newly established bourgeoisie was that the overcoming of feudalism should not lead to a mass entry of the lower classes to decision-making centres, and by extension to challenging capitalist relations of exploitation and domination. It was for this reason, in any case, that there was so much panic over the French Revolution which, though bourgeois in its content, at the same time, highlighted a demand for democratic transformations of the old regime (Sotiris 2011). In fact, it would be popular struggles that would create the conditions for the establishment of universal suffrage and the functioning of representative institutions, irrespective of the fact that in a number of ways these processes are structurally truncated (inequality in political influence, "loopholes in the law",[1] transfer of real power from parliament

[1] On the subject of these "loopholes" Poulantzas says: "The State often transgresses law-rules of its own making by acting without reference to the law, but also by acting directly against it. It is very discursiveness, each juridical system allows the Power-State to disregard its own, laws and even enters an appropriate variable in the rules of the game that it organizes. This is called the higher

to the executive and the administration). Consequently, there should be nothing surprising about this course towards authoritarian statism. In capitalism *too* the political superstructure is contingent on the class struggle.

What Are the Characteristics of Authoritarian Statism?

The key element is that there is a transformation of relations of representation into management at all costs of matters of a "fundamental public interest", which sometimes involves management of public finances, sometimes initiation of a war against terrorism, sometimes handling of an internal enemy. In any case, what it is selected is the adoption of a series of emergency measures of extreme content which, while supposedly imposed for the maintenance of order, are gradually transformed into a new form of order (Agamben 2005; Zizek 2009).

Emergency measures are imposed in a state of exception. Exceptional regulation establishes a regulatory framework to cover a crisis situation in such a way that it can function as a process of transition/restoration from "problematic" to "healthy" reality, a transition, however, that will differ from the previous normality that led to the current failure (Belantis 2013). The state of exception can only function restrictively, inhibiting the exercise of certain rights. It is a regime of suppression (exclusion) that always targets a specific segment of the population that is designated as a permanent public enemy, though an attempt will be made to maintain that it is a framework for universal application. The segment in question is presumed to hold a number of rights whose exercise contributes to reproduction of the "problematic" situation. Thus, in order for regularity to be restored, they have to be deprived of them for the sake "of public interest"

---

interests of the State (raison d'Etat)—which, strictly speaking, entails both that legality is always compensated by illegalities 'on the side', and that state illegality is always inscribed in the legality which it institutes … Every juridical system includes illegality in the additional sense that gaps, blanks or 'loopholes' form an integral part of its discourse. It is a question here not merely of oversights or blind-spots arising out of the ideological operation of concealment underlying the legal order, but of express devices that allow the law to be breached … The state-institutional structure is always organized in such a way that both the State and the dominant classes operate at once in accordance with the law and against the law … illegality and legality are themselves part of one and the same institutional structure" (Poulantzas 1980: 84–85).

(Belantis 2012c). The institutionalization of emergency regulation establishes a new basic law parallel to the existing Constitution. In other words, the question is not raised of repealing the relevant provisions of the Constitution but a legislative "para-Constitution" is instituted which comprises the basic regulatory framework for the entire duration of the exception regime. But the length of time that the regime of exception will remain in force and the procedures prescribed for it to be lifted are usually forgotten. For the regime of exception to be imposed unhindered by the distortions brought on by the mediation of the political element, there is a series of changes which, when combined, lead to the state of emergency.

The first change is associated with transformations in the functioning of parties. Undoubtedly, something that has emerged since the early 1980s is the progressive convergence in the programmes of liberal and social-democratic parties. It is the period when differentiation of their programmes as different forms of bourgeois management and integration of the dominated classes into the strategy of the bourgeois power coalition gradually comes to an end (Belantis 2012b). But now a "break in the continuity" is to be observed. It is not enough for party formations to formulate the same positions. They must also consent to policies that ensure the dominating classes' institutional incapacity of intervention at the political level. This means suspending the functioning of parties as vehicles for communication of the demands of the dominated classes. It is achieved through the nationalization of parties, that is, through eliminating their autonomy in relation to the state's executive power. The State mechanism as a whole could continue to prescribe central bourgeois strategy but now the functions of integrating the dominated classes had been removed from the parties (Belantis 2012a). Thus, governments are formed that are instruments for organizing the dominant political bloc, side-lining and/or adulterating the mediations of representation and electoral legitimation without, however, formally abolishing them (Kouvelakis 2011). To put it somewhat differently, in the new form of parliamentary democracy popular demands will not be mediated even disconnectedly. All that will be conducted will be negotiation of intra-bourgeois character.

On the basis of the above, we can understand the second change concerning the transition from the interventionist-arbitrational state to the state as headquarters for economic restructuring (Sakellaropoulos 2007). The State no longer attempts to smooth social contradictions, in the interest, of course, of the long-term reproduction of capitalist social relations, but focuses on designing policies for altering the correlation of power to the advantage of ruling class forces. To this end, a contraction takes place of the relative autonomy of the capitalist state vis-à-vis the bourgeoisie, resulting in limitation of the corresponding autonomy of the Ideological Mechanisms (as a result of the impossibility of forming a positive imperative for the dominated classes) vis-à-vis the administrative mechanism that performs basic management of the State (Belantis 2012b).

The third change has to do with further delegation of powers by the parliament and the Executive either to the head of government, that is to say, to the Prime Minister and his entourage of technocrat advisors and/or to transnational organizations such as the European Union (EU) and the International Monetary Fund (IMF). Parliamentary institutions are considered ill-qualified for handling a multitude of issues, and parliamentary deputies are there simply to ratify the decisions of transnational bodies and the heads of government.

The fourth change is related to the overall reorganization of the party system: the emergence of new parties, the decline of older parties, unprecedented governmental alliances imposed by the "dynamic of things".

The fifth has to do with the hardening of repressive mechanisms. As D. Kaltsonis observes: "the security forces have been strengthened both numerically and in terms of material and technical infrastructures … New mechanisms have been created and new methods of organization and action adopted … Legislation provides new possibilities for police forces" (Kaltsonis 2014: 185). And this is why the only sectors in all developed capitalist countries where massive recruitment[2] continues are the security forces.

[2] For Greece, it is indicative that the number of people in the security forces rose from 30,000 in 1974 (1.03% of Labour Force) to 150,000 in 2013 (3.1% of Labour Force).

The Role of European Monetary Union (EMU) and the EU

The direction that has been described is in perfect accord with the role and strategies of the EMU and the EU, whose policies constitute a specialized variant of authoritarian statism verging on ordoliberalism. Ordoliberalism is an ideology for implementation of State policy whose starting point is the assumption that the economy is developing in a context where many partners are participating and society should be inculcated with the notion that the existence and reproduction of this game is something of fundamental importance. The role of the State is to underwrite its operational rules and ensure compliance with them (Foucault 2008: 201). The power of the State must be strengthened and a framework must be created for the market to function, but this cannot be done "freely", as perceived by classical liberalism and, to a significant extent, by neo-liberalism. The fundamental objective is to intervene in society so that at all times the mechanisms of competition can play the role of regulator (Foucault 2008: 164). The market is not a natural phenomenon but a product of historical evolution as well as the specific form of capitalist state. Consequently, competition and markets are internal and structural elements of the State and it must ensure that they operate properly. A point of convergence with neo-liberals is that market is not held responsible for the devastating social consequences of its actions (Burgi 2014: 20). What is of concern is that there should be a network of social protection so that any individual within its ambit should be provided with incentives to return (Foucault 2008: 205).[3] So, the issue is neither income redistribution nor improvement of social conditions, nor the achievement of full employment, but rather the perpetual reproduction of capitalism in conjunction with preservation of a section of the population in order for it to be able to work, when and if conditions allow (Foucault 2008: 207). But it is questionable whether these people will be able to enjoy the same freedom as others, given that they have fallen into this disadvantageous situation (Hayek 2001: 124).

[3] And as Burgi aptly observes, the question is shifting from what policies are effective in addressing unemployment and poverty to what the threshold is for a minimal social protection network (Burgi 2014: 23).

Implementation of these guidelines in the EU and the Eurozone is a recent development. On March 25, 2011 the ruling classes of the countries participating in the EMU agreed on the so-called Euro Pact. In accordance with the Pact, each State would be required to present a long-term plan for gaining the confidence of the financial markets. An annual "stability and convergence programme" setting out its deficit, revenue and expenditure targets, the strategy to achieve these objectives and the timetable for its implementation was drawn up at the national level. In order to achieve this, each member state would implement a series of structural adjustments.[4] Supervision by the EU bureaucracy has become suffocating: Each national budget draft is presented to the European Council prior to examination by the national parliament and the recommendations of the European Commission must be incorporated into it.

As far as labour costs are concerned, they will be closely monitored and will be compared with the corresponding figures for the Eurozone countries as well as those of the EU's main trading partners. If it is judged that the wages are not compatible with competitiveness, their level will be reconsidered. Similarly, as indicated in the quotation, the viability of the pension system will be under constant and close scrutiny targeting to align retirement age with life expectancy and accordingly reducing early retirement schemes.

At the same time, it is envisaged that a mechanism will be established to act as a deterrent to the growth of debt. The mechanism will be binding and will operate automatically whenever the deficit exceeds a speci-

[4] In the conclusions of the European Council of March 24 and 25, 2011, inter alia, it says: "These new commitments will thereafter be included in the National Reform and Stability Programmes and be subject to the regular surveillance framework, with a strong central role for the Commission in the monitoring of the implementation of the commitments, and the involvement of all the relevant formations of the Council and the Eurogroup ... Each year, concrete national commitments will be undertaken by each Head of State or Government ... Member States commit to consult their partners on each major economic reform having potential spillover effects before its adoption ... Progress will be assessed on the basis of wage and productivity developments and competitiveness adjustment needs ... Each country will be responsible for the specific policy actions it chooses to foster competitiveness, but the following reforms will be given particular attention: ... review the wage setting arrangements, and, where necessary, the degree of centralisation in the bargaining process, and the indexation mechanisms ... ensure that wages settlements in the public sector support the competitiveness efforts in the private sector ... labour market reforms to promote "lexicurity ... aligning the pension system to the national demographic situation, for example by aligning the effective retirement age with life expectancy ... limiting early retirement schemes".

fied threshold. This will be effected through legal commitments (constitutional regulation or a framework law).[5]

Also proposed is further reduction of employers' insurance contributions but the key priority is development of a common unified enterprise tax base.[6]

A few months later, at the December 2011 Summit, all members of EU apart from Britain agreed to the "Treaty on Stability, Co-ordination and Governance in the Economic and Monetary Union". This was a clear step towards further defence and shielding against the "people as enemy" if we bear in mind that it included a constitutional enactment[7] of balanced budgets,[8] which means that with the appearance of deficits,[9] mandatory reductions in social spending will automatically be triggered and public debt reduced each year so that the 60% target becomes feasible. And it is easy to see where the sums for these reductions will come from (wages, pensions, social spending). Whenever a member state violates the prescribed limits, a series of sanctions will come into force, that is to say a cut in funding but also the possibility of punitive measures[10]! The key

[5] Correspondingly "Participating Member States commit to translating EU fiscal rules as set out in the Stability and Growth Pact into national legislation. Member States will retain the choice of the specific national legal vehicle to be used, but will make sure that it has a sufficiently strong binding and durable nature (e.g. constitution or framework law".

[6] "Developing a common corporate tax base could be a revenue neutral way forward to ensure consistency among national tax systems".

[7] In the preamble to the specific Treaty it states "that compliance with the Contracting Parties' obligation to transpose the 'balanced budget rule' into their national legal systems, through binding, permanent and preferably constitutional provisions, should be subject to the jurisdiction of the Court of Justice of the European Union, in accordance with Article 273 of the Treaty on the Functioning of the European Union; ... that Article 260 of the Treaty on the Functioning of the European Union empowers the Court of Justice of the European Union to impose a lump sum or penalty payment on a Member State of the European Union which has failed to comply with one of its judgments ... that the European Commission has established criteria for determining the lump sum or penalty payment to be imposed in the framework of that Article".

[8] As indicated in Article 3 of the Treaty "the budgetary position of the general government of a Contracting Party shall be balanced or in surplus".

[9] 0.5% of GNP is the prescribed ceiling for the deficit.

[10] It is stated clearly in the introductory report that in the event of a State having a deficit of over 3%, it must "if necessary, compel a Member State to reduce a deficit which might be identified". How could that be done? According to Article 3 of the Treaty "in the event of significant observed deviations from the medium-term objective or the adjustment path towards it, a correction mechanism shall be triggered automatically. The mechanism shall include the obligation of the Contracting Party concerned to implement measures to correct the deviations over a defined period of time".

political decisions on the economy and the drafting of national budgets will be required to have the pre-approval of the EU bureaucratic mechanisms.[11]

Obviously, all of this is not happening by chance. It is part of a concerted effort not only to have the crisis managed but also to have a new model of accumulation. The countries in which the transnational economic surveillance mechanisms are involved are just the beginning of a process whereby transnational organizations will, in various ways, co-ordinate with national states to enforce the new economic model. It is a process of interarticulation of international and national institutions, the basic issue at stake being the transfer of a huge amount of wealth from labour to capital, with a view to restoring profits to pre-1973 levels. The institutions and the rules are constantly revised once fiscal targets are not met. The interaction of transnational and national policies contributes to this.

From this viewpoint, the transformation of the Greek state is not an exception but just a foretaste of what is programmed to happen throughout Europe in the near future.

Authoritarian Transformation of the Greek State

Changes in the Internal Operation of State Mechanisms

Authoritarian statism assumes idiosyncratic and specialized features in the Greek case due to the intensity with which the economic crisis has

---

Automatically means the adoption of the reversed qualified majority, that is Commission's proposals for sanctions can only be rejected with two thirds of the votes of member states in the Council against them (Vassalos 2018: 76).

[11] According to Article 8 "The European Commission is invited to present in due time to the Contracting Parties a report on the provisions adopted by each of them in compliance with Article 3(2). If the European Commission, after having given the Contracting Party concerned the opportunity to submit its observations, concludes in its report that such Contracting Party has failed to comply with Article 3(2), the matter will be brought to the Court of Justice of the European Union by one or more Contracting Parties ... the judgment of the Court of Justice shall be binding on the parties to the proceedings, which shall take the necessary measures to comply with the judgment within a period to be decided by the Court of Justice".

affected the Greek social formation. The shift of power from the summit of the executive in centres inaccessible to popular control is even more pronounced given that it becomes the uphill of the Troika, which exercises an executive and supervisory function in managing not only public finances but also labour relations. This involves a series of decisions initially taken by a very limited number of people (most of them not elected), and then going to the Parliament for formal ratification via the emergency procedure, thus making there any discussion prohibitively risky under the bugaboo of party discipline. A characteristic feature of this is the continual resort to extraordinary legislative acts without the existence of conditions of "unforeseen need" referred to in the Constitution, given that they are arrangements for the organization and operation of fiscal services, wage cuts and pensions, the standing down of employees (Kassimatis 2012), and when in many cases the House *is* in operation and can legislate on the basis of the normal procedure. Through this practice each government tries to avoid possible desertions by deputies belonging to the government's majority, but this is not the only reason. There is also the fact that prevailing case law holds that legislative acts, in opposition to presidential decrees, are not easy to challenge by direct judicial control and in fact the only body that can exercise control over their constitutionality is the President of the Republic and, as a result, their possible referral by the President would lead to a deep political crisis.

At the same time, some decisions never come for ratification in the Parliament, as was the case with the loan agreement of the first Memorandum, while amendments, also called "updates", are decided by the Minister of Economy without Parliament's approval.[12] Parliament is not informed of the progress of the negotiations and in cases where consensus is sought it finds itself presented with *faits accomplis*. The existence of this new rung on the ladder serves as an aid to the adoption and implementa-

[12] It is characteristic that in accordance with the first Memorandum, the Finance Minister not only signs the approved drafts of the agreements but also negotiates and signs the quarterly revisions and agreements of the Memorandum, about which he simply informs the House. In the second Memorandum, there was a provision for the recapitalization of the banks before the relevant agreement was concluded. After being signed it was to go to the Parliament as information (Kotzias 2013: 313–314; Kaltsonis 2014: 175, 176).

tion of the measures, since it prevents, or to be precise attempts to delay, social reactions from introducing similarly intense, and synchronized, material consequences into the hard core of the State (Markantonatou Maria 2012).

A number of other practices that are becoming more and more common with the passage of time also contribute to downgrading of the role of Parliament: the Prime Minister assumes further and further competences, which are integrated by osmosis into the lenders' bureaucracy,[13] the Cabinet meets very rarely, many questions submitted in the context of parliamentary control are never discussed, the overall presence of the Prime Minister and the ministers in the Parliament is downgraded.

Another very important aspect of authoritarian statism is the violations of the Constitution that have taken place in recent years. In this category, there are violations of the Constitution as a whole and violations that have to do with individual provisions of various conventions. In general terms, one very serious violation is the non-ratification by Parliament of three loan agreements (the first and second Memoranda and the Medium-Term Programme) as prescribed under Article 36 Paragraph 2 of the Constitution, as they were not a conventional State loan agreement (Katrougalos 2013a: 176).

At the general level, there is also a violation of Article 48 of the Constitution, with both constitutional and political implications. The article in question foresees the possibility of emergency situations in the event of war, coup d'état or revolution, and can be extended every 15 days following a decision by the Parliament. But what we have instead of that is an ill-defined extension of the state of emergency that arises out of the country's budgetary situation. As D. Belandis observes, everyday life adapts to the emergency of unlimited duration. The "emergency" thus

[13] One characteristic example is the provision in Article 7 of Law 3839/2010, which states that "acting in the context of the Constitution and its laws, the Prime Minister, through a decision published in the Government Gazette, on matters of urgency and major national concern may, by way of exception from any general or specific provision and in compliance with the general principles of Community law: (…) entrust directly to natural or legal persons the conduct of studies or the provision of services and determine the subject and time of delivery of the study or service". The second paragraph of the article in question is interesting: all public sector services are made available to these persons, given that they "are obliged to provide the abovementioned studies, committees and working groups with all information and data required" (Kaltsonis 2014: 178).

replaces popular sovereignty, which is allegedly the fundamental principle of the Constitution (Belantis 2012a).

In this context when the Council of State considered the Athens Bar Association's appeal against the constitutionality of the first Memorandum and stated that it was operating within constitutional legitimacy, its justification was based on the "law of necessity" and in particular on the possibility of bankruptcy of the country if the measures were not immediately enacted. This decision, however, highlights the problem of the argument about the dialectical relationship between "permanent" and "temporary". Social rights *may* apply in periods of normalcy. By contrast, in circumstances of exception, of unspecified duration, significant restrictions must be imposed, which may border on suspending social rights (Belantis 2012c). Above and beyond that, there are specific violations arising out of the implementation of every relevant agreement. Thus, according to Article 14 Paragraph 5 of the Loan Facility Act, that is, the first Memorandum, Greece has irrevocably and unconditionally surrendered any immunity[14] that the Greek state might claim to benefit from, along with its assets in all legal proceedings[15] related to the Agreement (Kassimatis 2010: 21–22). This violated the fundamental principle of respect for the sovereignty of the State, drawing into question the sovereign rights and indeed the very substance of the country (Kassimatis 2010: 25). As noted by G. Katrougalos, this is a clause that has no precedent in the constitutional history of Greece. It constitutes a de facto abdication of economic sovereignty and a violation of the principle of popular sovereignty, notwithstanding the fact that under international law legal immunity has been codified in the United Nations Convention on the Judicial Immunity of States and Their Assets (Katrougalos 2012: 218–219). It is quite characteristic that there is no such provision in the loan contracts of other countries under a Memorandum regime (Katrougalos 2013b: 9).

[14] Under Article 14 Paragraph 5 "The Borrower hereby irrevocably and unconditionally waives all immunity to which it is or may become entitled, in respect of itself or its assets, from legal proceedings in relation to this Agreement, including, without limitation, immunity from suit, judgement or other order, from attachment, arrest or injunction prior to judgement, and from execution and enforcement against its assets to the extent not prohibited by mandatory law".

[15] As indeed is mentioned at point 11 of the Form of Legal Opinion written by the Greek side "Neither the Borrower nor any of its property are immune on the grounds of sovereignty or otherwise from jurisdiction, attachment—whether before or after judgement—or execution in respect of any action or proceeding relating to the Agreement".

In Article 4 a provision was included committing, for the benefit of the creditors, the entirety of Greek public property, movable and immovable, in money and in securities, rights and sources of national wealth, and prohibiting the concession of any priority of "any other creditor or public debt holder" (Kassimatis 2010: 219). Violations were also entailed in the agreement of October 26, 2011, the so-called Medium-Term agreement. As observed by D. Belantis the overall package of measures including large wage cuts in the public and private sectors, redundancies, changes in labour relations limiting rights, institutionalization of reserve labour, firings of employees working under contract in the public sector, restrictions on collective bargaining, large reductions in pensions: all this is in direct conflict with Article 25 of the Constitution, which is informed by the principle of the social state, the rule of law and the social rights derived from it (the right to work, the right of access to social security, the right to free negotiation etc.; Belantis 2011: 13). Above and beyond the Greek Constitution, K. Chrysogonos argues that lowering the minimum wage in the private sector violates Article 4 (1) of the European Social Charter, which safeguards the right of workers to remuneration that ensures a decent standard of living. Specifically, the European Social Rights Committee resolved through its decision of May 23, 2012 that a 32% reduction in wages for young people under the age of 25 contravenes this provision by lowering the minimum wage below the poverty threshold for Greece, which has been set at 580 euros per month (Chrysogonos 2013: 54).

The agreement on PSI (private sector involvement) violates two basic principles of the Greek Constitution on a number of individual and social rights. Imposition of a charge on bondholders violates the principle of equality vis-à-vis public burdens (it affects a particular category, the bondholders, irrespective of their current financial situation (Chrysogonos 2013: 76) and does not provide for some form of compensation and tax relief for whatever damage is sustained[16] (Chrysogonos 2013: 53–54), thus depriving them of the right to a dignified living and contravening

[16] It is worth noting the dimensions of the loss suffered by bondholders which at the most conservative estimates amounted to 53.5% of the original face value of the bonds but in reality was much greater because the new securities were of longer duration and at lower interest rates (Chrysogonos 2013: 73).

the relevant provisions of the Constitution (Article 2 (1); Chrysogonos 2013: 77). There is also an infringement of tax law since haircuts involve treatment for bondholders who are natural persons that differs from the treatment administered to bondholders who are legal persons under public law (for which special favourable tax arrangements were introduced) and to banks (for which arrangements were made for recapitalization and financial support) (breaching the principle of equality [Article 4 of the Constitution]) (Chrysogonos 2013: 107).

On the basis of point 13 of the Long-Term Agreement, the property of the Greek state was mortgaged, with particular reference to the *Helios* energy programme for the securing of the Greek alternative energy sources. The term "public state property" includes among other things marine and water resources, forests, ports, basic energy resources, public buildings, control of the telecommunications network, military equipment and so on. The Agreement clearly contravenes Article 1 Paragraph 2 of the Constitution, where it is explicitly stated that the ownership, use and exploitation of public property are a fundamental means for the exercise of national sovereignty (Belantis 2011: 14–15).

Apart from that, the second Memorandum, which includes the abolition of all family and multi-child benefits and their replacement by the single family's support allowance to be granted on the basis of income criteria, breaches the provisions of Article 21 Paragraphs 1 and 2 of the Constitution that provides for the protection of the family and of multi-child households (Chrysogonos 2013: 56).

Law 4093/2012, which was voted in the context of application of the third Memorandum, includes a significant number of pension rulings that violate Article 73 Paragraph 2 of the Constitution, which prescribes that pension bills should be specific and not attached to laws regulating other matters (Katrougalos 2013b: 11–12).

Moreover, with the amendment that was inserted into an unrelated bill (Article 54 of Law 4178/2013) on dealing with arbitrary construction, in violation of Article 74 (5) of the Constitution, which prohibits this practice, an opportunity was provided for abolishing public instrumentalities through Presidential Decree (Kaltsonis 2014: 177).

But above and beyond the unconstitutionality of the agreements as a whole and in part, the attempt to implement the policies they entail has led to further unconstitutional practices. The recruitment of rail workers in the public transport sector, who were on strike, in January 2013, and a few months later secondary school teachers, who were on strike too, employing the baseless argument of risk to public health, the social life of the country and public order, contravenes Article 22 Paragraph 4 of the Constitution, which prohibits any form of forced labour, permitting by way of exception the requisition of personal services for purposes of national defence or urgent social need in the event of natural disaster or danger to public health. But this strike did not involve the whole country. It only involved Attica. There was no disaster, no threat to public order. Nor was public health threatened, since there was no issue of dissemination of specific noxious infectious or contagious diseases (Chrysogonos 2013: 60–61).

Another important parameter in the whole context of authoritarianism is the stepping-up of repression. The State fortifies itself against the people as enemy. This entrenchment is not confined to run-of-the-mill police repression of demonstrations. There is a significant qualitative and quantitative upgrading of all relevant practices. The use of physical and chemical repression has proliferated. In "unruly" areas such as Keratea in Attica and Skouries in Chalkidiki[17] organized campaigns of repression have been unleashed in an attempt to break the will of struggling residents, when a strike exceeds the State's and the Capital's margins of "tolerance" then police invade the occupied factory (Halyvourgia), and at the same time police forces become a permanent presence in all urban centres. In addition, the repression of migrants and refugees is taking place through a variety of practices: confinement in concentration camps, constant checks, even physical torture at police stations. On the other hand, and this may be the most important, there are signs of a tendency towards blurring of the boundary between the army and the police (Belantis 2013), as typically exemplified by the Kallimachos and Talos exercises in 2011, where the army was trained to crack down on protesters.

[17] In Keratea there were many months of protests by residents against the installation of a sanitary landfill site. In Skouries, there were also strong reactions against the operation of a gold mining plant.

One last (but not least) issue is the numerical reduction in representation. An attempt is being made to limit the number of elected delegates to the representative bodies at all levels for the sake of "efficiency", both through already institutionalized provisions and through planning for the future. Thus, the Kallikrates local government law has reduced the number of mayors from 910 to 325 and 57 prefectures have been replaced by 13 regional governors.

The Direct Involvement of the Troika and the Creditors' Mechanisms in the Operation of State Institutions

It should be made clear that Greece's association with the EU, the European Central Bank (ECB), the IMF and their mechanisms is not limited to violations of the Constitution and the implementation of certain guidelines but has acquired another dimension: there has been an organic intervention of this kind which amounts to a break from the past operations of the Greek state. In other words, not only there is an intense external pressure from the Troika to implement the Memorandum measures, but the external institutional intervention is being internalized directly into the Greek state. This does not mean that the policies being imposed through the direct presence of Troika representatives do not correspond to the interests of sections of Greek monopoly capital and that the only winners are the "foreign" capitalists. What is happening is that the extraordinary situation of the Greek economy and the impossibility of an alternative political solution emerging from the dominant strata have enabled sections of Greek and foreign monopoly capital (and their political representatives) to create an alliance against the "people as enemy", who are the key opponent, but *also* against the secondary antagonist: un-competitive capital (which appears similarly incapable of formulating an alternative policy). The fact that elements of the Greek state's independence are being subverted in this way is the price paid by the part of the Greek bourgeoisie that benefits from that process. To put it somewhat differently, what is involved is a heterogeneous alliance in action, with loss incurred through implication of foreign institutional actors in the operations of the Greek state but with gain ensured by transfer of a large mass of surplus value to the dominant sector of monopoly capital and liquidation of non-competitive capital.

Let us look at it more concretely. As we have said, the issue is not merely one of pressure from lenders to implement the "rehabilitation" programme, the content of which has been designed by themselves, through threats to stop funding. Nor is it just the fact that the creditors are always very well supplied with inside information on the specificities of the Greek administration. The main issue is the direct intervention in the functioning of Greek state, which in itself changes the position and the role of Greece in the international division of labour (see below).

The first example is to be found in the constitution of the so-called Task Force headed by the former German diplomat Reichenbach, with initial participation from Germans, Swedes, Dutch people, French people, Austrians. Its objective in its first year of operations was to supervise the public sector. In fact, what was done was control of public health, tax evasion, the land registry and even the management of defence finances (Kotzias 2013: 334), with the committee being responsible not only for control of expenditure but also for its collection (Kotzias 2013: 341). At the end of 2012 its cadres came from 20 EU countries and new areas of activity had been added, such as entrepreneurship and justice, but there was specialization in previously covered areas such as in the tax office where the Finance Ministry installed specialists from Germany, Belgium, France and the Netherlands (Kotzias 2013: 335). At the decision-making level this group, having obtained access to the entirety of Greek economic data, has acquired a say in spending cuts, staffing, administrative structures and so on (Kotzias 2013: 337). Of course, this takes the form of "advice", but in order for loan instalments to be disbursed, implementation of such advice is taken as a criterion (Kotzias 2013: 340).

The second case has to do with the intervention of four German ministries in the workings of their Greek counterparts. The most typical case is the Ministry of Decentralization, where a regime of control over municipalities and regions has been established under the "German-Hellenic Assembly" headed by German Deputy Minister of Economic Co-operation Hans-Joachim Fuchtel. The latter has called for restructuring of the local labour markets with a view to creating areas of low labour cost that might attract foreign investment. In the same context he sought cheap labour to be trained in Germany, and he was particularly interested in the management of rubbish as a raw material. At the level of financial management, the policy being promoted is one of removing local government revenues from the State budget, something that is bound to lead to the generation of new debt (Kotzias 2013: 346–347). To address this, plans are being made to hive off municipal services to private individuals, fire staff, which increase municipal taxes. At the same time, under the privatization policy, municipalities are obliged to proceed with expropriations in order to reinforce the TAIPED (Public Utilities Development Fund). If the local government institutions fail to deliver the expected results then, in line with the provisions of the Memorandum and the relevant legislative act of November 2012, a series of rigorous measures are provided for. If a local authority fails three times to implement the recommendations made, the local authority in question will be subjected to a special regime of reorganization. Above and beyond that, apart from the measures involving the German Ministry of Finance, similar interventions are also on matters by the German Ministries of Economy, Technology, Environment and Health, concerning central administration, health and the use of renewable energy sources. The basic vehicle for this "assistance" is the German company Deutsche Gesellschaft fuer die Internationale Zusammenrabelt-GIZ. Since December 2013 the company has maintained offices in Athens and, as stated on its website, its Greek section has the task of elaborating policy road maps for the relevant German ministers in their dealings with their Greek counterparts (Katsaganis 2014).

The third case involves TAIPED, the fund that manages the divestiture of the country's public wealth. The shares of this fund belong to the Greek government, but the creditors have secured a robust presence here too: on the board of directors three members are appointed by the Greek government but there are also two representatives of the EU and the ECB. Moreover, alongside the Board of Directors a seven-member committee of experts has been established, three of whom are representatives of the lenders (Kotzias 2013: 349–350).

The fourth case is that of the (bankrupt) Greek banks, where commissioners serving the interests of the creditors have been installed and control each decision taken by the board of directors of each bank. This is despite the fact that it is the Greek government that has taken over the bank debts. When the banks are resold, their debt from the recapitalization will be counted as part of Greek government debt (Kotzias 2013: 338).

The fifth case is the creation, through the second Memorandum, of a special fund into which the proceeds of the Greek state will be channelled at all times, even if Greece is faced with a humanitarian crisis (Kotzias 2013: 312).

The sixth and most recent case concerns the provision in the third Memorandum according to which from January 1, 2017 the General Secretariat for Public Revenues, which until then had been under the civil administration of the Ministry of Finance, was transformed into an Independent Administrative Authority. This means that it is no longer subject to control by the Ministry of Finance but enjoys full operational and organizational independence. The impact of this change is very important as this Authority has the exclusive prerogative of interpreting tax legislation, setting collection targets and ensuring means of forced recovery from taxpayers (Valavani 2016: 123). Correspondingly, in matters of recruitment, dismissal, evaluation and remuneration, employees depend on the Administrator of the Authority, outside of the jurisdiction of the Civil Service Code. At the same time, in the meetings of his Board of Directors, he participates as a specialist, without voting rights, appointed by the EU so that it may be informed directly of the state of public revenues from the perspective of the creditors. Last but not least, the competences that have been assigned to this new Authority (such as the Public Investment Programme and the NSRF) cannot be transferred to the Ministry of Finance or other government bodies through a later regulatory administrative act (Valavani 2016: 124–125).

The Direction of Things

We explained that the transformations of the Greek state in the period of the crisis are associated with a more general and international course towards authoritarian statism in conjunction with the implementation of a state of exception since the Troika intervened in Greek affairs. The question that remains to be answered is whether all the changes described represent a qualitative break in the configuration of the Greek state.

The debate was opened by N. Kotzias, who argued that Greece has been transformed into a "debt colony". This means a State that is formally independent, as there is no international agreement that puts it under the control of another State, but because it has concluded a number of unequal agreements, it has lost the essence of its sovereignty. The control imposed on it is imprinted within its institutional system (Kotzias 2013: 286–287). Thus "internal institutions are called upon to implement decisions taken by third parties—parties that reconcile the internal policy and agenda of the debt colony" (Kotzias 2013: 288). This is what distinguishes it, according to Kotzias, from the colonies of the past: the debt colony is being prevailed upon by the Centre to limit its costs and finance its defence and security itself. In the case of Greece, the lenders first defined their objectives and means of achieving them, along with sanctions for the contingency of the other side's failure to achieve them, and the Greek policy staff undertook implementation. That settled, the updates of the Memoranda are agreed, as we have seen, exclusively between the lenders and the Minister of National Economy, and then the House, and sometimes the Council of Ministers, are also called upon to ratify them retrospectively (Kotzias 2013: 311). In the event that issues arise in relation to this debt, they will be settled on the basis of English law,[18] and because the English courts are regarded as being not very strictly against the borrowers, provision was made for litigation to be heard on the first loan agreement at the Court of Justice of the EU[19] and the latter in the Luxembourg courts.[20] This is because the European

[18] "The choice of English law as governing law for the Agreement is a valid choice of law binding the Borrower in accordance with Hellenic law" as mentioned in point 9 of the Form of Legal Opinion, accepted by Greece.

[19] In accordance with point 10 of the Form of Legal Opinion "The Borrower has legally, effectively and irrevocably submitted to the exclusive jurisdiction of the Court of Justice of the European Union in connection with the Agreement and any judgement of this court would be conclusive and enforceable in the Hellenic Republic".

[20] In accordance with Article 15, Paragraph 2 of the Master Financial Assistance Facility Agreement that is included in the second Memorandum "The Parties undertake to submit any dispute which may arise relating to the legality, validity, interpretation or performance of this Agreement and each

Court is an institution of the creditors but also the courts of Luxembourg are considered particularly strict in the application of English law, whereas the Greek courts are under an obligation not to apply regulations that contravene the Greek Constitution (Katrougalos 2012: 219–220).

As far as we are concerned, we think that question of national independence of any State should be seen in the context of the imperialist chain which is the result of uneven development and in which all national formations participate in which the capitalist mode of production predominates. The concept of national sovereignty is *relational* and is determined by the position of a national formation within the chain. It is the class struggle that contributes either to upgrading the position of a State or to corresponding downgrading. So, what is basic is not whether for a number of reasons a State loses elements of national sovereignty, but whether it is a qualitative turn, contributing to a substantial change in the form of the State. In other words, its transformation into an entity is characterized by extended loss of national sovereignty.

On this question and in the case of Greece, our response will be one of positive agreement with N. Kotzias. But we believe that the term "debt colony" raises the problem that a colony must be part of an empire, something accepted by Kotzias, but we do not think that the concept has the analytical stringency that is required by a theory of the international capitalist system. The reason for this is that the older Empires (the ancient empires of the East, the Roman Empire, the Byzantine Empire and the Holy Roman Empire) were based on pre-capitalist production relations. These relations made territorial expansion necessary, including some forms of direct government or political control, necessary for ensuring a surplus for the imperial State. The colonial empires of the modern era, although based on the capitalist social relations that prevailed at the centre, included some forms of territorial expansion and direct governance symptomatic of a transitional form,[21] in the sense that they corresponded to conjunctures of contradictory and competitive coexistence of capitalism with other

of its Facility Specific Terms (including the Annexes and Schedules thereto) to the exclusive jurisdiction of the courts of the Grand Duchy of Luxemburg".

[21] As quite rightly observed by Panagiotis Sotiris: "What else is slavery in the modern era than the attempt in the absence of a 'free' labour force that will work for capitalist agriculture, to get one, if necessary by violence. Similarly, what more were the great colonial empires than attempts to extend

ways of production, within a trajectory towards emergence of a purely capitalist international system (Sakellaropoulos and Sotiris 2005: 31).

Our position is that, with some qualifications, the concept that might be used would be that of the quasi-protectorate. The result would be commencement of a series of military interventions (Kampuchea, Eastern Slavonia, Bosnia, Kosovo, East Timor, Afghanistan and Iraq) that lead to military control in some areas that will be completed in at some other time while in others it is still going on.

What are the key features of the new protectorate states? To begin with, there are four major differences from the past: (1) Governance is not assumed by a colonial country, but by an international organization or an international alliance. In this sense protectorates are not colonies; (2) no direct forms of colonial government are created but local governments co-operate with representatives of the international community; (3) there is no attempt at extra-capitalist extraction of wealth to serve primary accumulation in the Metropolis; (4) although local governments are maintained, the scope of foreign intervention is such that it covers a very wide range of issues. Of course, there are elements of continuity with the old protectorates. The inhabitants of these regions are considered immature in the management of their own affairs and paternalistic intervention is required from external actors, who instil in the local inhabitants, the rules and values that are deemed suitable by the Western imperialists.

Does Greece belong in the above category? The reality is that there was no military occupation in Greece or control of its foreign policy. As strange as it may seem, there has been no radical reorientation of any of the basic issues of Greek foreign policy (Greek-Turkish, the Cypriot question, the FYROM name issue). In this sense, it could be said that Greece is a case of national sovereignty being lost over issues with a bearing on the internal organization of the State and its financial functions. This is why we use the term "quasi-protectorate". It is a protectorate of a new form where the burden of foreign intervention focuses

capitalist production relations and forms of accumulation by violence, within the context of expanded reproduction of European capital" (Sotiris 2003).

on the economic functions of the State. But this is only a partial answer. In fact, this is an on-going institutional construct, an experimental terrain within the overall framework of managing the economic crisis. What we have is an overall strategy of capital and imperialism aimed at transforming the State structures of the weakest national formations into sites for overexploitation of labour power and liquidation of non-competitive capital. The institutional transformations that take place are a meeting point for all the social forces that benefit from the process. The movement unfolds within a State structure weakened by the institutionalized presence of popular demands but increasingly resembling a mode of management of ruling class interests impenetrable to class struggle. This new form of hybrid state will not, in other words, be confined to subordinate and insufficiently competitive national formations. The start will be made in Greece and other "peripheral" states will follow[22] after the signing of the EU Stability Pact. The idea, indeed, is to extend this pattern as a model, to the imperialist centres as well, where it will assume the character of a victory against "people as enemy". So, the basic strategy is not one of subordinating a country but of administering a crushing defeat to the people as enemy. The fact that the strategy proceeds along the quasi-protectorate path is simply a development facilitating the ultimate goal of annihilating popular conquests internationally.

[22] Here too our view differs substantially from that of N. Kotzias, who thinks that "Greece is being treated in one-dimensional fashion as country whose entire being is circumscribed by the fact of owing money, for whom the primary criterion for decision-making and action is the interests and demands of its creditors" (Kotzias 2013: 312). In fact the situation is not a triangular schema of entrepreneurs, states and "imperial" administration (i.e. the bureaucratic machinery of the European Union) as Kotzias with post-modernist logic assumes. It is an attempt to overthrow the previous model of accumulation for the benefit of the most powerful sectors of monopoly capital, a strategy mediated by the corresponding political personnel in each national formation. The real problem is the crisis and the reason for it varies: in some places it can be the debt, in others the banking system, and in any case the outside economic interventions have taken place for different reasons in each country. But the question is not just one of conflict between a post-modern imperial coalition and "debt colonies" of a new type. It is class struggle (both between bourgeoisie and working class and intra-bourgeois) but it is also antagonism between capitalist formations within the imperialist chain.

References

Agamben G., 2005, *State of exemption*, Chicago: Chicago University Press.

Belantis D., 2011, "Legal and constitutional aspects of the 'new agreements'", *Outopia* vol. 97, pp. 13–16 (in Greek).

Belantis D., 2012a, "Weimar days" http://www.rednotebook.gr/details.php?id=5068, accessed on 11/11/2012 (in Greek).

Belantis D., 2012b, "On the parliamentary state of emergency and its connection with the fascist threat (8 theses on a question for discussion)" http://ektosgrammis.gr/index.php?option=com_content&view=article&id=1777:%2D%2D%2D%2D%2D%2D%2D%2D%2D%2D%2D%2D%2D%2D8%2D%2D%2D%2D%2D%2D&catid=117:ektosylhs&Itemid=516, accessed on 9/11/2012 (in Greek).

Belantis D., 2012c, "Theses on the contemporary "state of emergency"" http://rednotebook.gr/details.php?id=4701, accessed on 15/11/2012 (in Greek).

Belantis D., 2012d, *Towards the state of emergency: the weakening of legal forms*, mimeo (in Greek).

Belantis D., 2013, "Neo-liberalism, fascism, and the "state of exception"" http://rednotebook.gr/details.php?id=10676, accessed on 12/2/2014 (in Greek).

Burgi N., 2014, "Introduction", in Burgi N. (ed.) *La Grande Regression. La Grece et l' avenir de l' Europe*, Lormont: Le Bord de l' Eau, pp. 15–52.

Chrysogonos K., 2013, *Getting around the constitution in the age of the memoranda*, Athens: Livanis (in Greek).

Foucault M., 2008, *The birth of biopolitics. Lectures at the college de France 1978–1979*, New York: Palgrave Macmillan.

Hayek F., 2001, *The road to serfdom*, London and New York: Routledge.

Kaltsonis D., 2014, *Law and Society in the 21st century*, Athens: Topos (In Greek).

Kassimatis G., 2010, *The Loan Agreements of Greece with European Union and IMF*, Athens: Athens Bar Association, http://www.constitutionalism.gr/html/ent/817/ent.1817.asp, accessed on 10/11/2018 (in Greek).

Kassimatis G., 2012, "A silhouette of the lawless lending regime", Pontiki 29/12/2012 (in Greek).

Katrougalos G., 2012, *The crisis and the way out*, Athens: Livanis (in Greek).

Katrougalos G., 2013a, "The legal exit from the crisis", *Outopia* vol. 102, pp. 174–180 (in Greek).

Katrougalos G., 2013b, "Memoranda, individual rights and democracy: the eclipse of the constitution", *Outopia* vol. 103, pp. 7–13 (in Greek).

Katsaganis D., 2014, "Five German ministries active in Greece", *Kefalaio* 29/3/2014 (in Greek).
Kotzias N., 2013, *Greece, debt colony. European empire and German primacy*, Athens: Patakis (in Greek).
Kouvelakis S., 2011, "Movement time, political time" http://anasynthesi.gr/index.php?option=com_content&view=article&id=324&Itemid=1, accessed on 20/3/2014 (in Greek).
Markantonatou Maria, 2012, "The fiscal crisis state and the rhetoric of state of emergency, economic warfare and the retreat of sovereignty", *Theseis* vol. 118, http://www.theseis.com/index.php?option=com_content&task=view&id=1172&Itemid=29, accessed on 7/11/2012 (in Greek).
Poulantzas N., 1980, *State, power, socialism*, London and New York: Verso.
Poulantzas N., 1984, *State, Power, Socialism*, Athens: Themelio (in Greek).
Sakellaropoulos S., 2007, "Towards a declining state? The rise of the headquarters state", *Science and Society* vol. 71, no 1, pp. 7–32.
Sakellaropoulos S. and P. Sotiris, 2005, "Returning to imperialism. An intervention on the views of Panich and Gindin concerning construction of the informal American empire", *Monthly Review* vol. 26, pp. 22–38 (in Greek).
Sotiris P., 2003, "Empire: new theoretical model or reproduction of old contradictions?", *Theseis* vol. 85, http://www.theseis.com/index.php?option=com_content&task=view&id=835&Itemid=29, accessed on 7/5/2018 (in Greek).
Sotiris P., 2011, "The age of post-democracy" http://aristerovima.gr/details.php?id=2939, accessed on 11/11/2012 (in Greek).
Valavani N., 2016, *The third memorandum, overturning of an overturning*, Athens: Livanis (in Greek).
Vassalos Y., 2018, "Consolidation of autocratic rule in the EU and opposition: the parallel processes of the Troika's emergence and the economic governance reforms and how they could be overthrown", in Sotiris P. (ed.) *Crisis, movement, strategy: the Greek experience*, London: Brill, pp. 68–87.
Zizek S., 2009, *First as a tragedy then as a farce*, London and New York: Verso.

8

The Reaction of the Dominated Classes 2010–2015

What has been said about the policy and the content of the Memoranda, their economic and social outcomes, and the transformations in the State, inevitably elicited reactions from the dominated. These reactions were extremely forceful, up until SYRIZA's election victory of January 2015. The retreat of the movements that followed, particularly after the agreement by the SYRIZA-ANEL government, will be the subject of Chap. 10.

At the social level in particular, the evolution of popular reactions corresponded to the pattern that Stathis Kouvelakis characterized as prolonged popular war, enlisting a term coined by Mao. It is a combination and alternation of multiple forms and levels of struggle within which ever broader layers of society are activated and the given context of political and social power relations challenged and transformed. It is a process including clearly insurrectional features whose ultimate goal is to overturn the overall balance of forces (Kouvelakis Stathis 2011a). In the Greek case, every adoption of new austerity measure led to new social reactions even more acute than the previous wave.

The first period of mobilizations started on May 5, 2010, when, following announcement of the first Memorandum, a wave of hundreds of thousands of people deluged all the country's major cities in protest. Peak

S. Sakellaropoulos, *Greece's (un) Competitive Capitalism and the Economic Crisis*,
https://doi.org/10.1007/978-3-030-14319-0_8

of the reaction was an attempt by the workers to move on Parliament. This was, in the same year, followed by further days with pan-Hellenic strikes, but without the massiveness of May 5. It is a development mostly explicable by agitation over how such massive nation-wide mobilizations as those of May 5 had failed to forestall the adoption of the first Memorandum, despite the vote against the Memorandum by three PASOK deputies (Sakorafa, Oikonomou, Dimaras). Their immediate proscription foreshadowed the coming spectacular transformations of the party system (at the end of 2010 V. Papachristos would also be expelled because he did not vote for the bill on changes in work relations). So, it had begun to seem obvious to all that the Greek social formation was passing through a new phase in which social reactions needed a "paradigm change" if they were to be effective. This feeling coexisted in uneasy contradiction with the fact that in many sections of the population, there was still a perception that however harsh the measures, they were something temporary and would be over once the Greek economy began to recover, as it would soon. This dipole (new forms of struggle, illusions about return to the previous economic status) would be felt both in local elections, where PASOK would again be the party with the most votes (see Chap. 8) and during the mobilizations of the following period. A survey of the new traditions of struggle might well include the occupation of the Ministry of Health by striking health workers, the first appearance of the "Den Plirono" (I'm not paying) movement and the long-term campaign by the inhabitants of Keratea against the establishment of landfills in their area.

The second period of protracted mobilization was between May 25, 2011 and July 15, 2011, when the so-called Indignados movement or Movement of the Squares unfolded in conjunction with very significant and massive strike activity. It is something truly unprecedented in Greek political history and can be interpreted from the fact that the projected new measures were forcing ever broader sectors of Greek society into poverty and deprivation and, on the other hand, were showing that a different type of mobilization was required to counter such a large-scale attack from capital.

On the afternoon of Wednesday May 25 after thousands of calls had been issued through Facebook, thousands of people occupied Syntagma

Square, similar invitations coming from another 38 points in key cities (the White Tower in Thessaloniki, Plateia Georgiou in Patras, Plateia Eleftherias in Heraklion). The most pessimistic believed that this particular mobilization was an imitation of those of Tahrir Square in Egypt or Puerta del Sol Square in Madrid and would not be able to be sustained. But this was quickly refuted. On the first day, it is estimated that 25,000 to 30,000 people participated at Syntagma, 5000 to 7000 in Thessaloniki, 3000 in Patras, but on the following days more and more people came and in all the public squares of Greek towns and cities,[1] there were similar occupations. Not long afterwards, there were occupations of squares in Athenian municipalities, albeit not on an everyday basis, but functioning as a "complement", as it were, to Syntagma.[2] The upshot was that the Greek people made the acquaintance of an unprecedented form of mobilization that took place on a daily basis. Certainly, Syntagma Square played a key role because it is the central square of Athens, the capital of the country, which is home to about half the population of Greece. In spatial terms, it is situated opposite the Parliament and surrounded by a variety of government buildings. In that sense, its occupation and the principle of maintaining a permanent presence in it symbolize direct confrontation with State power and continuous unremitting struggle.

The movement united around demands such as the fall of the government, the cancellation of the Memoranda and non-payment of the debt

[1] The areas where the Indignados made their presence felt were Aegina, Andros, Arta, Veria, Volos, Giannitsa, Drama Evros, Kozani Rhodes, Zakynthos, Herakleio, Thessaoniki, Thebes, Ierapetra, Ikaria, Ioannina, Kavala, Kalamata, Kastoria, Corfu, Kefalonia, Kiato, Corinth, Lamia, Larissa, Megara, Mytilene, Xylokastro, Patras, Molaoi, Katerini, Preveza, Ptolemaida, Pyrgos, Rethymnon, Santorini, Sitia, Syros, Tinos, Mykonos, Chania, Milos, Halkida, Stylida, Amfissa, Lefkada, Karditsa, Arachova, Aliartos, Livadeia, Sparta, Alexandroupoli, Komotini, Agrinio, Edipsos, Tripoli, Trikala, Nafpaktos, Igoumenitsa, Edessa, Nafplion, Aigio, Gargalianoi, Samos (Bresia 2011: 92) It is interesting that mobilizations did not always take place in squares but also in areas that were regarded as symbolic of the town: for example, the White Tower in Thessaloniki, the Public Market in Chania (Bresia 2011: 95).

[2] Neos Kosmos, Aigaleo, Galatsi, Gyzi, Nikaia, Vari, Voula, Vouliagmeni, Vyronas, Keratsini, Glyka Nera, Elliniko, Argyroupoli, Exarcheia, Korydallos, Zografou, Ilioupoli, Kaisariani, Kallithea, Neos Kosmos, Ampelokipi, Galatsi, Gyzi, Nikaia, Vari-Voula-Vouliagmeni, Vyronas, Keratsini, Glyka Nera, Elliniko, Exarchia, Korydallos, Zografou, Ilioupoli, Kaisariani, Kallithea, Agia Paraskevi, Maroussi, Nea Ionia, Nea Heraklion, Nea Smyrni, Pallini, Papagou, Patissia, Piraeus, Perama, Peristeri, Nea Filadefia, Haidari, Halandri, Holargos-Papagou, Petralona, Kolonos and so on (Bresia 2011: 92–93).

and direct democracy predominated as a decision-making process. The slogan "we don't owe anything, we are not selling anything. we are not paying" conjoined refusal to recognize the debt with opposition to privatization of public institutions and the sale of public property by the Hellenic Republic Asset Development Fund. The demand for democracy arose to convey the need for collective decision-making processes in contrast to an ever more downgraded parliamentary process that exemplified the abandonment of even the mediated presence of the lower classes in the domain of politics (Kouvelakis Stathis 2011c). Institutions of equal rights of speech ("isigoria") were introduced through inclusive assemblies and an attempt was made to establish collective processing of proposals and decisions.

That said, each *plateia* had its own peculiarities. In Syntagma, there was the separation between the "upper" and "lower" *plateia.* The upper plateia was frequented by a group of less politicized *indignados* coming from a more conservative background, reacting spontaneously and waving Greek flags in a practice that inaugurated people's participation in mobilizations for the first time, freed from the mainstream parties for which they had voted until then, turning the political crisis into a national crisis. In other words, these people were radically challenging the ability of the upper "crust" to govern. They showed that "greek people, was in the squares and in the streets, having seceded from the institutions and the people who supposedly represented them and acted in their name" (Kouvelakis 2011b). At the same time, the visibility of the Greek flag was a sign that sections of the popular strata realized how the presence of the creditors meant loss of elements of national sovereignty, which in addition to international humiliation of the country and its population had tangible material effects for ordinary people. So, importance should be attached to the element of self-determination within the national formation in such a way as to ensure that life could be lived in an environment of dignity and social justice (Sotiris 2012). Essentially this is the first step towards a potential social alliance of the subordinated lower classes. In contrast, in the lower *plateia* one would find the people of the Left, with the exception of the KKE.[3] They were attempting through the people's

[3] The KKE had chosen not to participate in these mobilizations, judging that they fell far short of posing a challenge to the capitalist system.

assembly to introduce a clearer identity and an orientation into the mobilizations. Correspondingly, in Patras the presence of the student Left was more pronounced, in Heraklion there was a stronger participation of the anarchist milieu, and in Kozani there was a pronounced attendance of the folksy Right and so on (Bresia 2011: 95).

Local problems arising out of implementation of the Memorandum also developed outside of Athens: the sale of the harbours in Corfu and the gold mines on the Evros in Thrace, the underfunctioning Thebes hospital. Movement practice also differed. Unlike in Athens where the accepted position was that activists should remain in the square to reinforce the symbolic aspect of permanent presence and opposition to State power, in other towns and cities there were protest marches and occupations of public buildings (regional councils, ministries), not to mention gatherings for manifestation of rejection of visits by ministers and parliamentarians (Bresia 2011: 97). In the case of Athens, the occupation could be sustained because it was supported by unprecedented actions of creating infrastructure. Within a few days of the first gathering structures necessary for the presence, survival and protection of the protesters on a daily basis had been organized: awnings and tents had been erected, a kitchen, a pharmacy, a first aid group, a radio station, a website and cultural activities. Moreover, working groups were organized, such as cleaning crews, legal support groups, security services, communication groups, gender protection groups and artistic expression groups (Kavoulakos and Gritzas 2015: 343).

In any case, the "squares" movement was part of a process of repoliticizing an entire society as well as a meeting point between a number of different currents. An important role in it was played by the big demonstrations that were organized at this time. They culminated in the demonstration of June 5, 2011, which is estimated to have been attended by between 360,000 and 600,000 people in Athens and around 40,000 people in Thessaloniki. The two-day pan-Hellenic strike on June 28 and 29 in the context of the Athens mobilization involved more than 60,000 people on the first day and approximately 100,000 on the second day. All in all, according to one survey, in this two-month period approximately 2,600,000 people (29% of the adult Greek population) participated in at least one mobilization (according to the Public Issue No. 92 barometer). But the adoption of the new austerity package (Medium-Term Programme)—with only the PASOK M.P P. Kourouplis voting against it while G. Lianis had left a few days earlier—led to a gradual petering out of the mobilizations.

The next mass mobilizations took place in the autumn of 2011, with occupations of ministries as an important mode of intervention, culminating in the two-day nation-wide strike on October 19 and 20. This action may well have been the most wide-ranging ever seen by the public sector, as is understandable because the new measures on salaries and the undermining of permanent tenure through the introduction of standby employment[4] were milestone events if seen against the previous mode of functioning of the public sector. On the first day in particular, the number of demonstrators, approximating 500,000, probably surpassed the figure of June 5. (In any case Public Issue that month in its political barometer No. 96 estimates that 25% of the adult population participated in some form of mobilization).

A few days later as the Papandreou government celebrated the approval of the Medium-term loan by the European Union, there was a qualitative change in the character of popular reactions. On October 28, major mobilizations took place during parades,[5] some of which were cancelled, notably that in Thessaloniki where in the midst of an uproar of disapproval the President of the Republic himself, Karolos Papoulias, was forced to leave, with subsequent cancellation of the parade, something unprecedented in Greek history. In our opinion, this in itself represents a turning point in the political consciousness of Greek workers. On the day when the Greek bourgeois state seeks upgrading of its legitimation through parades, the Greek people challenge this ritual. It amounted to direct rejection of the terms of ruling class hegemony, clearly demonstrating that social dissatisfaction was assuming ever more aggressive forms, with the tacit implication that national independence was not to be secured through symbolic ceremonies but through articulation of specific strategies that would thwart surrender of national sovereignty, or elements of it.

---

[4] The new measures on salaries included wage cuts for civil servants; the institution of standby employment meant reduced pay for the workers with permanent tenure which had been considered as "redudants" for as long as it was needed to be dispatched to another position.

[5] October 28 is a national holiday in Greece in remembrance of the outbreak of the Greek-Italian war of 1940.

At the same time throughout the autumn of 2010–2011 and the winter of 2011–2012, the so-called movements of disobedience against payment of the new real estate property tax continued their expansion and the first social solidarity structures began to be created (see below). One very important struggle was that of workers at the "Halyvourgia" steel plant who were demanding retraction of redundancies and had embarked on a protracted strike. Meanwhile, mobilizations were proceeding in the milieu of the mass media (*Eleftherotypia* newspaper. ALTER television station), with experiments conducted in self-management. Other examples of self-organization are not only the case of the factory of VIOME but also the creation of co-operative restaurants and cafes by unemployed people. Throughout the period from 2010 to 2013, there were very dynamic struggles at Skouries in Halkidiki against expansion of the activities of the Hellas Gold company, given that implementation of the project in question would mean destruction of more than 300 hectares of forest, with the environmental impact also expected to wreak havoc with the health of residents, not to mention the effects on fishing, logging, construction and tourism (Louka 2012: 76–77).

The decision by the two largest parties (PASOK and ND) to conclude a second Memorandum and undertake even more unpopular measures triggered new mobilizations in February 2012, culminating in the February 12 rallies which in overall numbers country-wide must have concentrated the largest number of demonstrators seen in Greece since 1974.

Subsequently, and up until the May election, the issues were put on hold but action against the property tax continued. The movement did not conduct any intervention on March 25 in Athens[6] because of tight policing of the parade by the forces of suppression, but protests were held in the provinces against the parades.

Following the elections and ensuing lull in the summer of 2012, the Samaras government's adoption of the medium-term fiscal strategy framework triggered strikes and demonstrations on November 6 and 7. The magnitude of the reactions was perceived as being comparable to

[6] March 25 in Greece is celebrated as the beginning of the Greek revolution against the Othoman occupation and the creation of the Greek independent state.

those of the immediately preceding period (it is estimated that in the two months of October–November 2012 about 2,150,000 people participated in the social mobilizations) (Mavris 2014). Although this seventh package of measures was approved in the Parliament, the governing majority suffered very serious losses: there were now 153 votes in favour compared to the 179 who had supported the vote of confidence for the Samaras government the preceding June.

The next major turning point was the mobilization against the abolition of Greek Radio and Television (ERT), with the related dismissals, in the summer and autumn of 2013. The government's snap decision to close ERT had the effect of creating a very strong support movement. The violence of the government's move, literally from one hour to the next, made it clear even to the most sceptical that the country had moved into a state of emergency. The government's mistake was to believe that public opinion would attach significance to the lack of objectivity often attributed to ERT and to the "privileges" enjoyed by its employees. Here there was a twofold mistake. On the one hand, it very quickly became evident that the beneficiaries of privilege were a handful of staff members (consultants, non-permanent staff, etc.) linked through special status to governmental centres, and on the other that the credibility of ERT had recently had restored. Also left out of account was the political history of Greece and the crucial role in the nation's historical consciousness played by freedom of the press. In a country that had experienced participation in two world wars, the national schism of 1916,[7] the dictatorship of Metaxas (1936–1940), the German occupation (1941–1944), the civil war (1947–1949), the violence of the post civil war State, the Colonels' dictatorship (1967–1974), the abolition of public television and radio was no formal administrative matter. This was also the attitude in the countries of Western parliamentary democracy, which is why there were vehement reactions from abroad. Obviously if within the space of a single day a public organization or a public enterprise had ceased operations and 2650 employees had been dismissed, as occurred

[7] In 1916, for a brief period, Greece split into two "states", in one of which, in Southern Greece, power was in the hands of King Constantine and in the other, in Northern Greece, it was the Prime Minister Eleftherios Venizelos who ruled.

with ERT, there would still have been reactions but they would not have enjoyed the public support that was extended to ERT. That is because this unprecedented action was experienced by broad social strata as a combination of an attack on labour rights, abolition of a public good and restriction of the functioning of democracy. But the mobilizations in solidarity with ERT would not have continued for approximately five months if in this period it had not functioned as an experiment in self-management by a public organization and in pluralistic projection of news and programmes that hitherto had not been made available to the public.

The government took this decision in part as a way of providing the Troika with an example of high-speed reform with measurable results (redundancies) and in part to demonstrate its ability to open a breach in the public sphere, nudging it in the direction of greater authoritarianism. But it had not counted on the magnitude of the reaction, nor on the cost it itself would be required to pay, with the departure of DIMAR from the governmental coalition (see Chap. 9).

The result was that the governing majority from the 179 seats it had held after the June 2012 elections, henceforth, after the losses sustained from voting the third Memorandum and from implementing the ERT decision, fell to a slim margin of 152–153 seats.

The next two years (2014 and 2015, up until the Referendum) would see a significant downturn in the mobilizations. People seemed to be expecting more comprehensive political change, at the same time adopting a perception that the individual issues triggering such mobilizations could only be vindicated through sweeping political change. In the first months of government by the alliance of SYRIZA and the Independent Greeks, there was another social lull, to be interrupted by the rallies called in response to the referendum proclaimed for July 5 (see Chap. 10). In the week preceding the referendum, the supporters of "yes" and "no" summoned two gatherings, each in Athens, both massive but by general consent the rally of the supporters of "no" was possibly the largest to have been held in Athens since 1974.

In any case between 2011 and 2015, there were 27,103 demonstrations and meetings, in other words 15 per day on average, symptomatic of the dynamic that had been created. To take it year by year: in 2011, there were 5910 demonstrations and meetings throughout Greece, the following year 5654, in 2013 6231, the year after that 5198, and in 2015 4110 demonstrations and meetings. The overall corresponding figure for strike meetings between 2011 and 2015 was 1717,[8] while the specific numbers were 356 in 2011, 409 in 2012, 373 in 2013, 323 in 2014 and 256 in 2015 (Papanikolopoulos 2016: 13).

Within this general context of militant mobilization, it should not be overlooked that the emergence of practices of social solidarity to counter the rapid degradation in living conditions was, and is, of the utmost importance. One early form of this was collective catering as a socializing factor, a practice primarily involving a politicized milieu already participating in a variety of initiatives. Their range may not have been very great but they set the tone, lending an aura of collegiality and solidarity, an important point of departure for further practices conducive to solidarity. The soup kitchens serving a significant section of the population, particularly the more vulnerable groups, were a prevalent innovation. They were soon joined by the social groceries, which in some cases evolved into co-operatives. Their aim was to enable working and lower middle-class families to have access to cheap, good-quality food and household goods. The experimental element was the attempt to generate relations of equality between co-operative members, contributing to elimination of the networks of intermediaries. Urban vegetable gardens and food distribution structures were developed subsequently and the "no middlemen" movement established whereby, in collaboration with citizens' initiatives, producers distributed their products directly to consumers at much lower prices than those in retail outlets. A similar system started to operate with social pharmacies, with donations from citizens funding the collection of medicines. Psychological support units also began to operate and some hospitals took to accepting uninsured patients, in addition to conducting free medical examinations.

On the other hand, the collapse of public health structures, coupled with rapid increase in the number of unemployed and uninsured workers, created a very serious gap in primary care services. In response to this

[8] The form of action that predominated in these mobilizations was the strike, with 832 strikes recorded, followed by work stoppages (488 instances) and rallies (231 recorded) (Papanikolopoulos 2016: 15).

situation, a number of social clinics (Thessaloniki, Volos, Elliniko, Exarchia, N. Smyrni) began to be established with a view to providing primary medical services by doctors and nurses free of charge, in contrast to the rundown of the public health and the high cost of recourse to the private sector (Karakioulafis 2014: 94).

Another form of social solidarity was provision of free lessons, either as remedial teaching (coaching) or in preparation for entrance examinations to the university for the children of families afflicted by the crisis, and similar practices began to make their appearance among accountants, electricians and so on. This soon expanded into a host of other activities: dance lessons, photography, visual arts, music, foreign languages and so on. But mutual help structures such as time banks, exchange bazaars, mutually supportive trade and various forms of co-operatives (co-operative cafes and restaurants) made their appearance. Finally, there should be mention of collective artistic projects (artists' groups, self-managed conservatories).

All in all, it is estimated that around 500 alternative projects were launched throughout Greece in the 2011–2014 period. In particular for Attica which, including as it does both Athens and Piraeus, is the country's largest prefecture, the relevant research by Kavoulakos and Gritzas indicated that in the spring of 2014 there were 68 social clinics and social pharmacies, 19 social grocery stores, 71 co-operative schools and conservatories, 58 groups organizing markets without intermediaries, 47 collectives operating social kitchens, 84 time banks, 23 self-managed urban vegetable gardens and 140 social co-operative enterprises.

One point that should be noted is that all of these ventures were significantly different from the civil society's NGOs' counterparts. The reason for this was that they were usually informal in character, without legal status, based on self-organization, challenging the prevailing social and economic practices and values by incorporating into their operations a range of qualities such as solidarity, reciprocity and egalitarianism (Kavoulakos and Gritzas 2015: 345–346). In other words, all this movement that arose after the time of the squares had not only a clear political signature, but it also served as precursor to a greater social change that was expected to take place in the foreseeable future.

References

Bresia M., 2011, "Is all of Greece a town square?", in Giovanopoulos C. and D. Mitropoulos (eds.) *Democracy under construction. From the streets to the squares,* Athens: A/synechia, pp. 91–100 (in Greek).

Karakioulafis C., 2014, "Santé et éducation: victimes des politiques d'austérité", *Chronique internationale de l'IRES* vol. 148, pp. 83–103.

Kavoulakos K. and G. Gritzas, 2015, "Movements and alternative locations in the Greece of crisis. A new civil society", in Georgarakis N. and N. Demertzis (eds.) *The political portrait of Greece. Crisis and deconstruction of the political,* Athens: Gutenberg/National Centre of Social Research, pp. 337–358 (in Greek).

Kouvelakis Stathis, 2011a, "The invisible end of a winter. Towards the second phase of the politico-social confrontation", *Epochi* of 25/3 (in Greek).

Kouvelakis Stathis, 2011b, "Crisis hour. Six theses on the revolt", *Dromos tis Aristeras* of 11/6 (in Greek).

Kouvelakis S., 2011c, "Movement time, political time", http://anasynthesi.gr/index.php?option=com_content&view=article&id=324&Itemid=1, accessed on 20/3/2014 (in Greek).

Louka M., 2012, "Cassandra mines: when the gold does not shine", *Ektos Grammis* vol. 30, pp. 75–77 (in Greek).

Mavris G., 2014, "The fluctuations in SYRIZA's influence in the 2012–2014 post-election period", *Efimerida ton Syntakton of* 25/2/2014 (in Greek).

Papanikolopoulos D., 2016, "The syndicalist dynamic 2010–2015", *Enimerosi* vol. 232, pp. 2–28 (in Greek).

Sotiris P., 2012, "The age of insurrections and the left (thoughts on the "squares", politics and left strategy in a landscape of surprises and overturns", *Theseis* vol. 120, http://www.theseis.com/index.php?option=com_content&task=view&id=1193&Itemid=29, accessed on 20/3/2014 (in Greek).

9

The Crisis of the Party System

From May 2010 to the 2012 Elections

In the first year of the Memorandum, the severity of the crisis, the unprecedented measures that had been adopted, the major social protests that took place, above all the gathering of May 5, the resignations of the three PASOK deputies, the autonomous popular dissatisfaction, all made it clear that the country had entered a new historical phase.

From May 2010 onwards, the mainstream media played a decisive role in sidelining reactions and assisting implementation of this Memorandum policy. The main argument adopted was that the crisis is neither global nor European but Greek, purely and simply (Pleios 2013) and attributable to the distortions of the past (high wages, low productivity, a defective political system, a bloated public sector, clientelistic relations, hyperconsumerism).[1] It is characteristic that the international crisis

---

[1] "And just when Greece was ready to start on the difficult path of modernizing its productive, i.e. entrepreneurial, structures, it was swept by a *tsunami* of populism that installed small and medium businesses in the role of 'class' allies of farmers, workers and oppressed State employees, in that order!" Article of M. Papadimitriou in *Kathimerini* of 12/9/2010, cited in Lialiouti and Bithymitris 2013: 159.

S. Sakellaropoulos, *Greece's (un) Competitive Capitalism and the Economic Crisis*,
https://doi.org/10.1007/978-3-030-14319-0_9

appears to parallel the corresponding Greek crisis, not intersect with it.[2] An attempt is made to construct a framework of collective guilt, where the negative developments are attributable to the mistakes of Greek society, where the present situation is a kind of catharsis for the sins of the past, and where no alternative is available, so that everyone should accept the *fait accompli.*[3]

In the meantime, between June and November 2010, there was a downturn in workers' mobilizations and it became evident that popular dissatisfaction would be expressed in the outcome of the local elections. Both the mass media and the Prime Minister himself, G. Papandreou, had lent the aura of a referendum to these elections. It is a perspective that is reinforced by the fact that New Democracy (ND), the major party of the opposition, up to that point, and for another year, was to be numbered—at least in words—among the anti-Memorandum forces.

The result of the first round of the regional elections, from which more secure conclusions might be drawn on the potentialities of the political parties, resulted in PASOK's emerging as first party, with 34.6% and 1,884,310 votes, followed by ND with 32.6% and 1,774,778 votes, the KKE with 11.0% and 596,977 votes, SYRIZA with 4.5% and 244,990 votes, LAOS (populist wright) with 4.0% and 220,550 votes, the Ecologists-Greens with 2.8% and 154,331 votes, DIMAR with 2.1% and ANT.AR.SY.A (Far Left) with 1.8% and 97,499 votes (Vernardakis 2011: 56).

Of course, if one sees the situation statically it would be possible to say that the result was satisfactory for PASOK. Two regional leaders of its influence (in Crete and in the South Aegean)[4] were elected from the first round of the elections; in five other regions, PASOK's candidates emerged

[2] "The European Union and the member-states that comprise it are not responsible for all these distortions. Responsibility lies with Greece, its peculiarities, and the inability of the country's political system to function in such a way as to set an example for citizens". Article by K. Iordanidis in *Kathimerini* of 27/6/2010 cited in Lialiouti and Bithymitris 2013: 158.

[3] "The goal we must remain committed to is 'almost an accounting task'. The government is 'free' to concentrate on a single objective. Greece is short of precious time to organize its defences. Let us hope that it will not dissipate its strength in stupid, purportedly 'ideological' but in fact small-minded political betrayals". Article of M. Papadimitriou in *Kathimerini* of 6/6/2010, cited in Lialiouti and Bithymitris 2013: 156.

[4] The country is divided into 13 regions.

first and Dimaras, who left PASOK and who was among the three PASOK deputies to vote against the first Memorandum, came third in the Attica region, the largest in the country, and was excluded in the second round (Gemenis 2012: 111–112). This defeat of Dimaras was important because Mr. Papandreou had threatened that if Dimaras won the elections in Attica he, the Prime Minister, would call for new parliamentary elections. All in all, PASOK seemed to have won tactically and lost strategically, something that was to be confirmed in the immediate future. However, if the results are seen in terms of dynamics and trends, the conclusions that emerge are that within the space of a year PASOK lost 1.1 million votes and 9.3% of its support.[5] Such rapid deterioration in a governing party is an unprecedented development. And, of course, there can be no question of the vote being "relaxed" because of the municipal and local elections, because PASOK itself had proclaimed them "a referendum vote".[6] Interestingly, the leaks from PASOK were channelled either towards abstention or towards the Left (see below).

ND found itself with around 500,000 fewer voters, almost a full percentage point behind its vote in October 2009. At first sight, the result seems to have been due to the internal crisis that led to the expulsion of D. Bakoyanni from ND and the departure of four other deputies who were under her influence.[7] But this is a secondary factor. The basic problem was that ND had not managed to take advantage either of the radical decline of PASOK or of the anti-Memorandum stance it itself has adopted. So, the negative outcome was primarily a reflection of the indignation of a sizeable proportion of voters against the key players in the party system, and accordingly has to do with PASOK's drastic loss of

[5] The results of the 2009 national elections were: PASOK 43.92% and 3012.542 votes, ND 33.47% and 2,295,719 votes, KKE 7.54% and 517,249 votes, LAOS 5.63% and 386,205 votes, SYRIZA 4.60% and 315,665 votes, Ecologists-Greens 2.53% and 173,589 votes, ANTARSYA 0.36% and 24,687 votes.

[6] As George Papandreou said in the inter-channel interview, if the results of the elections are negative for PASOK "then the decision must be for the People".

[7] Dora Bakoyanni was a very important office holder in ND. When after the ND defeat in the 2009 parliamentary elections its then president K. Karamanlis resigned, D. Bakoyanni came second after Antonis Samaras in the elections for a new party leader. Bakoyanni subsequently disagreed with Samaras and in 2010 voted for the first Memorandum, which led to her expulsion. A few days after the local elections the five parliamentarians influenced by Bakoyanni formed the short-lived political party Democratic Alliance.

support also, with the difference that ND as a non-governing and anti-Memorandum party was less affected. As G. Mavris has argued, it was an uneven contraction, because the vote for PASOK was the worst since 1977. It obtained only 63% of the votes it had won in 2009, whereas ND's vote was slightly higher than what it had secured in the European elections of 2009 and 77% of its vote in the 2009 Greek elections (Mavris 2010).

Similar conclusions can be drawn for LAOS, which managed to stand independently in only six of Greece's 13 regions. The decline of more than 1 percentage point in its vote is attributable to the stance it adopted of supporting the Memorandum.

By contrast, the KKE saw an absolute increase in its vote in the order of 80,000 votes and 3.5 percentage points, a development due to the defection of a section of PASOK's electoral base. The outcome for SYRIZA seems contradictory. On the one hand, there was a marginal drop of around 0.1%, yet in absolute numbers the loss amounted to 70,000 fewer votes. Such loss may be explained by the split that led to the founding of the Democratic Left (DIMAR)[8], by the former president Alekos Alavanos independently running for office in Attica, and similarly, by Syriza's political officer in regional administration, Despina Spanoudi, independently running for office in Central Greece (Vernardakis 2011: 58). But be that as it may, it cannot conceal the stagnation of a party of the Left at a time when the entire political scene was shifting leftwards. And this was to be seen in the critical situation that was to be confronted by SYN/SYRIZA in the coming months.[9]

DIMAR achieved a vote that exceeded its strength in the united Synaspismos but was a long way from displaying a momentum that might enable it to become an autonomous presence in future.

[8] Recall that in June 2010 the so-called renewing wing of the Synaspismos, headed by F. Kouvelis, left the then Synaspismos and formed the Democratic Left.

[9] Very briefly, after the 2010 elections an internal confrontation began within the Left Coalition (Synaspismos), which was the largest component of SYRIZA. Almost all the groups (apart from the Synaspismos and the Ananeotiki Kommounistiki Aristera [Renewing Communist Left – AKOA] in SYRIZA, which at that time was a front formation, were evidently reconsidering their participation, with most joining together with Alekos Alavanos to form the "Metopo Allilengyis kai Anatropis" ("Front for Solidarity and the Overthrow"), from which however they gradually withdrew when at the beginning of 2012 the dynamism of SYRIZA became evident, elevating it after the elections in the May of the same year to the position of official opposition.

The vote for ANTARSYA was remarkable: for the first time a grouping of the extra-parliamentary Left succeeded in winning a national audience.

Last but not least, of particularly important, as will be shown later, is the fact that the Golden Dawn neo-Nazi party also acquired some dynamism. Its leader N. Michaloliakos stood as a candidate in the mayoral elections for Athens and received the non-negligible vote of 5.3%, taking advantage of the fact that LAOS did not put forward a candidate, instead of supporting ND's Kaklamanis (Georgiadou 2014: 195).

Another important parameter worth mentioning has to do with the rate of abstention in the first round, the second highest in the history of the country's elections. Only 5988,678 people voted (whereas in the prefectural elections of 2006 7,111,538 voted), and only in the 2009 European elections did fewer, that is, 5,261,355, people vote (Vernardakis 2011: 59). This is clearly an act of censure against the political system, which was reinforced by the unprecedented rise of invalid and blank ballots. Specifically, they totalled 9.1% of votes, whereas in the prefectural elections of 2006 the figure had been 6.6% and in the prefectural elections of 2002 the figure had been 6.1%. In all other recent elections, it had been just over 2%, with the sole exception of the 1999 European elections, where 4.2% of the ballots had been invalid or blank (Vernardakis 2011: 60).

Due to its nature, the second round[10] is not conducive to drawing precise conclusions, but one can stand in some respects: the rate of abstention rose to 43% of the real electorate, as against 27% in the first round and there was also a small rise in the percentage of blank ballots (10%). This development indicates that the overwhelming majority (G. Mavris estimates 77%) of voters who did not vote for one of the two-party-system candidates in the first round did not vote for them in the second round either (Mavris 2010). PASOK won in 8 out of the 13 regions, in most cases marginally, and the mayors who enjoyed its support wrenched, after many years, the municipalities of Athens and Thessaloniki from the Right, thus helping to sustain the notion that PASOK remained the first party, albeit

[10] Local elections are held in two rounds. The participants in the first round are the candidates who manage to get themselves on the ballot. If in the first round a candidate obtains 50% +1 of the votes, he is the winner. Otherwise a second round is held with participation only of the two leading candidates.

with very heavy losses (Vernardakis 2011: 60–61). We should bear in mind that in the 2009 national elections PASOK had won in all the regions, whereas now the candidates received an average of 50.8% in the second round, with ND candidates taking 49.2%.

In conclusion, the 2010 elections showed clearly that the party system that had prevailed since 1977 was on the way out, notwithstanding the temporary victory of PASOK. The two branches of two-partyism were suffering a major blow and the electoral audience was either seeking a solution to the Left or censuring the system as a whole, resorting to abstention and invalid or blank ballots. In any case, it had become apparent that the country was confronted with deep transformations. Their consummation was linked to whether the crisis and its consequences were going to be even more profound.

The ruling class sensed this subterranean current of challenge, and it made them uneasy. The attitude of the media made it clear how much concern there was that the prescribed course of implementing the Memorandum should not be disturbed,[11] not to mention the anxieties generated by ND's anti-Memorandum stance.[12] Consequently, what had to be done, as the evidence mounted that new measures would be necessary, was agreement between the two major parties, but that wasn't enough in itself. Solutions had to be developed outside the boundaries of run-of-the-mill parliamentarianism.[13] It was at this time, essentially, that

[11] "Its main deficit, however, is that of political leadership. We urgently need politicians who will ignore political costs and will not be constantly preoccupied with public relations projection. Determined politicians who can understand what it means to balance income and expenditure, who can work in a technocratic and professional manner and who are already well-established in society and in the market. Unfortunately the parties have few such people, which is why we need new blood to enter politics". Article in *Kathimerini* of 13/3/2011. (mentioned in Lialiouti and Bithymitris 2013: 162).

[12] "We hope for the good of the country that the people of New Democracy come to their senses and listen to their conscience. If at the end of May Mr. Papandreou has not achieved a minimum of national consensus, things will be bleak. If the parties have not overcome their obsessive ideological scruples about 'their' state, the Greek economy will surrender to its rapists .... The enemies of the nation will have won this round". Article by M. Papadimitriou in "*Kathimerini*" of 17/4/2011 (mentioned in Lialiouti and Bithymitris 2013: 153).

[13] "We need ... a strong emergency government. In a country at war". Article by K. Kallitsis in *Kathimerini* 13/3/2011 (mentioned in Lialiouti and Bithymitris 2013:154). Also: "There is a solution for everything, with Bonapartist characteristics: a small government of national salvation, comprised of politically aware technocrats and knowledgeable politicians with a uniform political outlook, who will commit themselves to achieving clear goals, will save the country and after will

suggestions began to be floated of arrangements along like the Papademos-type solutions, the banker who was eventually to become prime minister, and such a solution was accordingly adopted. All these attitudes reveal the depth of awareness of the crisis among the leaders of the ruling class, but also the single-mindedness of their endeavour, on the one hand, to transform the crisis into a transfer of wealth from the world of work to the world of capital and on the other to liquidate less competitive enterprises.

The movement of the squares and the events of October 28, 2011 would intensify the inherent contradictions, although there were evidently no significant changes other than the departures of the deputies Lianis and Kourouplis from PASOK as ND persisted in its anti-Memorandum stance, obliging Papandreou to attempt playing a Bonapartist role, announcing a referendum for early November.[14] But nobody in the ruling class wanted to take any risks with the way the situation was developing and Papandreou's shaky government accordingly collapsed. And it is worth noting how permanently reluctant European elites are to hold referenda, to the point where almost all European treaties are ratified by national parliaments. Confronted with this situation, the Papademos government was chosen as a solution for a "flight forward" for capital, despite the uncertainty about how long he would remain in office. It was an

---

each go his/her own way". Article of K. Kallitsis *Kathimerini* of 17/4/2011 (mentioned in Lialiouti and Bithymitris 2013: 154). Also "Unfortunately, it turns out that only if foreign operatives take matters entirely into their own hands is there any hope of being saved .... This is not the first time Greece has been placed under the guardianship of foreigners .... There will be cries of protest, but it will not be so tragic in terms of national dignity if the supervision of the foreign functionaries is more direct, with the installation of commissioners in the non-existent Greek state machine". Article by A. Stagos in *Kathimerini* on 15/5/2011 (mentioned in Lialiouti and Bithymitris 2013: 164).

[14] In November 2011, Papandreou proposed a referendum to approve or reject the decision of the EU summit the previous October. The agreement included a 50% "haircut" of the Greek debt and an additional €130 billion aid package to Greece. Under the agreement, private individuals accepted on a voluntary basis a 50% reduction in the value of the Greek bonds they held. The agreement was accompanied by a budgetary adjustment programme with a duration until 2021, and establishment of a permanent surveillance mechanism for continuous monitoring of implementation of the reforms in Greece. The referendum proposal encountered reactions both in other European countries and within Greece, and it did not take place. Papandreou withdrew his proposal and resigned from the prime ministership. A coalition government was formed with the support of PASOK, ND and the People's Orthodox Alarm (LAOS), with the former vice-president of the European Central Bank, Lucas Papademos, as prime minister.

attempt to establish post-modern forms of political power, where direct delegation to a representative of business would replace the refracted mode of political representation that the functioning of bourgeois parliamentary democracy embodied. At the same time, ND's participation in the Papademos government signalled the incorporation of this party into the Memorandum strategy, the elimination of elements of autonomy at the political level and a fundamental challenge to the basis for the reproduction of the bipolar political system.

Subsequently, with the further upsurge in the social mobilizations triggered by the attempted implementation of the new measures, the crisis worsened and peaked on the evening of February 12, 2012, with the major mobilizations against the second Memorandum and the departure of dozens of deputies from the parliamentary groups of PASOK, ND and LAOS. So, within the space of two and a half years, there were very significant changes of composition in the forces of the parties' parliamentary groups. About 30 deputies left PASOK and ten resigned, disagreeing with the austerity measures; about 15 left ND for the same reason, and departures due to disagreement were also registered in LAOS, which for a long time had consented to the austerity measures. The situation was unprecedented: more than 60 deputies elected in 2009 no longer, in February 2012, belonged to the party through which they had come into public life.[15]

The dynamic of the February 12 mobilizations and the parliamentary regroupments they brought in their wake shed a revealing light on the legitimacy deficit, and the country went to elections, though this was not something bourgeois officialdom was anxious to see, aware that it would entail a significant strengthening of the anti-Memorandum forces. In reality, the ruling elite would have liked the Papademos government to remain—that is, a government headed by a person of the banking establishment enjoying the support of the three largest parties who might implement with impressive clarity the agendas of the most powerful

[15] Concerning PASOK it is significant that the first Memorandum was voted (May 2010) by 156 of its 160 deputies, the mid-term Memorandum (June 2011) by 154, the Papademos government's (November 2011) by 148 and the second Memorandum (February 2012) by just 129 deputies. Correspondingly, there were 20 deputies in ND who did not vote for the Memorandum on February 12.

monopoly circles (Greek and foreign). But the lack of legitimacy of this governmental schema was very evident. As noted by Giannis Mavris, public opinion polls revealed obvious disapproval of the second Memorandum (79% of citizens were against the Memorandum in February 2012) and from the beginning of 2011 the demand for elections was continually growing; in April 2012 it reached the figure of 67%. Calling elections was a consequence of the insistence of those "underneath" and the forced agreement of those "on top" in the face of the possibility of an uncontrolled social explosion. It was therefore agreed that elections would be held in May 2012.

The 2012 Elections

The May elections marked a total overturn of the two-major-party based political system that had prevailed in Greece from 1977 onwards, with alternation of PASOK and ND in government. ND emerged as first party, but with only 18.85% of the vote, a fall of 14.62% from the national elections of 2009 and a loss of 1,100,000 voters. SYRIZA came second, with 16.78%, a rise of 12.18% and an increase of almost 750,000 in the number of voters (and it should be taken into account that 2009 was before the split that led to the founding of DIMAR). In third place was PASOK, with 13.18% and an unprecedented 30.74% fall in its support, with a loss of over 2.1 million voters. Next came the new party, the Independent Greeks, with 10.6% and 670,000 votes,[16] followed by the KKE (Communist Party of Greece) with 8.48% (a rise of 0.94%) and after them Golden Dawn, with 6.97% (6.68% higher) and 420,000 more voters, then the new party DIMAR with 6.1% and 386,000 votes, the Ecologists-Greens with 2.93% (up 0.4%) and 13,000 more votes and after them LAOS with 2.90% (down 2.73%) and a loss of 200,000 votes. They were followed by the new party Democratic Alliance with 2.55% and 161,000 votes, Recreation now of Thanos Tzimeros with 2.15% and 136,000 votes, Drasi (action) of Stefanos

[16] Independent Greeks (ANEL) was founded in April 2012 by 10 former deputies of ND, led by P. Kammenos, who refused to vote for the second Memorandum in February 2012.

Manos with 1.80% and 114,000 votes[17] and ANTARSYA (revolt) scored above 1% with a 0.83% rise to 1.19% and 50,000 more votes.

The outcome of the May 6 elections clearly reflected the depth of the social crisis, the social polarization and the unmistakable political crisis. There was the collapse of PASOK, which returned to the electoral percentages of 1974, punished for the policies it had followed. And this was significant because we are speaking of the disintegration of a milieu that had been dominant for over three decades in the broader popular strata, playing a key role in their representation and incorporation into bourgeois strategy. Then there was the forceful censure of ND, which failed to achieve more than 19%, marking the worst performance in its political history. At the same time, the aggregate result for the two parties fell to a historical low point: 32.20%,[18] meaning a loss of 3.3 million votes and the greatest electoral shift in the post-dictatorship period, to say the least. PASOK received the support of 33% of its 2009 voters and ND 49% (Stathopoulos 2014: 66).

Up until 2012 the two-party scenario was self-sustaining. Dissatisfaction with one party led its voters to support the other, in both directions. ND's decision to participate in the Papademos government had a corrosive effect on the two-party system. It helps to explain the fact that total electoral percentage for the pro-Memorandum parties clearly put them in the minority. Moreover, the historically high percentage vote for parties that remained outside Parliament (19.03%) was higher than the percentage

---

[17] The two parties of Thanos Tzimeros and Stefanos Manos are perceived to represent extreme neoliberal views, and this would lead them to collaboration in the next elections, of June 2012.

[18] It is worth recording the words of G. Mavris, who observes: "In Greek political history a percentage of bipartisan influence of this order has been recorded only once, 62 years ago in the first post-civil war elections of 1950. In those elections, (note that a proportional representation system was used) the aggregate vote for the two largest parties, the People's Party, led by K. Tsaldaris and the Liberal Party, led by S. Venizelos, accounted for 36.4% of the votes. If we also count the third party of that era, i.e. National Progressive Centre Union of N. Plastiras, the cumulative percentage of the three largest parties was close to 52.5%. In today's line-up of party forces, even though no straightforward analogy applies, the first two parties (ND and SYRIZA) in aggregate accounted for 35.6% and the first three (with PASOK) only 48.81% of the electorate. This fragmentation of political forces was deeper even than what had emerged in the Parliament of 1950. It was so dramatic that it sometimes seemed like an ideological-political equivalent of the corresponding fragmentation of political forces that was to be observed at the first post-civil-war elections. That was the result of occupation and civil war. This later version was the political and electoral result of implementation of the Memorandum" (Mavris 2012a).

for the first party, and along with the abstention registered the increased alienation of the electorate from the political system. The Left, for its part (SYRIZA, KKE, ANTARSYA), took 26.4% achieving the highest vote it has won in parliamentary elections in Greece, exceeding even the result of 1958.[19]

Sorting these results by category, one could end up with a number of different groupings. The first includes (a) the purely pro-European and pro-Memorandum forces (*New Democracy*, *Drasi* (Action), *Dimiourgia Xana* (Recreation now), which received about 38% of the votes; (b) anti-Memorandum and pro-European forces (DIMAR, SYRIZA, Ecologists-Greens, which won almost 26%; (c) the Left-wing forces (KKE and ANTARSYA), which received less than 10%. Their position was not only against the Memoranda but also for exit from the Euro and the European Union (EU); (d) the right-wing anti-Memorandum milieu (Independent Greeks and LAOS[20]), which received slightly over 13%; (e) the special case of the Nazi Golden Dawn, with 7%.

In terms of electoral geography, SYRIZA recorded its highest percentages among public sector employees (22.1%), the unemployed (21.5%), university and technical college students (19.2%), private sector employees (18.9%) and self-employed people (17.8%). It also recorded very high levels of support in the working class municipalities of the capital. The conclusion is that its electoral sociology was very different from that of the pre-crisis SYRIZA and/or from the Communist Party of the Interior. The SYRIZA of 2012 represented a significant section of the popular strata, it projected a working class, younger-generation and to some extent petty bourgeois character. It should be noted that the aggregate support for the Left, SYRIZA and KKE was 30% among private sector employees, and at the lower levels of this category (the most proletarian strata) went as high as 45%; among public sector employees the figure was 34%, and at the lower levels the figure reached 52% (Vernardakis 2012a).

---

[19] At that time the party of the United Democratic Left, which was the legal vehicle for the outlawed KKE, received 22.4% and emerged as the second parliamentary force after the conservative party of Prime Minister Constantine Karamanlis.

[20] After voting in favour of the motion tabled by the Papademos government, LAOS did not support the second Memorandum but joined, albeit belatedly with the anti-Memorandum current.

By contrast, PASOK, which previously dominated these categories, found 10.6% support in the public sector, 7.7% from private sector employees and 4.1% from the unemployed. It suffered very big losses in working class areas of the Attica Basin, where it was sometimes relegated to fifth place. Even in the categories where it was over the national average (farmers 23.1%, public sector pensioners 25%, private sector pensioners 20.8%), in reality the contraction was over 50% of its previous influence (Vernardakis 2012a). In the new petty bourgeois strata (freelancers) that had been hit hard by the crisis PASOK's influence fell to 9.1% and ND's to 13.2% (Moschonas 2012: 6) This is a social category that also votes for Independent Greeks (12.9%) and Golden Dawn (8.7%). The latter emerged as first party, with 19.2%, among small and medium-sized entrepreneurs (trade and light industry), followed by Independent Greeks with 13.2% and ND with 9.6%. To convey the extent of ND's representation problem, it is mentioned that in the top business and employer strata it won just 10% of the vote.[21] Only among farmers did it manage to retain a high percentage: around 26.2%.

In terms of educational level, both PASOK and ND are under-represented among graduates of universities and technological institutes, with 10.6% and 14.3% support respectively. By contrast, they are over-represented among people with primary school education, with 21.4% and 29.5% support respectively. On the other hand, the three pro-European parties (Democratic Alliance, Drasi and Recreation now) enjoy a significant momentum in the educated section of the population, winning 11.2% support from graduates of tertiary education at a time when the Greek national average was 6.44% (Moschonas 2012: 7). SYRIZA too succeeded in securing a respectable 19% of the vote of higher education graduates (Stathopoulos 2014: 74). As for the age parameter, ND and PASOK present a profile of aged voters. ND was supported by 29.2% of those over 55 (making it second party in this category) but only 10.1% of those between 35 and 54 and 7.4% of the 18–34 age group. In contrast, SYRIZA was supported by 17.4% of the

[21] From this viewpoint, the example of Ekali (a very upper-crust district of Athens) is significant. ND took 31.6% of the vote there, but Drasi managed 21%, Recreation now 8.9% and Democratic Alliance 5.4%.

18–34 age group, 20.3% of the 35–54, 12.3% of those over 55 age group. The figures for ANEL were 12.4% of the 18–34 age group, 12.9% of the 35–54 age group, 6.7% of the over 55 age group. For Golden Dawn, they were 10.2% of the 18–34 age group, 7.8% of the 35–54 age group, and 3.7% of the over 55 age group (Koustenis 2014a: 120). So, we see that the two parties of the former bipolar system are supported by older voters, unlike the three parties brought into the foreground by the dynamics of crisis.

Above and beyond the collapse of the former bipartyism and the near-annihilation of PASOK,[22] the party that had put its stamp on history after the fall of the junta, the elections of May 2012 also highlighted the variety of dynamics unfolding within the country. The fact that ND did not do well with representing the employer strata, in contrast to the more purist liberal parties of Bakoyanni, Tzimeros and Manos, is symptomatic of the distance that had been created between these strata and their erstwhile political representation. My view is that this is attributable in part to the deterioration of the traditional political personnel who were being held responsible for the advent of the crisis but also to the failure of ND to adapt in time to the framework of the Memorandum policies. At the same time, the collapse of the two-party consensus highlighted the absence of a second full-blooded bourgeois party as alternative vehicle for exercising governance, either alone or in alliance with ND. In contrast, the consistency shown by the ND breakaway Independent Greeks, which remained in the anti-Memorandum camp, was rewarded, drawing away 15% from ND, 22% from LAOS and 11% from new voters (Stathopoulos 2014: 66). On the other hand, it was not only the quantitative dimension that illustrated the dynamic of the Left but also the qualitative: over-representation in the popular strata and in the younger age groups. One might claim, arguably, that one Greece was departing and another Greece arriving. This specific arrangement of parties corresponded to a political (not electoral) balance between the Memorandum and anti-Memorandum powers, a reduction in the influence of every type of bourgeois party and a great increase in the strength of the Left, with SYRIZA as its key component. SYRIZA derived the benefit from raising the issue of Left

[22] PASOK formed governments from 1981 to 1989, from 1993 to 2004 and from 2009 to 2011.

government. It was precisely this point that gave SYRIZA its impressive momentum[23]: the formulation of a clearly alternative orientation (not a proposal, because something like that would also require specialized content). By contrast, the KKE, which did not include this dimension in its policy, found itself within the space of a few weeks witnessing the overturn of an intra-Left correlation of forces that dated if not from the split of 1968[24] then at minimum from the first post-junta years. It is no coincidence that in the May elections 16% of the KKE voters chose to vote SYRIZA, with the resulting gap being filled by former PASOK voters. If one takes into account the dynamic that is evident in the results both for SYRIZA and for DIMAR, it is obvious that the 18,000 additional votes received by the KKE did not reflect a genuine political momentum, and this would be seen at the June 2012 elections (Eleftheriou 2014: 162–163).

Not only SYRIZA and ANEL had an impressive increase in strength but also the neo-Nazi Golden Dawn, which skyrocketed from 20,000 (0.3%) votes in the 2009 parliamentary elections to 440,000 (7.5%), electing 21 deputies. Characteristically, it is noted that it was supported by 9.1% of male voters, 9.3% of farmers, 8.9% of the self-employed, 9.1% of the unemployed, 9.5% of students and 9.0% of those with a middle-school level of education. Among young voters it emerged as second party, with 14% of the vote (Koustenis 2014a: 103; Stathopoulos 2014: 66). It therefore represented an amalgam of patriarchal phallocratic elements of the male population and social categories hit by the crisis and feeling intense insecurity and pessimism about the future (Koustenis 2014a: 108). In any case, it is arguable that there were five main reasons for this new development.

[23] Nineteen per cent of the electoral base of SYRIZA was comprised of former PASOK voters, 16% of former KKE voters and 16% of new voters (Stathopoulos 2014: 66).

[24] In 1968, the united KKE split into the pro-Soviet KKE and the Eurocommunist KKE (interior). In all the electoral contests that took place after the fall of the junta the KKE clearly had greater electoral strength than the KKE (interior). The evolution, more or less, of the KKE (interior) into the Coalition of the Left (1991) did not change this correlation. It was not until the elections of May 2012 that SYRIZA, the electoral front of the Coalition of the Left with other organizations of the extra-parliamentary Left and Left-wing Social Democrats, overtook the KKE in electoral strength.

The first reason has to do with the fact that the censure expressed against key political figures, as a consequence of the depth of the crisis and of the proletarianization of strata which until then were of petty bourgeois status, enabled the emergence of a hitherto marginal party. This party would promote itself as the sole vehicle for reaction against the "post-junta status quo", to which it indiscriminately consigned all the political forces that had been active since 1974. This development was facilitated by the joint support that PASOK and New Democracy extended to the Papademos government and by the second Memorandum, which played an important role, on a symbolic level, and beyond that (Koustenis 2014a: 107).[25]

The second reason derives from the first and has to do with the crisis of credibility experienced by the Greek Right in the course of the crisis. It started with the decision of LAOS not only to vote for the first Memorandum but also to participate in the Papademos government[26] in an attempt to turn from an anti-systemic protest party into a party of government, thereby spreading disillusion in its electoral base,[27] (when it decided not to support the second Memorandum, it had already entirely lost whatever credibility it had had) and continued with the decision by ND to participate in the Papademos government, in this way accepting the Memorandum framework. The establishment of the Independent Greeks was a late development, coming when the influence of Golden Dawn had already begun to grow (Mavris 2013d). The division of the right-wing vote marked the break-up of the social alliance that the ND party had rallied following the fall of the junta (Touliatos 2012: 52).

The third reason has to do with the shift to the right of the Papademos government's agenda: the sharpening of repressive practices, the focusing on the migration issue as the main problem of Greek society, the articula-

[25] It is characteristic that 36.1% of Golden Dawn voters had voted ND in the 2009 elections, 28.6% PASOK and 18.5% LAOS (Georgiadou 2014: 212). Correspondingly, ND lost 13.6% of its vote to ANEL and 5.2% to Golden Dawn (Georgiadou 2014: 199).

[26] For the quite noteworthy similarities between LAOS' electoral audience prior to its political collapse and the later audience for Golden Dawn see Koustenis 2014a: 105.

[27] It is characteristic that it attracted only 25% of its 2009 voter support (Stathopoulos 2014: 66) registering losses of the order of 14% even towards SYRIZA and DIMAR (Georgiadou 2014: 199).

tion of a discourse centred on Greek society's "lack of discipline", against which checks and barriers must be erected. All this worked to the advantage[28] of a party with the profile of Golden Dawn.

The fourth reason is linked to Golden Dawn's self-projection as a provider of "solidarity", exclusively for Greeks: food distribution, finding work for the unemployed in the place of immigrants (but on the terms of overexploitation that apply for immigrants), assistance for the elderly and so on.

The fifth is related to the fact that due to the catalytic involvement of the lenders in the country's economic and political developments, it had been possible for Golden Dawn to elaborate a frame of reference conflating migrants and lenders into an integrated external enemy, a visible distillation of all that is hostile to the nation (Koustenis 2014a: 107; Voulgaris and Nikolakopoulos 2014: 23).

If we want to focus now on the different perceptions that emerged, we could say that two basic contradictions came to the forefront (Memorandum/anti-Memorandum and bourgeois parties/Leftist parties) and two secondary ones (Europeanism/anti-Europeanism and the fascism[29]/anti-fascism divergence).

The non-formation of a government, leading to new elections in June 2012, was the unsurprising outcome of all the above contradictions. It

---

[28] Specifically, on the immigration issue it is worth noting that in parts of Athens with dense concentrations of migrants, Golden Dawn obtained its highest levels of support: Plateia Vathis 12.1%, Plateia Attikis 11.6%, Plateia Amerikis 11%, Metaxourgeio 10.9%, Kolonos 10.2%, historical centre 10% (Mavris 2013d).

[29] Bear in mind that basic elements of the discourse articulated by Golden Dawn share common ground with Nazism. There is a condemnation of all that might be called the political "establishment" along with a quasi-metaphysical projection of the conviction that the solution will come from the Golden Dawn when Greek society effects its traditional return to the triptych Homeland—Religion—Family (Paraskeva-Veloudogianni 2012: 42). It is redolent with the neo-romanticism of the Nazi ideology of return to an ideal German past. Golden Dawn also articulates simplistic Manichean schemes, which are sometimes associated with already formulated conspiracy theories and the elaboration of a mystic schema in which Golden Dawn is the central axis against everything else and all others are complicit in, or tolerant of, the implementation of these conspiracies (conspiracies against Greeks, with Zionism playing a key role etc.). This, as in the case of classical Nazism, does not signify a socially subversive project but rather a more intensified capitalism with greater autonomy of the party-state. In fact, the Golden Dawn professes a kind of paternalistic capitalism where its party will oversee the elimination of the "distortions" of the post-junta settlement: "corrupt politicians", the "left-wing state", "lazy civil servants", the "rotten political system" (Kousiantas 2012).

should not be forgotten that, as already mentioned, the dynamic of grass-root mobilizations was what necessitated the May 2012 elections. This dynamic found expression in the electoral result, with the rise of the Left and the collapse of the bipolar party system. It was not conducive to facile governmental coalitions, so that even DIMAR did not consent to forming a government. On the other hand, the extraordinary rise of the Left was particularly troubling for the ruling class, not to mention the international imperialist centres. Bear in mind that SYRIZA went to the elections with a fairly radical programme,[30] whereas the KKE and ANTARSYA continued their opposition to the EU and the euro.

My position is that the Greek ruling class and the international imperialist centres were not prepared to accept cancellation of the Memorandum, let alone agree to the formation of a Left-wing government. In other words, the strategy of the Greek and foreign ruling class dictated that any deviation from the framework of the Memoranda, which even the Independent Greeks advocated, would lead to significant shifts in more radical directions, since the overthrow of the Memoranda would take place under pressure from the grassroots, enjoying legitimacy from an electoral result. For precisely these reasons an unprecedented attack began, coming largely from abroad, against the likelihood of an electoral victory of the Left.

It is worth devoting a little more time to this. In an interview with *Kathimerini* shortly before the June elections, the chairman of the Federal

[30] It is worth mentioning on the subject of wage losses that in the SYRIZA election programme of May it says "we can, without irrationality and fragmentation, within a period of two years regain the wage levels that were secured in 2009, making unemployment benefits available to everyone, locals and immigrants, until they find work, and gradually increasing it, for the first two years, to 80% of the last salary". On the issue of debt, the possibility of halting repayments and writing off most outstanding debt was considered within the framework of possible solutions. As regards major productive units, the May programme stated: "The financial system can and should become public". The demand was raised for "returning to the public the enterprises and agencies that had been partially or totally privatized (Public Power Corporation, Greek telecommunications, Greek Railway Organization, Hellenic Post, Athens Public Water Authority, public transport system). Also promoted was retention or return to the control of the state of essential production units critical to the development of the economy, such as ports, airports, highways, shipyards, mineral and energy resources. The search for and exploitation of minerals and energy for as long as, and in so far as, they are needed, must be regulated by the State, with democratic control and in consultation with local communities. For this to happen public bodies are needed for the management of mineral and energy resources".

Reserve Bank of Germany Jens Weidmann said: "Failure to comply with the agreement will mean termination of funding. And this may have implications for the country's prospects of remaining in the eurozone". The blackmail is clear here: any deviation from what has been agreed will take Greece out of the European Monetary Union (EMU). Correspondingly, Britain's Prime Minister David Cameron pointed out in a statement that "we need to send a very clear message to the Greek people: either you will stay in the euro with all the commitments that implies or, if you opt for something else, you are actually voting in favour of leaving". Here the blackmail is even more relentless and it is not only about the implementation of what has been agreed but also about the composition of the government itself. The President of the Commission Baroso said, more indirectly, that the EU "wants Greece to stay in the euro zone", implying that there could be some choices that will put Greece outside of it. Similarly, EU President Van Rompuy issued the reminder that "we want Greece to remain in the euro zone, but respecting its commitments". Here too we have a mode of expression that is all insinuation but the message is patently threatening. The same could be said of the content of the statements by Hollande, President of the French Republic: "We should warn them that if there is the impression that Greece wants to distance itself from its commitments and abandon all prospects of recovery, there will be eurozone countries that will prefer to end Greece's presence in the EMU".

One thing that should be noted is the number of officials who make statements directly interfering in Greek political affairs. This is something unprecedented but at the same time indicative. It could be explained by the fact that a prospective Left-wing SYRIZA government would be an anomaly in Europe and could comprise an unfortunate precedent. As was pointed out, Greece was something like a test case for how to make an effective response to the international economic crisis. The possibility of an overthrow of this orientation caused concern among the international political and economic elites. Juncker therefore made a point of getting in first: "If the radical Left wins, the consequences for monetary union will be unpredictable". Merkel's position was similar: "We will speak with any elected government. What I can do, though, is warn anyone who is elected that I am against any exiting from the EMU. The internal cohesion of the European Monetary Union will be jeopardized". At the same time, she issued a reminder that if Greece violates the Financial Stability Pact it will be brought before the European Court of Justice.

The truth is that SYRIZA was going to the June elections with a much more modest programme.[31] Nevertheless, what the Greek and other European elites feared was the momentum that could have been created by a victorious outcome for the Greek Left. Within the short time between the squares movement of June and the October mobilizations, the October 28 protests, the demonstrations on February 12, the party defections of the second Memorandum, the results of the May elections,

[31] First of all the party leadership tried to calm fears that SYRIZA would follow policies of rupture with the EMU and the European Union. In the presentation of the electoral programme, it was stated that "we should reorient European resources to supporting unemployment, low incomes" or, as G. Dragasakis said in the same presentation, "redesigning the NSRF and increasing its absorptive capacity. A European investment financing program in EU member states to address the recession. Greece, like the other eurozone countries facing liquidity problems, needs to be strengthened, either through non-interest-bearing financing from the European Investment Bank or through alternative funding within the European Union".

On the issue of debt, A. Tsipras stated "the new government ... [will] demand renegotiation of the loan agreement. In particular, with regard to a sustainable response to the country's sovereign debt crisis, it will seek a European solution. Without a common European solution to the problem of accrued debt and development finance, Greece cannot at the same time achieve fiscal adjustment and a primary surplus, paying interest on accumulated debt, and financing public investment and public policies. This is an unresolved equation. This is why we will demand a new debt renegotiation with the aim of drastically reducing it, or a moratorium on debt and the suspension of interest payments, until conditions for stabilization and recovery of the economy are established".

As for salaries, social spending and property tax, the positions that were adopted were very moderate: "Unemployment benefit will be provided for twice as long as the present period (two years) .... The government will abolish special charges (real estate taxes) for small and medium income brackets, and first and foremost for the unemployed, for those on low pay, for people living on small pensions and those on the poverty line", "There will be an immediate freeze on cuts to social spending, salaries and pensions to put an end to marginalization through low incomes and to the downgrading of the middle class".

But on the question of nationalizations too it was moderation that predominated: For example, for natural and mineral wealth a special insurance fund would be created to which all rights on this wealth would be transferred. Thereafter "nationalization and then socialization, i.e. placement under public and transparent social control of banks that have been recapitalized through the Financial Stability Fund. A freeze on privatizations of Public Organizations of strategic importance for the national economy that have been passed on to the celebrated Special Fund, with gradual restoration, depending on the potential of the economy, of the publicly controlled strategic enterprises that are either in the process of privatization or have already been privatized (the Public Power Corporation, the Hellenic Telecommunications Organization, the Greek National Railways, the Hellenic Post Office, the Athens Water Supply and Sewerage Company, the public transport system)". Here too the difference from the May programme is obvious.

it would have been difficult for the SYRIZA government to pursue a policy of even mild management of austerity. The momentum in question significantly complicated prospects for anything like that. So, it was not the content of SYRIZA's programme that aroused such widespread concern but rather the social dynamics that within such a short time had overturned so much of the status quo. The greatest problem for the ruling class was that it had no positive project to offer to the impoverished and subjugated social classes, so that it was obliged to resort to the weapon of fear of the unknown.

Within this context of widespread alarmism over what would happen following a possible victory of SYRIZA, the June 2012 elections were held. ND secured first place with 29.66% (an increase of 10.81%) and 630,000 additional votes. It was followed by SYRIZA with 26.9% (an increase of 10.1%) and 594,000 more votes. Next came PASOK with 12.28% (down 0.90%) and 78,000 fewer votes. Then Independent Greeks with 7.5% (3.1% down) and 209,000 votes, followed by Golden Dawn with 6.92% (a marginal reduction in the order of 0.05%) and 15,000 fewer votes. DIMAR follows with 6.26% (an increase of 0.15%) and 1000 additional votes, KKE with 4.5% (a 3.98% reduction) and 259,000 fewer votes, Recreation with 1.59% (a fall of 2.36% from the aggregate vote in the previous elections for the parties of Thanos Tzimeros and Stefanos Manos, which were now on a single ballot) and 150,000 fewer votes, and LAOS, with 1.58% (a fall of 1.32%) corresponding to 86,000 fewer votes.

What should be noted is that despite the widespread interest in these elections there were 260,000 fewer voters than the number that had participated in the May 6 elections, with the result that the electorate was smaller than for any national elections of the last 20 years: just 6,216,582 people. The actual figure for abstention was 24%, reversing a key element of Greek political culture, which was mass electoral participation. It should be noted also that this is a continuing phenomenon, given that by comparison with the 2009 election there was an 829,024 decrease in participation. The decrease from 2007 was 1,138,444 and from 2004 1,356,786 (Vernardakis 2012a).

ND's victory seems to have been greatly facilitated by the barrage of statements from foreign leaders that were made in the last days before the election, braking the momentum that SYRIZA's had acquired at the start of the second pre-election period. At the same time, the surprise caused for the ruling class by the May results gave way to a rallying process. ND attracted conservative voters who had previously opted for other conservative formations (LAOS, Democratic Alliance, Recreate Greece and, to a certain extent, Independent Greeks.) At the institutional level, it made itself evident with the disbanding of the party of D. Bakoyanni, who returned to ND, not to mention the amalgamation, confronted with the centrifugal tendencies of their voters, of the parties of Thanos Tzimeros and Stefanos Manos.

In terms of electoral geography, a key factor in the success of ND was the attitude of the non-active population, as the party of A. Samaras gained the support of 42%[32] of pensioners and 37% of housewives, not to mention 36% of the rural vote. Among employees its influence was more limited (21% among public sector employees and 19% among private sector employees), but it also did quite well with employers (35.9%) and farmers (35.3%). In any case, it is to be noted that ND recorded the highest increase between the two elections among the economically secured (from 26% to 38%) (Mavris 2013a). On the contrary, among the unemployed it won only 17%. As for the age categories, ND predominated among the elderly: 48% of the over 65 s, 33% of those between 55 and 64, whereas among the young between 18 and 24 it received only 11% of the vote and among tertiary and technical students only 12% (Mavris 2012b: 103). As for geographical distribution, the class factor in the vote was evident from the fact that the conservative party predominated in the northern and north-eastern municipalities of Attica and the south-eastern coastal zone, that is to say in areas inhabited by the bourgeoisie and upper strata of the petty bourgeoisie (Ekali 70.1%, Psychiko 58.3%, Papagou 49.05%, Glyfada 33.84%, Aghia Paraskevi 32.20%, Cholargos 32.04%).

SYRIZA for its part won the vote of 34% of private sector employees, 33% of public sector employees, 37% of the unemployed, 39% of ter-

[32] The data cited here is based on research carried out by Public Issue (Mavris 2012a), but in some cases (e.g. internal categories of private sector employees) we are using data from VPRC research (Vernardakis 2013a). In any case because there cannot be absolute accuracy in the context of a sample survey, all data should be treated as indicative.

tiary and technical students and 42% of the middle classes downgraded as a result of the crisis. As far as age categories are concerned, it took 37% of the votes of young people aged between 18 and 24 and only 13% of those of people over 65 and 18% of pensioners. We note that the older the voters, the lower the percentage of votes, and vice versa. In rural areas, it secured 22% of the votes and in Attica 31%. On the basis of spatial distribution, its influence in the economically less privileged areas (western and south-western municipalities of Athens and Piraeus) ranged between 35% and 40% (Nikaia 37.68%, Egaleo 37.15%, Keratsini 36.67%), whereas in the bourgeois districts of north-eastern and south-eastern Attica it ranged between 6% and 11% (Psychiko 11.80%, Ekali 6.54%, Filothei 10.88%). In the western districts of the city of Athens, mainly inhabited by lower-income and working class people, SYRIZA obtained between 29% and 34% of the votes, whereas in the bourgeois districts and the old city centre its vote was below 25% (Mavris 2013a). Overall in Attica it remained the first electoral force, with a 4.3% lead over ND, but this was 3.5% lower than in the May elections (Stathopoulos 2014: 69).

PASOK managed to keep its vote mainly in the country's rural areas, where it won 16% votes. On the contrary in the urban centres, it was wiped out, winning a total of 11% votes and in Athens it struggled to secure 8.5% votes. Among employees its vote fell from 44% in 2009 to between 7% (for private sector employees)[33] and 10% (for wage earners in the public sector). Among the unemployed it gained 5% of the votes. It is characteristic that in the working class areas of the western suburbs and Piraeus its vote did not exceed 10% (Peristeri 8%, Egaleo 9%, Nikaia 7.9%, Keratsini 8%) when in 2009 it had been over 43%. At the opposite pole, among employers and entrepreneurs it was over-represented (17.2%). In terms of age groups, PASOK secured 20% of the vote among pensioners, 21% of those over 65, 14% of those aged between 55 and 64, and these two age categories comprised two-third of its electors. In contrast, it received only 5% of those aged between 18 and 24 and just 8% among tertiary and technical students (Mavris 2013b). Generally speak-

[33]According to VPRC data, PASOK secured 1.6% of votes among skilled workers and 4.5% among unskilled workers and those working on flexible schedules.

ing its age distribution shows similar tendencies to those of ND and opposite to those of SYRIZA. The older the voter the higher the percentage vote for PASOK.

For DIMAR it could be said that its highest influence is to be found in the upper and middle strata of the north-eastern suburbs: Vrilissia 10.2%, Pefki 9.8%, Holargos 9.4%, Nea Smyrni 9.4% and Chalandri 9.3%. In contrast, in working class areas it took only a little over 5% of the votes (Drapetsona 5.7%, Perama 4.9%, Aghia Varvara 5.1%) quite different from the average in the capital. This electoral geography leads us to the conclusions that while SYRIZA appears to be PASOK's successor in terms of electoral geography (working class, popular strata), DIMAR attracted the upper layers of those who participated in the social alliance historically represented by PASOK (Mavris 2013c). Thus, according to VPRC data, it received 7.7% of the votes of freelance professionals, 7.7% of the votes from wage earners, 11.1% of the votes of skilled workers. The age distribution of its voters is interesting. The highest percentage (10%) is in the youngest age group (18–24 years old). There is also over-representation of tertiary and technical students, who account for 11% of the vote. In contrast, the lowest percentage of its voters is in the age group over 65 years. (5%), thus presenting some similarities with the age distribution for SYRIZA. This must be due to the hopes of educated youth that the modernizing and anti-Memorandum discourse of DIMAR, implemented in State policy, will create opportunities for upward social mobility.

Golden Dawn received 13% of the vote among young people between 18 and 24 and 16% of the votes of those between 25 and 35. This shows that it has a momentum in the younger generations and in particular those who are already trying to join the labour market. By contrast, the party is under-represented among older people (only in the 45–54 age group do they attain the national average), something that can be explained both by memories from the German occupation and by recollections from the dictatorship that these age groups would have. In terms of employment, the potential of Golden Dawn is illustrated by the support it receives from sections of the private sector, but this happens in an unequal way. It received 24.5% of votes from unemployed workers and employees in a flexible work regime (making it the second party after

SYRIZA), 20.3% from employers/entrepreneurs (second party after ND), 12.6% from middle management in the private sector, 12.2% from the unemployed, 11.1% from specialized workers and 10.2% from wage earners in the private sector. The high percentages in sections of the working class[34] can be explained by the insecurity felt by part of the working class with reason to fear unemployment and by Golden Dawn's ability to demonize another weak element in the working class, the immigrants (Vernardakis 2013a). By contrast, among tertiary and technical students it takes 7% of the votes, among pensioners 3%, among housewives 3% and among public sector workers 6% (Mavris 2012a: 103). But it should be noted that although its percentages are high in a broad range of private sector professions, its vote is predominantly a grassroot vote. This means that its voters are in the lower ranks of each particular social category and therefore live in lower-income neighbourhoods.

Independent Greeks (Anexartiti Ellines) show high percentages among the unemployed (11%), among the 25–44 age group (10%), among women (9%), among those with financial difficulties (9%) and among housewives (9%). The percentage vote from them is low among pensioners (5%) and among the over 65 s (5%) (Mavris 2012b: 103).[35] It is interesting that they have particular influence in low-income areas: Aigaleo 8.30%, Perama 9.65%, Stavroupoli 10.31% and Menidi 12.71%. In other words, they are the folksy section of the conservative Right, which on account of the crisis has severed the relations of representation that existed between New Democracy and itself. But, on the other hand, a more ideologically oriented segment of its electorate which opted for ANEL in the May elections subsequently returned to ND.

Beyond its decline, the Communist Party of Greece (KKE) does not display any remarkable distinctiveness over previous elections in its electoral geography. It appears very weak among employers/entrepreneurs

[34] From this viewpoint the very good results it achieved in working class areas of Athens are indicative: B' Piraeus 9.3%, Salamina 13%, Tavros 11.1%, Perama 10.9%, Renti 10.3%, Kamatero 9.9% (Mavris 2013d).

[35] VPRC data show even more pronounced low-income characteristics to the point where their electoral geography looks like that of a Leftist party. From employers/entrepreneurs they receive only 1.6% of the vote, but from specialized workers 11.1%, from school pupils/students/soldiers 10.7%, from the unemployed 9.6%, from middle managers in the private sector 9.3% and from unskilled workers/ employees on flexible work schedules 9.1% (Vernardakis 2013a).

(1.6%) and freelance professionals (2.8%). It is over-represented among the unemployed (6.8%), middle managers in the private sector (6.5%), private sector employees (6.1%) and low-income areas (Nikaia 8.51%, Peristeri 7.21%, Egaleo 6.77%) (Vernardakis 2012b).

We can conclude overall that there has been a historically unprecedented short time-span between the two elections. The inability to form even temporary, short-lived governments reveals the depth of the contradictions that have emerged within the party system and, on the other hand, the criticality of the question (which has been posed urgently even from abroad) of the course the country is on.

It should also be noted how volatile relations of representation have been, given that since 2009 about 2/3 of the electorate have shifted their vote. Between May and June an estimated 30% of voters changed in their party allegiance. In 1989–1990, when coalition governments were also formed, it is not estimated that more than 8% to 10% did this. Of course, this massive shift at the June elections has to do with the fact that because of the brevity of the intervening time these elections did not seem like new elections but rather like the second round of a single electoral process, even if the smaller parties were not in a position to consolidate their performance of May. The two largest parties, which together had attracted the vote of about one in three voters, were subsequently supported by nearly three out of five voters. There was a dispersal at the first election and a relative rallying in the second, which was, however, in no way reminiscent of the 1977–2009 "classical" period of two-party predominance.

The intensity of the class struggle as it evolved from May 2010 to February 2012 was also reflected in the polarizations that emerged—(a) social polarization: on the one hand, wage earners, the unemployed, the self-employed, and on the other hand entrepreneurs, housewives, farmers; (b) polarization by age: on the one hand, people up to the age of 55 and on the other the more elderly[36]; (c) geographical polarization: on the

[36] The question of generations is very important. We should not forget that high rates of youth unemployment were also prevalent before the advent of the economic crisis. When the crisis struck, they exploded. Beyond that, even obtaining a degree sometimes complicates access to the labour market rather than facilitating it. In any case, the hunt for additional qualifications and certificates is never-ending. At the same time, young people are the ones who enter production under the worst conditions because of Memoranda commitments, in a framework that is then used as a lever for the generalized removal of basic labour rights (lower basic salary, absence of insurance, flexible employ-

one hand, big urban centres and on the other the provinces, but also polarization in Attica (especially in the June elections) between the centre and the low-income suburbs against the northern suburbs; (d) political polarization, which takes three forms: (1) between Memorandum and anti-Memorandum axes, (2) between Left and Right, (3) between anti-fascism and the fascist deviation. The emergence of this last-mentioned bipolar arrangement is interesting because it replaces the post-junta dichotomy between Right-wing and the totality of anti-Right-wing progressive forces (Vernardakis 2013a). The prevailing social polarization played an important part in this development.

In terms of party politics, ND won the elections on the strength of the high levels of support it enjoyed among older people, in the business and employer strata and among self-employed farmers. In contrast, the differences between urban centres and the countryside did not play a decisive role in the final developments. ND's victory was achieved thanks to a social alliance of employers, middle-ranking farmers and the non-active sections of the population. SYRIZA, for its part, was supported by an alliance of workers in employment (especially in the middle and lower economic categories), the unemployed, small industry and small-scale professionals (Vernardakis 2012b). In other words, those who were seeing their lives deteriorating rapidly, and some of them still had not much more to lose. This was also reflected in the geographical distribution of the vote, in which ND was under-represented in the lower petty bourgeois and lower-income areas and over-represented in the urban and upper-bourgeois areas, with the image for SYRIZA being exactly the opposite. To put it somewhat differently, one of the key parameters of ND's electoral success was the rallying of the bourgeoisie, something which had not applied in the May elections. On the basis of this rallying of forces a social bloc was established with participation of factions of the upper petty bourgeoisie (traditional and new) but also farmers and pensioners. In other words, it was an alliance of sections of those who had

---

ment, arbitrary prolonging of working hours). All this contributes to a situation where young people are forced to wait longer years and grow older before being able to gain their independence from their family. Thus a "cheated" generation is created which gradually realizes that although it has conformed with all the requirements imposed on it, the expectations created are not going to be satisfied (Gaitanou 2011: 58).

benefited from the crisis, or who judged that the end of the crisis would put them in a more advantageous position, with those who feared—because of an impending victory of the Left—losing the security they possessed, along with traditional voters such as the middle agrarian strata. In this light the subsequent formation of the three-party government would be based on a political alliance between those not being affected, those for whom the effects would be limited and those afraid of losing everything. To this would contribute the influence of PASOK on the upper petty bourgeois strata and DIMAR on the middle petty bourgeois strata.

From the 2012 Elections to the 2014 Elections

The fact that in the June elections, where ND came first, it failed to win parliamentary autonomy (it won 129 seats, not 151) led to a fever of consultations to form a coalition government, given that a third consecutive recourse to the polls was thought to be inviting paralysis of public administration and the economy. What was of interest was the formation of a government with a large majority so that all the painful measures agreed with the lenders could be approved without friction.

From the outset the target that was set was formation of a three-party government including ND, PASOK and DIMAR. The last-mentioned was regarded by the Greek elite as a rather moderate Leftist party with a strong pro-European orientation, which is why it was judged that it would co-operate without any particular difficulties with the two major bourgeois parties. Indeed, DIMAR agreed to participate in such a government with the president of ND, A. Samaras, as Prime Minister and with the support of 179 deputies (129 from ND, 33 from PASOK and 17 from DIMAR). This government, with three-party collaboration, was to continue until the closure of Hellenic Radio and Television in June 2013, when DIMAR dissented and left the government. The other two parties remained until the January 2014 elections (see below).

Let now look more closely at the political stance of each party separately from the formation of the Samaras government until the 2014 dual elections (local government and European elections).

As already mentioned in the previous chapter, between June 2012 and May 2014 there were two very important social mobilizations: the first concerned the reactions to adoption of the new package of measures in November 2012 and the other the support movement for ERT, Hellenic Radio and Television), namely in June and July 2013. Beyond that there were a number of individual social struggles (teachers, local government workers, Metro employees, university administration, cleaning workers, doctors in the State insurance institution), which fell short of leading to a general crisis of the political and party system, as, for example, the movement in the squares had done. But this cannot obscure the equally evident reality of gradual reduction in the parliamentary strength of the government, which started as a three-party formation of 179 deputies and after the split over ERT became two-party, with dwindling support in parliament that by April 2014 had fallen to 152 deputies.

In reality throughout this period two tendencies coexisted at the grass-root level. One was a desire for extrication from the Memoranda and the consequences of the social crisis they brought in their train and the other was the fear that the opposition did not embody a coherent alternative project and ultimately things could get even worse.

This shortcoming reflected on the influence of SYRIZA and the Left wing as a whole as registered in the period under review. An important role in this was played not so much by the government's public relations policy, which constantly spoke of new economic successes—it was clear from the relevant chapter how stale this argumentation was, the conflict between the extremes (Golden Dawn and SYRIZA), which would be leading the country to disaster if it weren't for the moderate governance of ND, the demonizing of A. Tsipras through references to his religious beliefs, (whether he was married) and so on. The real problem was that social struggles, despite their lengthy duration and the self-sacrifice of their participants, did not lead to specific victories, highlighting the dimension of how only a central political victory would contribute to the satisfaction of the relevant demands. But this also presupposed the existence of an alternative plan. The case of Cyprus, where following the collapse of the banks the preliminary haircut of deposits was rejected in Parliament only to be voted for subsequently through fear of a general collapse of the Cypriot economy, exerted an intimidating influence on significant sections of the Greek population.

On the other hand, the dynamics of the continuing crisis did not leave even the dominant parties untouched. From its initial anti-Memorandum stance and the announcement of renegotiation ND then shifted to a position similar to that of the PASOK of the time that it enjoyed parliamentary autonomy, that is, full compliance with the creditors' requirements. This put an end to such independence as the conservative party had enjoyed from the most powerful branches of Greek and foreign capital. Correspondingly, PASOK's decision to participate in government, and also to remain in government after the abolition of ERT, further exacerbated the government's internal conflicts, highlighting the identity problem it was called upon to manage at a time when the distinction between Right and progressive forces had ceased to have any meaning, given PASOK's record of collaboration with ND since December 2011. Characteristic of the diminution of its leverage, above and beyond its use of another name for the May 2014 European elections, where it presented its candidates under the name of Elia, the Olive Tree coalition, is the fall in its number of active members and supporters, from the 236,151 people that had participated in the election, in March 2012, of E. Venizelos, who succeeded G. Papandreou, to the proceedings a year later, in March 2013, at the party congress where there was participation of only 112,016 individuals. The results of this political and organizational decimation were that PASOK in 2014 would include only party cadres attached to the State apparatus along with a very narrow entourage of historical supporters (mostly elderly) (Mavris 2013b).

DIMAR, for its part, was required, because of its implication in the three-party government, to face a weakening of its position as an anti-Memorandum party, a stance in which it had persisted until the June 2012 elections. As C. Vernardakis aptly observes, DIMAR had failed to operate as a veto player inside the government (Vernardakis 2013a). In our opinion DIMAR had suffered what SYRIZA and ANEL were to suffer later when they were in government: the attempt to defy the provisions of the Memorandum without a default on payments, debt cancellations, preparations for a break with the lenders and an attempt to find an alternative path outside the European Monetary System and the EU would lead either to acceptance of the Memoranda or to political contraction. It was precisely this that DIMAR failed to manage, and although these oscillations may have led to its departure from the Samaras government, they had also greatly weakened it.

Even though in the first period after the June elections SYRIZA appeared to have a clear lead over New Democracy, this was shrined by the end of 2012, but even its reinstatement at the head of the polls, after a while, was not enough to stabilize a wide margin between them. This development, which contradicted prevailing assessments of how fast the difference would open in favour of SYRIZA, can be explained by two factors. The first is that the leadership of SYRIZA chose not to establish structures of resistance and solidarity vis-à-vis the policies of the Memoranda. It inserted the forces of the party into the enclaves of resistance where they emerged but it did not proceed to a coherent and co-ordinated effort to develop a movement for continuing challenge of the Memoranda and the government. Essentially it opted for the policy of gradual attrition of the government, perhaps secretly hoping that in that way it would avoid having to manage crucial phases of the Greek crisis. Within this problematic SYRIZA regarded as positive any stirring of the movement that was working to the detriment of the government, but it did not take the lead in externalizing it. The second reason had to do with the inability to articulate a coherent alternative programme. This was to some extent also attributable to the major disputes within the party between the majority who wanted the country to remain in the EU and the euro and the minority that rejected this preference. But it would be a mistake to restrict consideration only to this parameter. In fact, the real problem had to do with the contradictions brought to light by SYRIZA's predominant orientation. This is because the issue was not technical (a committee to draw up a governmental programme) but deeply political: how can there be delinkage from Memoranda involving such high levels of debt while continuing with funding from abroad and remaining in the EMU and the EU? The embarrassment was perceived by the electorate, and support for SYRIZA began to lose some of the momentum it had had at the beginning of its rise, and distrust began to emerge in public opinion as to how far it wished, but was not able, to do what it was promising.

The dynamics of the emergence of Golden Dawn (Chrysi Avghi) was linked, on one hand, the conservative voters' emerging reactions to the policy of ND and on the other hand to the steady line it had pursued since securing a place in the parliament. It did not appear to be integrated into the political system continuing a policy of denouncing everything, at the same time carrying out an escalating series of military-type attacks against opponents, in particular immigrants and Left-wing people. The governing centre watched all this with some embarrassment, to a certain extent exploiting the shift of the political agenda to the Right. But successive terrorist attacks such as the attack on KKE members in Perama, the bullying of the mayor in Meligalas (15/9/13) and, above all, the murder of the anti-fascist singer Pavlos Fyssas by a member of Golden Dawn G. Roupakias (17.9.13) induced the State to carry out a total about-face. It had finally registered that an ever more extreme military-style intervention by Golden Dawn was in progress which, given the dissatisfaction over the social crisis, was enjoying a considerable level of tolerance if not approval from broad layers of Right-wing voters. The State responded by arresting the leader and the parliamentarians of Golden Dawn, relegating it to a peculiar status of semi-illegality. But the fact that, despite all this repression and the revelations that followed of the practices that had been adopted by Golden Dawn, its popularity remained high, suggests that the problem ran quite deep.

The Independent Greeks suffered significant losses, with ¼ of their initial parliamentary support not voting for them this time. This, in our opinion, reflected a problem of strategy that Panos Kammenos' party had to face. With the great majority of its members and supporters coming from the conservative Right, and nevertheless declaring that it could not ally itself with any force supporting the Memorandum, it necessarily left open the option of collaboration in government with SYRIZA, something that was not readily accepted internally. At the same time, inability to produce a clear plan of exit from the crisis only served to heighten its inherent contradictions.

The KKE had to recover from initial shock at being overtaken by SYRIZA. Its acquisition of the status of representative of a substantial proportion of the popular masses, something achieved at least from the beginning of the post-dictatorship period, was lost within a few weeks in the spring of 2012. After the May elections the argument employed by the party leadership was that, irrespective of SYRIZA's drawing power, the KKE's electoral strength had risen, but it could not be repeated in the June elections when SYRIZA found itself scoring over six times the figures for 2009 (when it was together with DIMAR) while the KKE lost almost half of its votes, the overwhelming majority of which went to the party of A. Tsipras. Following these developments, attempts were made to overcome the embarrassment by shifting to an ultra-Left rhetoric with its key element the refusal to participate in any Left-wing government, thus investing in probable defeat of any government based on SYRIZA.

The 2014 Elections

The Predictions

> The gradual contraction of the movement climate of 2012–2014 encouraged the feeling that "second rank" elections such as those for local government and the European Parliament, programmed for the end of May 2014 could have other implications, functioning as a basic parameter for continuation or termination of the policies under implementation.

The probability of a cliff-hanging outcome would be emphasized repeatedly throughout the pre-electoral period. But precisely because it had become abundantly evident to the power centres *also* what the character of the election was likely to be, they had taken the precaution of implementing a number of reforms that would put a damper on any possible SYRIZA victory. It was within this logic that they forced through a number of changes whose central objective was to create a new institutional reality as much as possible "cordoned off" from the entry into it of class struggle priorities. The right to vote in local elections was accordingly abolished for certain categories of citizens (immigrants and expatriates) and a number of restrictions were introduced concerning the citizens living far away from the place where they have the right of vote. The introduction for the first time in Greek history of the simultaneous holding of European, regional and municipal elections could only sow confusion in voters' minds because so many different issues were at stake, and this too was perceived as a way of downgrading the importance of elections (Mavris 2014a: 10). To aid and abet this approach it was decided that the first round of the local elections would take place a week before the European elections, thereby reducing participation in the latter. It had in any case been shown through the experience of the 2010 elections that one in five voters in the first round of the elections did not participate in the second (Mavris 2014a: 10).

Given the acuteness of the crisis, unlike in 2010 when it had not yet been felt, in such extent, the requirement that voters should move three times within the space of a few weeks (because of the preceding Easter celebrations) was particularly arduous. Two successive electoral contests were held, the first serving as preparation for the second, to the advantage of the government side. The calculation was that the field of self-government was not a privileged terrain of electoral confrontation for SYRIZA, as opposed to the central electoral theatre of the European elections. The reason for this was that local-self-government comprised a network tied to the structures of the old political system (see below). At the same time the rapid electoral rise of SYRIZA had not left it with enough time to develop relations of trust and representation at the local level.[37] There was also the question of the difficulty of making alliances in the second round given the collaboration that existed between pro-Memorandum candidates with links and a base in the local communities and a record of having managed the available resources, as opposed to SYRIZA candidates, who in many cases merely reflected the influence that the party had exercised in an earlier period. (Mavris 2014a: 8); additional inhibitory factors were the absence of convergence between the various forces in the anti-Memorandum coalition. Given all this, the Samaras government calculated that manipulation of this kind would enable the autonomous dynamics of the first round to generate a climate of failure for SYRIZA through displacement of its candidates by pro-Memorandum candidates, which would affect the outcome of the European elections also.

In other words, the central aim of the government was to secure a cloudy and indecisive outcome in the triple elections. The very great like-

[37] In contrast to the past, where the Communist Left was based on its grounding in local society, subsequently consolidating its presence at the central political level.

lihood of a SYRIZA victory in the European elections would be offset by the results of the municipal and regional elections. We should bear it in mind that the point of departure for the pro-government forces was very high on the basis of the 2010 elections so that there was a very wide margin for loss. Specifically, PASOK and ND together controlled 54.4% of the municipalities of the country, whereas SYNASPISMOS and DIMAR controlled only 4.5%.[38]

This whole plan should be seen in the context of what we have already pointed out vis-à-vis the sealing off of State institutions from representative procedures. The unclear result, with the help of the media of course, as a component in entirely different elective processes, would lead to the conclusion that no clear electoral trends have emerged, and therefore no indisputable disapproval of the government, which should therefore complete its term.

The Local Government Elections

About 6,088,121 people participated in the first round of the municipal elections, a smaller number than those in June 2012 (6,216,798) and May 2012 (6,476,818) but a larger number than in the first round of the 2010 local elections (5,988,678). In the 2014 elections, 38.44% abstained and 7.13% cast spoilt or blank ballots. In 2010, 39.12% abstained and 9.10% cast spoilt or blank ballots. So, there was a marginal 0.7% increase in participation and a significant 2% decrease in blank and spoilt ballots. The result in the regional elections was characterized by marked contraction in the influence of ND from 32.6% to 26.2%, with the influence of SYRIZA rising from 4.5% to 17.8%, Golden Dawn skyrocketing from 0.2% to 8.1%, the KKE vote falling from 11% to 8.8%, ANTARSYA rising from 1.8% to 2.3%, the Ecologists-Greens going down from 2.8% to 2.1% and the in any case much reduced vote for PASOK not being calculable with precision because that party did not submit any official candidacy.

[38] The others are regarded as "independent" but apart from certain mayoral candidates in island municipalities, the political identities of most "independents" are linked to ND and PASOK (Mavris 2014a: 5).

Of course, the above figures have to be viewed with all due consideration for local specificities because, as calculated by C. Vernardakis, approximately 35% of votes go to personalities who do not belong directly to a party but rather to local socio-economic alliances. In this context it could be observed that the entire Centre-Left (PASOK-DIMAR[39]-The River[40]) performed quite satisfactorily, with seven candidates making it to the second round of the regional elections, as against five for SYRIZA, not to mention the two largest municipalities (Athens-Thessaloniki). These developments can be interpreted as a reflection of the fact that the Centre-Left milieu includes a host of cadres with significant experience in local government. They are a kind of "deep state" (Belandis 2014) involved in the administration and management of European funding but also human resources, the construction of clientelistic networks and the establishment of relations with sections of the local, and not only local, bourgeoisie.[41] Here the impact of the transformation in the party system was delayed. Relations of representation broke down much more slowly, precisely because these administrators of citizens' everyday life, at a time when it was under permanent attack, were not regarded as responsible for the Memorandum policies being pursued. It was this apparent independence, together with administrative experience, not in solving problems but in "permanent management of need", to cite D. Belandis' perceptive formulation, that prevented the

[39] After its participation in the Memorandum government DIMAR is to be included in the Centre-Left, not the Left, current.

[40] The River was established in the spring of 2014 by the journalist S. Theodorakis, and espouses pro-Memorandum positions.

[41] But there is no justification for concluding that the electoral survival of "independent" pro-Memorandum candidates has been primarily due to clentelistic relations. As D. Belandis very perspicaciously observed: "It would be wrong to argue that the phenomenon is exclusively, or even primarily, a reflection of clientelism, notwithstanding the already widespread prevalence of clientelistic relations. Links of this kind supplement and underwrite habitual administrative practice and are integrated into broader relations of social representation but do not explain them or provide a comprehensive interpretation for the Centre-Left's presence in the local administrative sphere and local government. In the final analysis what is of central importance is the 'perceived' or even real bureaucratic and administrative proficiency or even 'more-than-adequacy' of the Centre-Left authorities. Thanks to the long-term experience in management, this sufficiency acquires technocratic or quasi-technocratic characteristics. It therefore comes to be considered that the daily life of the populations and their management depends on the sufficiency and stability of the centre's 'administrative chieftains'" (Belantis 2014).

dynamic of the 2012 elections from spreading into this area too with the same vigour. In essence it was a process that sought to preserve the terms of political representation of the past by making some "necessary" adjustments, that is, for a substantial part of the State apparatus to continue to function without being affected by the changes in the correlation of forces taking place at the central level. It was not just a question of left-over administrative cadre from past power relations seeking to survive but rather an attempt to curb the popular dynamic that might emerge from the institutions of local government. In this sense there was nothing accidental about the promotion accorded by the mainstream media to the initiative of the five Independent mayors (Kominis, Boutaris, Filios, Skotiniotis, Dimaras) as non-party figures and devoted servants of their local communities.[42] Let's reiterate: it is not merely a matter of bourgeois political personnel with specialized skills deriving from previous relations of representation. It is an aggressive move illustrating aspects of authoritarian statism: capable management of bourgeois power at the local level, a distancing from politics and parties and therefore a break from some facets of traditional representative democracy.

It is in this context that an interpretation might be offered of the predominant presence of numerous Memorandum candidates in the first round of the municipal elections,[43] not to mention the regional elections. But there are other aspects that also require emphasis: One is the unmistakable contraction of ND's sphere of influence, especially in the regional elections (−6.4%). Another is the timidity of PASOK's moves, as if it were trying at all costs to avoid a clear registration of results. There was a fall (−2.2%) in the vote for the KKE as a result of its leadership's decision to refuse collaboration with any other grouping on the Left, a policy that

[42] In November 2013, the Centre-Left oriented mayors of Athens G. Kaminis, of Thessaloniki G. Boutaris, of Patras G. Dimaras, of Volos P. Skotiniotis and of Ioannina F. Filios published a joint declaration centred on three points: (a) independence from party tutelage; (b) innovative solutions for day-to-day management and improvement of quality of life; (c) rational management of competences and resources and redefinition of relations between municipalities, the State and business enterprises.

[43] Of the nine largest municipalities in the country (Athens, Thessaloniki, Piraeus, Peristeri, Patras, Larissa, Volos, Ioannina, Heraklion) it is only in Patras that an anti-Memorandum candidate achieved the highest vote, namely K. Peletides, who was supported by the Communist Party, and only three SYRIZA candidates (in Athens, Volos and Larissa), managed to come second.

was received with some scepticism by its voters. It is worth noting the rise in the vote for Golden Dawn also, despite its embroilment with the Fyssas murder.

The second round was characterized by partial success of the Left-wing forces, a result of the overall dynamics that apparently developed between the two rounds. SYRIZA managed to win in Attica as well as in the Ionian region, with SYRIZA support electing 19 mayors, along with four others supported by the KKE. The fact that governmental slates lost the largest region but also a number of important municipalities (Keratsini—Drapetsona, Patras, Halandri, Haidari, N. Philadelphia, N. Ionia, Kaisariani, Vyronas, Aigaleo, Ag. Paraskevi, Kozani, Larissa)[44] in many cases overturning significant differentials, reflects a certain achievement in mobilizing the population on the Left. In any case our view is that the result in the second round cannot be seen in isolation from the result of the election to the European Parliament.

The Elections to the European Parliament

In the European elections SYRIZA emerged as the first party, with 26.6% and 1,518,068 votes, followed by ND with 22.7% and 1,298,713, votes, Golden Dawn with 9.4% and 536,910 votes, PASOK with 8% and 458,043 votes, the River with 6.6% and 377,438 votes, KKE with 6.1% and 349,255 votes, Independent Greeks with 3.5% and 197,701 votes, DIMAR with 1.2% and 68,873 votes, LAOS with 2.7% and 154,027 votes, Greek European Citizens with 1.4% and 82,350 votes, DIMAR with 1.2% and 68,873 votes and the Union for our Country and our People with 1% and 59,431 votes. There was a 60% turnout (5,942,196 votes) and 3.8% (225,724) informal votes/blank or spoiled ballots. If we compare the results with those of June 2012 it emerges that there was a 2.5% (274,602 votes) fall in participation. As for the party vote, SYRIZA saw very slight (0.32%) reduction (−136,414 votes), ND a very significant 6.94% fall (−526,784 votes), Golden Dawn a substantial 2.47%

[44] Naturally, as explained, this is a partial tendency confined to the municipal level. Of the nine largest municipalities only two were won by a candidate from the Left: Patras by the KKE candidate Peletides and Larissa by the SYRIZA-supported candidate A. Kalogiannis.

rise (110,886 votes), PASOK a 4.26% fall (−297,621 votes), the KKE a 1.61% rise (72,028 votes), LAOS a 1.1% increase (56,928 votes), whereas DIMAR was wiped out electorally, falling by 4.15% (316,113 votes). The newly established parties (The River, Hellenic European Citizens,[45] Union for our Country and our People[46]) can be seen, for various reasons, as having made a successful first electoral appearance. Of course, this comparison is only valid with the caveat that they are subsidiary elections. They are not elections for a government. They express a real tendency but also include options that would not easily be replicated in polarized parliamentary elections. The second reservation is that they cannot properly be equated with the results of the 2009 European elections, given that since then tectonic changes have taken place in the Greek social formation, with each new conjuncture introducing something different. So, these results can only be compared to the most recent ones, of June 2012, while of course bearing in mind that what is involved is a different order of elections, so that any conclusions drawn can be no more than relative.

With analysis of the results as the point of departure it emerges that this specific election result together with the content of the political conjuncture yields a number of different dichotomous political axes.

The first axis is the classic three-way Right-Centre-Left split (including in the Centre PASOK/the Olive Tree coalition, DIMAR and, the River and on the Right Golden Dawn: in June 2012 the Right secured 47%, of the vote, the Centre 20% and the Left 32%. In May 2014 the Left vote was at 35%, the Centre dropped to 18% and the Right to 42%.[47]

[45] The Hellenic European Citizens were founded a few weeks before the elections by the Greek German G. Hadzimarkakis, former Europarliamentarian of the German FDP, adopting moderate anti-Memorandum positions.

[46] The Union for our Country and our People was founded at the beginning of 2014, primarily by seceding ND parliamentarians disagreeing with the Memorandum policies of the Samaras government.

[47] If we take into account the average from all the electoral contests between 2007 and 2014 (2007 national elections, 2009 national elections, 2009 European elections, May 2012 national elections, June 2012 national elections, May 2014 European elections) we find that the Right scores an average of 43.9%, so that in the latest European elections its vote was 1.9% below the average. The Centre, with an average of 31.6% vote, was 13.6% below the average and the Left, with 22.5% in European elections also, achieved a vote 12.5% higher than average. (A special thanks to Alexander Rekleitis for this useful information).

The second axis pertains to the stance vis-à-vis the Memorandum. In June 2012, the political groupings declaring themselves opposed to the Memorandum (including DIMAR and the Ecologists-Greens) obtained 54% of the vote and those in favour 45%. In May 2014, the anti-Memorandum groupings were at 55% and the pro-Memorandum 40%. The difference is that in the anti-Memorandum current the most ambivalent forces (DIMAR and Ecologists-Greens) in 2012 comprised about 1/3 of the total in the milieu of the centre but in 2014 only 10%. By contrast, on the Right in 2012 the anti-Memorandum current comprised 34% but by 2014 this had risen to 43% (Antoniou 2014). This means that there was a shift in the centre in a more pro-Memorandum direction and an opposite trajectory on the Right towards more anti-Memorandum orientations.

Another distinction that can be drawn has to do with the attitude towards the EU. Whatever differences exist within the party formations in relation to this criterion, we can divide the parties into three main categories: (a) those who think that the EU is basically on the right track (i.e. the pro-Memorandum groupings, together with DIMAR), (b) those who think that the EU is on the wrong track but can be got onto the right track (SYRIZA, ANEL, LAOS, Ecologists) and those who argue that the EU is by its nature headed in the wrong direction (KKE, ANT. AR.SY.A, smaller organizations of the extra-parliamentary Left). In 2012, the first category obtained 43.5% of the votes and in 2014, 41.5%, the second 36.2% in 2012 and 36.4% in 2014 and the third 5.3% in 2012 and 8.5% in 2014 (Golden Dawn is not included in this category). We note that there is a slight but real shift towards declared anti-EU parties, but it does not represent a dynamic tendency.

Inside the Right the balance of forces of June 2012 was 31% for the neo-liberal tendency, 9% for the so-called patriotic right and 7% for Golden Dawn. In 2014, the balance was recorded as 24%, 9%, 10%. This is despite the contraction in the vote for ANEL because of the strengthening of LAOS and the creation of new parties like Hellenic European Citizens and Union for our Country and our People.

On the other hand, in the milieu of the Centre differences seem to be diminishing (due to the fall of PASOK and DIMAR and the dynamic emergence of The River). As a result the first discussions get under way for the establishment of a unified Centre-Left. The significance of the attitude towards the Memoranda seems to have declined and this milieu acquires post-modern and neo-liberal features.

Let see now what is happening in each party separately.

As far as SYRIZA is concerned, one key aspect of the results is that its share of the total Left-wing vote fell from 84% to 76% (without, of course, its ceasing to be the dominant hegemonic force) due to its limited but real losses to the Left, but in the context of an overall higher vote for the Left. This should be correlated with the fact that considerable losses were sustained by certain social categories: younger people, the unemployed, students, employees in the private sector.

Thus, according to data made available by Public Issue (Mavris 2012a, b) SYRIZA's influence in the 18–24 age group declined from 37% to 29.3%, in the 25–34 age group from 33% to 26.6%, in the 35–44 age group from 32% to 27.5% in the 45–54 age group from 34% to 31%. By contrast, in the higher age groups there is a significant rise: In the 55–64 age group the figure goes up from 27% to 29.9% and in the over 65 age group from 13% to 18.4%. Among the unemployed it drops from 37% to 30.9%, among students and scholars from 39% to 28.4%, among wage earners in the private sector it falls from 34% to 29.5%. In contrast, an increase is recorded among salaried employees in the public sector from 33% to 40.3%, among pensioners from 18% to 21.3% and among housewives from 23% to 28.5%. Corresponding results emerge from examination of the geographical criterion behind voting. There has been a marginal rise in the SYRIZA vote in urban areas (from 13% to 13.8%), a marginal fall in the higher sections of the middle class (from 27.6% to 27.1%), a real fall (from 32.2% to 30.2%) in the middle class overall and a significant fall in working class areas (from 37.5% to 33.8%).

This data shows that while SYRIZA managed to emerge as first party, with a real difference from ND, it does not have a dynamic of its own. It won because ND lost its power of attraction, not because it succeeded in maintaining, much less increasing, its existing alliances while *also* further penetrating into other social strata. Indeed, the opposite is the case. The most detailed data provided by VPRC (Vernardakis 2014) indicates losses even in the hard core of the working class (low-ranking office staff, unskilled labour, specialized workers, casual employees) where SYRIZA drops slightly from 32.5% to 31%.

ND shows a very significant decline in its influence, bringing it closer to May 2012 than to June 2012. This is due to its decline in all social categories where there had been some dynamism. Among housewives, support fell from 37% to 30.3%, and among retirees support fell from 42% to 31.4%. In the 55–64 age group support fell from 33% to 20.8%. Even in the strong category over the age of 64 there was a decline from 48% to 40.2%. Geographically, in the semi-urban areas support went down from 36% to 26.6%. Its vote in a series of urban municipalities point to a rift in its links with bourgeois layers: thus, the average vote for ND in Vouliagmeni, Voula, Psychiko, Filothei, Ekali fell from 57.1% to 47.9%.[48] In suburbs with residents from the upper levels of the petty bourgeoisie (Ag. Paraskevi, Halandri, Vrilissia, Maroussi) the vote went down from 31.8% to 25.7%. In contrast, the decline was less extreme in areas with a lower petty bourgeois population (Elliniko, Zografou, Galatsi, Vyronas) where the figure was 19.5%, down from 24.4%, but also in working class areas in the capital (Kamatero, Keratsini, Nikaia, Rentis, Peristeri, Aigaleo) where there was a decline from 18.2% to 14.7%. The conclusion for ND was that it had experienced a major defeat highlighting the legitimacy problem that had been created by its policy. It had become an ageing party that had already lost the support of the popular strata by the spring of 2012, which is why the decline in its influence in these places was now proceeding more slowly. At the same time the liquidating functions for the weaker sections of capital that were being triggered by government policy were leading to losses of bourgeois strata also.

Golden Dawn showed that it has significant dynamic support among entrepreneurs and the self-employed (from 11% to 13.1%) and particularly among employers running their own business (13.8%), among farmers and stockbreeders (17.8%) and professional light industrialists (15.9%), among people aged 18–24 (from 13% to 18%), among students (from 7% to 18%),[49] a marginal increase among the unemployed

---

[48] I have taken these processed statistics from an unpublished paper by Stathis Kouvelakis.

[49] What is interesting is that while Golden Dawn does have notable influence among students and young people, because among older age groups it attracts people of a lower educational level over-

(from 12% to 12.9%). Its support is also increasing in working class areas (from 8.9% to 10.6%). The success of Golden Dawn can be attributed to the fact that it manages to combine two elements: on the one hand, it appears to certain strata of Greek society to be the most stable anti-systemic choice, particularly after the detention of its leader and parliamentarians for complicity in the Fyssas murder, on the other because it promotes a discourse expressing the basic outlines of the views prevailing among a significant part in the Greek citizenry (chauvinism, social conservatism, the need for autocratic solutions, patriarchy, racism). All of these will become components of the social soil of the crisis period and an accompaniment to the social decline of many sections of the community.

PASOK suffered a large-scale collapse, confirming that it is an ageing party, the only age group present in it in appreciable numbers being over 65 (16%) and retired (15%). It continues to enjoy the preference of a fraction of the most affluent social strata, favoured by 12.6% of those who are still managing to live comfortably and 11.2% of employers/entrepreneurs. But it has broken its relations with the strata whose support imposed its primacy for approximately 30 years. It secures votes from 2.3% of people employed in light industry, 2.7% of the unemployed, 3.9% of private sector employees, 4.9% of students, between 3.2% and 4.9% of the most dynamic ages: 18 to 54.

The KKE increased its influence, succeeding in repatriating a section of its former voters who had chosen SYRIZA in June 2012, but without effectively challenging the hegemonic position of A. Tsipras' party within the Left. The KKE is of significance for the first post-dictatorship generation aged between 45 and 54 (8.5%), for tradesmen (8.1%), for the unemployed (8.2%, up from 4%). In geographical terms there is a marked increase in working class areas (up from 6.8% to 9.6%). But the question remains of its limited leverage on the Left as a whole and the impossibility of its impressing on a wider audience.

The River put up a remarkable performance for a party that was founded just two months before the election. But it should not be over-

all, it is shown as having 15.5% support among middle-school graduates and only 4.4% among graduates from institutions of higher education (Koustenis 2014b: 104).

looked that its success is to a large extent linked to the support it has received from the media as catalyst party for reconstruction of the Centre-Left. It draws support in age groups 25–44 (9.1%) and 45–54 (8.2%), among those with higher education (9.1%), employees in the private sector (11.5%), students (11.2%), and among those who live comfortably and/or have a record of achievement (9.1%).[50] It is also evident that it was voted for by the most prosperous strata: according to VPRC in the private sector's highest echelon The River won 12%, in the urban districts of Athens 8.6% and the same proportion in the corresponding upper bourgeoisie. In essence, The River came to cover a very important systemic need: to contribute to a certain centripetal tendency towards a transcendent political centre, a kind of political construct that will agree to seek compliance with neo-liberal policies through developing a politicized apolitical discourse where "everyone is to blame for what happened" and "the time has now come for radical breaks". Even though essentially this line of reasoning is no different from the sundry variations of "we all had our snouts in the trough" that the officials of the two-party mainstream like to expound, it nevertheless becomes more persuasive when heard from people and groupings not implicated in governing the country in previous years.

ANEL showed a sharp downturn, continuing with a stronger downward trend in the June 2012 elections. Even in the high-profile social categories in June 12, it experienced a significant decline: In the 25–34 age group it fell from 10% to 3.4%, among the unemployed from 11% to 5.9%, among those who were surviving with difficulty from 9% to 3.9%. The reason for this electoral defeat has to do with the party's incapacity to develop a more deep-seated political discourse beyond opposition to the Memoranda. This made them more susceptible to distracting input from ND, whence the great majority of ANEL cadre had originated, or from SYRIZA, the largest anti-Memorandum party.

[50] It is characteristic that according to data from VPRC The River won 12% of the vote from senior executives in the private sector.

The First Period of Government by the SYRIZA-ANEL Coalition (January 2015 to September 2015)

SYRIZA's electoral victory in the 2014 European elections was merely a prelude to the even greater victory it was to achieve in the January 2015 Greek parliamentary elections. Essentially the period from June 2014 to December 2014 was nothing more than a time of anticipation for when SYRIZA would become the government. There were no popular mobilizations of any importance. The Samaras government tried to introduce some relief for citizens from the excessive burden of taxation but it was obvious that political developments would be determined by the outcome of the election for the new President of the Republic. Under the Greek Constitution the President of the Republic, who is Greece's head of State, is elected every five years by the Greek parliament. If no candidate succeeds in winning 200 votes in the first two rounds or 180 votes in the third, national elections are called and the new parliament can elect a President with a simple majority. The President up to that time Karolos Papoulias had served two terms and was not permitted by the Constitution to serve a third, so a new President had to be elected. Seeking to clear the terrain, New Democracy proposed Stavros Dimas, Vice-President of the party and for a period European Commissioner for Employment and the Environment. PASOK agreed with this choice, but all the other parties opposed it. Finally Dimas won 160 votes in the first ballot and 168 in the second and the third, with the result that he was not elected President and elections were called. These developments were in accordance with the strategy of the opposition parties (SYRIZA, ANEL, KKE, Golden Dawn), who, on the one hand, thought that a pro-Memorandum government should not continue to be in power and on the other aspired, especially the first two, to becoming the government themselves. DIMAR, for its part, did not participate in the Presidential vote, but it was obvious that there were diametrically opposed views on what they ought to do, a sequel to earlier disputes over whether or not they should leave the Samaras government in the summer of 2013.

The elections were held on 25th January 2015 and the results were as follows for the parties to be represented in the Parliament SYRIZA received 36.34% (+8.57%), ND 27.81% (−1.85%), Golden Dawn 6.28% (−0.64%), KKE 5.47% (+0.97%), ANEL 4.75% (−2.76%), PASOK 4.68% (−7.60%). It should be noted that the former Prime Minister and former President of PASOK G. Papandreou stood for election with his own party, the KIDISO (Movement of Social Democrats), taking only 2.5% and failing to enter the Parliament. Abstention reached 35.13% (−2.40%), and spoiled and blank ballots 2.36% (+1.38%).

SYRIZA had undoubtedly scored a very great electoral success, the more so when one bears in mind that within five years it had achieved a 700% increase in its electoral influence. But, that said, the KKE could be regarded as satisfied that it increased its influence, despite the dynamics favouring SYRIZA, and ANEL too should be included among the winners, despite the steep decline in its influence: with the 13 seats it secured it was well positioned to be a potential governing partner for SYRIZA, which had won 149 seats and had not secured a majority (see below). As for the rest, there was obvious, though unequally distributed, punishment from the electorate for their participation in Memorandum governments. PASOK would be found to have lost 90% of its support since 2009 (or in any case 85% if one factors in the party of G. Papandreou) paying the penalty for having supported all the Memorandum governments from 2010 onwards. LAOS had barely made it over the 1% mark and was again denied representation in the Parliament. DIMAR, which had scored 6.3% in 2012, collaborated with the Green Party and won a mere 0.5%. The reduction in the influence of ND was very limited, something contributed to by the political repatriation of ANEL voters, for which the main motivating factor was the possibility of a radical Left party forming a government. This also affected the size of the vote for Golden Dawn.

The election campaign was characterized by intense conflict. Of the two major parties, SYRIZA called on voters to vote for it so as to "abolish the Memoranda by one law". ND warned that a SYRIZA win would lead to Greece leaving the EMU and the EU. The climate of social and economic insecurity that was fomented by ND, but also by the other pro-Memorandum parties (PASOK, The River) influenced certain social categories such as retirees and housewives, where the conservative party was over-represented, taking 36% and 34.5% respectively. But the greater part of Greek society was not persuaded by the danger-mongering, believing that there *could* be another way to extricate the country from the politics of harsh austerity. There was in any case nothing coincidental about the fact that 52% of ND's electoral base was comprised of pensioners and 11% of housewives. This reflected lack of dynamism on the part of ND as a bourgeois party and it was exploited by The River, who won their highest vote in the true blue bourgeois areas of Attica, Psychiko (13.6%), Filothei (13.5%). Ekali (11.7%) (Mavris 2015), whereas among the employer/entrepreneurial strata it suffered a 16.5% decline and among the self-employed a 12.1% decline by comparison with 2012.

SYRIZA's victory changed, but only slightly, the trend that had emerged in the 2014 European elections. The party of A. Tsipras had undoubtedly won the vote of a large proportion of the popular strata. But it was not possible to find any clear evidence of over-representation as it had been in 2012. In other words, SYRIZA had more of a popular audience than in May 2014 but a more limited popular audience than it had had in June 2012. It may with 38.7%[51] of the vote have been the first party for those aged between 18 and 24 but this percentage exemplified 6.6% over-representation[52] by comparison with the national average, whereas in 2012 for the same age category there was 37.5% over-representation.

Correspondingly, the same applied for voters aged from 25 to 34 and 35 to 44 where SYRIZA again emerged as first party, with 31.7% and 39%, but the degree of over-representation in the first category fell between 2012 and 2015 from 22.7% to −12.7% (in other words here there is under-representation) and in the second from 19% to 3.6%. The same is true for students, where SYRIZA may have achieved an impressive 42.3% vote but the degree of under-representation came down from 45% to 16.5%. Among the lower classes, for workers in the private sector, SYRIZA won 39.5% of the vote and for the unemployed 44.3%

[51] The figures are taken from the Public Issue exit poll of January 2015.

[52] The degree of over-representation results from the proportion in certain social categories of voters as against the national percentage.

but over-representation in the first category fell from 26.4% to 8.7% and in the second from 37.5% to 22%. The only exception is with public sector employees, where the SYRIZA vote was 44.3% and the over-representation ratio remained virtually the same, rising slightly from 22.7% to 22.9%. The conclusion is that SYRIZA continued to represent the political choice of young people but their level of support was growing to a lesser extent than that of other age categories.

Interestingly, grassroot voters and young people who did not vote for SYRIZA did not go to some particular party but dispersed to various electoral formations. Among young people aged between 18 and 24 ND increased its influence from 11% to 21.9%, among private sector employees from 19% to 22.9%. The ND vote among students rose from 12% to 19.5%; among the unemployed it rose from 17% to 24%. Golden Dawn increased its influence with civil servants from 6% to 8.8%. The vote for the KKE in the 25–34 age group went from 4% to 9.7%.

This fall in the proportion of young people and the popular strata among SYRIZA voters is linked to the strong presence of bourgeois and petty bourgeois layers, only slightly less than the national average, something which was clearly not the case in 2012. A closer look at those who voted for SYRIZA shows that 26.8% belong to the category employers/entrepreneurs, 34.9% are employers/self-employed, 32.9% are self-employed, 31.6% are pensioners and 35.3% are housewives. As a result, in the January 2015 national elections there was an increased presence of bourgeois and petty bourgeois strata in SYRIZA's electorate and a decrease in the weight of the popular strata and the youth.

Political Changes up to the Referendum of July 2015

Events moved very quickly immediately after election day. While everyone was expecting long drawn-out negotiations for formation of a government (given that SYRIZA needed two more seats to secure an absolute parliamentary majority), within a few minutes a SYRIZA-ANEL coalition government had been formed and immediately afterwards, A. Tsipras laid a wreath in the memory of the 200 Leftists executed by the Germans on May 1, 1944. Essentially it was an act that symbolized the formation of a government where the key partner was of Communist origin.

The outline of SYRIZA's policy, on the basis of which it was voted into office, was announced in a speech by A. Tsipras in Thessaloniki and signalled the end of austerity policies, renegotiation of the debt with a view to writing off a great part of it and paying back the rest in accordance with the rate of growth of the economy, discontinuation of the privatization programme and abolition of the real estate tax, an increase in the minimum wage, higher social spending for those living below the poverty line, restoration of the 13th pension payment, provision of free hospital care for the unemployed, an end to auctioning off of the primary residence.

But very soon it would become evident that things were going to follow a different, much more moderate, course, characterized by an effort to reach compromises with both the Greek establishment and, above all, with the lenders. The former type of compromise would be seen when, a few days after SYRIZA's election victory, Mr. A. Tsipras himself would propose for President of the Republic the former ND minister P. Pavlopoulos, a close associate of the former Prime Minister K. Karamanlis. This was a move that inserted a number of institutional limits into SYRIZA policy that could not be overcome. Any attempt to transcend these limits would trigger the resignation of the President of the Republic, and a subsequent profound political crisis, much more serious than the everyday bickering between government and opposition because there would be a clash between the government and the President of the Republic. It is interesting that finally Mr. Pavlopoulos was voted in not only by the totality of ND parliamentarians, from whence he originated, and by ANEL, but also by the totality of SYRIZA parliamentarians with the exception of Ioanna Gaitani, indicating that party origins did not comprise an inhibiting factor in the vote that brought him to office.

That said, starting from the negotiations with the lenders, the Tsipras government made it clear that it did not seek to write off the debt but simply achieve an "honest compromise", as it characterized the intended agreement. The prospect of retraction of the Memorandum commitments through a law with just one article simply disappeared from the governmental discourse. At the same time, it was proclaimed that Greece would not withdraw either from the euro or from North Atlantic Treaty Organization (NATO) (Katsourides 2016: 121–122). On both these points, the government directly contradicted older positions of the party on withdrawal from NATO and on the slogan "No sacrifice for the euro" (the latter formulation may not have amounted to a clear assertion of the prospect of exit from the EMU—as the Left wing of SYRIZA did—but neither did it exclude it). Last but not least, people who originally came from the Centre-Right and PASOK were appointed to key positions in the state apparatus. These were people who were not inclined under any circumstances to break with the European and Greek *status quo* (Spourdalakis 2016).

In this context the position on a joint agreement on cancellation of part of the debt was transformed into extension of the repayment time, depending on the rate of growth in the Greek economy (Mavroudeas 2015), with the issue of abolishing the Memorandum policies replaced by negotiations for the signing of a new agreement between Greece and the lenders. This was already clear from the February 20 Eurogroup communiqué where it was explicitly stated that Greece was demanding "extension of the Master Financial Assistance Facility Agreement (MFFA), which is underpinned by a set of commitments" and mentioned as well that "the Greek authorities reiterate their unequivocal commitment to honour their financial obligations to all their creditors in a full and timely manner" and that "the Greek authorities are also committed to ensuring the appropriate primary fiscal surpluses or financing proceeds required to guarantee debt sustainability in line with the November 2012 Eurogroup statement". At the same time there was a commitment to sabotaging—if not cancelling—the mandate from the elections for abolition of the Memorandum: "The Greek authorities commit to refrain from any roll-back of measures and unilateral changes to the policies and structural reforms that would negatively impact fiscal targets, economic recovery or financial stability, as assessed by the institutions". And the Eurogroup communiqué on the agreement concluded: "We remain committed to provide adequate support to Greece until it has regained full market access as long as it honours its commitments within the agreed framework". So, the goal was no longer abolition of the Memoranda but negotiations with the lenders for a more "flexible" agreement.

The point is that for as long as the negotiations lasted there was an interruption in the provision of loans to Greece which, as time passed, was facing a growing problem in servicing its debt, with corresponding diminution in its bargaining power. Finally, the Greek government on June 3, 2015 sent a 47-page proposal to lenders which had absolutely nothing in common with the initial governmental programme: gradual phasing out of early retirement, continuation of the privatization programme, restructuring of the way the debt is paid, increased value-added tax (VAT) on most products, retention of the special unemployment reduction tax on income over 12,000 euros, a *gradual* raising of the minimum wage. But not even this profoundly modified programme, not for cancelling austerity but for managing, it was accepted by the lenders, who demanded an additional €3 bn of fiscal measures, higher VAT so as to generate additional revenues of around one billion euros, along with retention of the content of the previous Memoranda and agreements (deregulation of the labour market, lowered labour costs, severe restrictions on recruitment to the public sector, compulsory mergers of public bodies), and for every legislative initiative of the government that would entail budgetary costs, advance approval of the lenders would be required.

The situation that had been created was stifling, as the Greek government was confronted not only with the problem of servicing the public debt but also with the fact that, owing to the fear that had gripped the ruling class over the direction events were taking, capital flight from Greek banks continued unabated throughout the first six months of 2015. It was dealt with through Emergency Liquidity Assistance, which was introduced by the European Central Bank until the announcement at the end of May that its increase had been checked, but the capital flight continued and Greek banks were led to suffocation. The confrontation peaked when on 25 June the lenders' side proposed to the Greek government a revised agreement whose content merely reproduced the Memorandum orientations of the most recent period. Specifically, among other things it provided for legislation to enable a company to proceed with mass layoffs, removal of the possibility of resuming collective bargaining (unless authorized by the lenders), 100% advance payment of taxes by companies and freelancers, € 900 million (0.5% of gross domestic product (GDP)) in cuts to social welfare expenditure, the financing of subsidiary funds to be provided only from the beneficiaries' *own* resources, the selling off of State-held shares in the telephone company OTE, a new reduction in public sector salaries, limitation of the Sunday day off for employees in shops, privatization of the Independent Transmission System Operator for Electrical Energy and so on.

It was in this context that A. Tsipras on Friday 26th June proclaimed a referendum to be held on July 5th on whether the Greek people accepted the lenders' proposals or not. There were two features that set the character of the nine days that intervened between the announcement and the conducting of the referendum.

The first was that due to the freeze on further provision of Emergency Liquidity Assistance and the risk that when the banks opened on Monday June 29 there would be an unprecedented flight of deposits (as soon as an hour after the announcement of the referendum citizens were flocking to most of the country's ATMs to withdraw the maximum amount allowed daily—from €580 to €800 depending on the bank), the government was forced to order temporary suspension of the operation of the banks and the Stock Exchange and impose restrictions, with the result that a citizen was not able to withdraw more than 60 euros daily from each bank account (one was able, however, to conduct electronic transactions up to the limits allowed by the capital controls). The result was that the referendum was conducted with the banks closed and with queues of depositors at the ATMs waiting to withdraw the 60 euros to which they were entitled.

The second has to do with the climate in which the "yes" and "no" campaigning took place. The "Yes" (accepting the lenders' proposals) was supported by ND, PASOK, The River, almost all the media, and the former prime ministers Simitis, Karamanlis and Mitsotakis, and corresponding interventions were made by several officials and foreign leaders. The "No" side was supported by SYRIZA, ANEL, ANTARSYA and Golden Dawn.[53] The KKE opted for an informal vote, judging that

[53] Characteristically we could cite President of the European Commission Jean-Claude Juncker's statement that "in the referendum Greek citizens are asked to answer whether they will stay in the

"NO" in the referendum will be interpreted by the Greek government as approval for its own anti-popular proposal (meaning the proposal of June 3).

Both sides held pre-election rallies in the intervening week but it was generally agreed that there were more people at the rally of the NO supporters on the Friday preceding the referendum in the central square of Athens, Syntagma Square, with A. Tsipras as the main speaker.

Perhaps the most basic feature of this particular week in terms of climate was the sharpening of polarization. Greece had been divided into two camps and the content of the dispute between them went far beyond the question of the referendum. In fact, it very much resembled a weaponless and violence-free, but very tense, replay of the 1947–49 civil war, but with the prospect of the Left winning this time. That was to be made clear by the result of the referendum itself: 61.3% voted "no" and 38.7% "yes", with a rate of participation of 62.5%. It was one of the most indisputable verdicts from a European referendum in recent years. What is most significant is that this 61.3% came from a country where the banks were closed, there were capital controls, the citizens were going once a day to ATMs to withdraw 60 euros, all the mainstream media and most foreign officials were supporting the "yes", warning and threatening with the untold disasters that would afflict Greece if the "no" won.

The content of the vote in the referendum bore the unmistakable stamp of class, as was highlighted by a number of factors: The first is that the political parties and the international conservative elite supported "yes". The second has to do with the fact that the employers (Association of Hellenic Industries, Commercial Association of Athens, Hellenic Exporters' Association, Association of Greek Tourist Enterprises) supported the "yes" by participating in its relevant defence committee (Mavris 2016: 9). The third is the polarization between different sections of society. The "no" was clearly in front in all age groups except the over 65 s, where "yes" won by 55.1%. The difference was more pronounced

euro or return to the drachma". This is an opinion that was shared by the governments of Germany, Italy and the France. The Council of Europe, in a statement, said that the referendum did not comply with European standards, because a period of at least two weeks was not left for debate. And on the day of the referendum European Parliament President Martin Schultz said that if the "NO" won in the referendum, Greece would have to introduce another currency.

among younger voters: 85% in the 18-24 age group, 72.3 in the 25–34, 85.2% among students. The figure for the unemployed was 72.3%, for civil servants 70.9%, for wage earners in the private sector 71.3%, for farmers 65.2%. By contrast, among pensioners "yes" won, with 52%, as it did also, marginally, among the self-employed, with 50.1% (Public Issue 2015). "No" was overwhelmingly in front in less affluent areas (Peristeri 70.3%, Keratsini 72.4%, Nikaia 72.5%, Perama 76.6%). Correspondingly, the "yes" triumphed in bourgeois areas (Ekali 84.6%, Psychiko 74%, Filothei 74%, Dionysos 69.8%) (Mavris 2016: 13).

Nevertheless, although the result has a clear conflictual dimension to it, both politically and socially, events were to take a quite different turn. Alexis Tsipras, very belatedly, made a laconic statement including, among other points, the following: "I am fully aware that the mandate you have given me is not an order to break with Europe but an endorsement for strengthening our negotiating power so as to reach a viable agreement … the Greek people answered the right question and at the same time changed the question of dialogue in Europe. It did not answer the question: 'in or out of the euro'. This question has to be removed, once and for all, from the discussion". And he concluded by saying that the next day he would ask the President of the Republic to call a meeting of party leaders.

These two points (convocation of the meeting of political leaders, clarification that there is no question of withdrawing from the EMU and ceasing payments as an alternative course of action in the event of failure of the negotiations) set the parameters within which Alexis Tsipras had decided to move. This is because the only reason for there to be a meeting of the leaders would be a tie or a marginal victory of "no" in the referendum, in which case Tsipras would seek a consensual solution. Not only did this not happen but the overwhelming majority in favour of "no" within a context of intolerable international pressures, with the banks closed and capital controls in place, reflected the majority's desire that the Greek government should act independently of the parties supporting "yes" and not hesitate to clash with the lenders so as to avert implementation of the proposal of June 25.

In contrast to all this, Alexis Tsipras and the government at its centre seemed not to know how to handle this whole situation and the dynamic of the 61.3%. The truth is that a section of the government was from the outset opposed to holding the referendum, seeing it as adventurist (e.g. Deputy Prime Minister G. Dragasakis or Minister of Finance G. Stathakis). But later developments have shown that the call for the referendum was a tactical move, more or less an exercise in damage control. It was judged that under the pressure that would be exerted either the "yes" would win or there would be a marginal victory of "no", so that the country would then be led to elections, without an agreement with the lenders, and with A. Tsipras adopting an attitude along the lines of "SYRIZA wanted to make the break, but with the referendum the people decided differently". When things did not turn out that way SYRIZA's inability to handle the situation became obvious. And this indecision had deeper roots, not unrelated to the Eurocommunist origins of the SYRIZA leadership team and the perception that the EU could be transformed into a Europe of the peoples. As a result, the issue was not to prepare for, at a minimum, a break with EMU, if not with the EU, in the event of failure of the negotiations: the goal was rather *the negotiations themselves*, given the perception that everything depended on maintaining a strong stance and putting forward coherent arguments, not adopting class strategies and changing the international balance.

In the above context, despite the vehement objections of the Left wing of SYRIZA led by Minister of Productive Reconstruction P. Lafazanis, the government brought a new Memorandum to Parliament. This third Memorandum included an array of measures such as the abolition of tax exemptions for farmers and advance payment of 100% of tax, not only for businesses but also for the self-employed. The measures also included an increase of VAT on restaurants and most food items, retention of the property tax, abolition of the tax law on triangular transactions, raising of the retirement age and pension cuts. Last but not least the Memorandum imposed the privatization of the Independent Power Transmission Operator, the continuation of the privatization programme and selling off of regional airports.

The reactions within SYRIZA against this spectacular about-face were not negligible. An internal party document circulated signed by 109 of the 201 members of SYRIZA's Central Committee. It said: "This agreement is incompatible with the ideas and the principles of the Left, but above all with the needs of the popular strata. This proposal cannot be accepted by the people and the members of SYRIZA". The party's youth wing condemned the vote on the third Memorandum, and in the parliamentary group the final version of the agreement was voted on August 14 by 118 of the 149 members, but adopted with ease (222 votes in total), given the support of ND, PASOK, The River and, of course, ANEL. The third Memorandum may indeed have secured passage in this way, but there was collateral damage: on the one hand, the government lost its majority in the parliament and on the other hand SYRIZA split, with the dissidents founding the Popular Unity Party[54] a few days later. The fall of the government led to elections being called for September 2015.

The September 2015 Elections

In the September election campaign, SYRIZA's rhetoric focused on two points: The first was that the acceptance of the third Memorandum constituted a tactical retreat and that any other option would have much worse consequences for the country and its people. Given the transnational character of the EU, progressive changes in other countries, such as a possible PODEMOS victory in Spain, would modify international power relations in a more positive direction. The second was that a "parallel" programme of reforms would be carried out that would alleviate the plight of the most vulnerable social classes as well as combating instances of corruption in the dominant elite who were to a significant extent responsible for the country's economic situation (Katsourides 2016: 125).

ND, PASOK and The River by contrast adopted a highly critical stance towards the government, arguing that valuable time had been lost in dead-end negotiations, with the result that a new Memorandum came, the cost of which would have to be paid by the Greek people. ND and PASOK in particular maintained that if the programme of the Samaras government had been continued, the country would gradually have extricated itself from the Memoranda. The KKE said that it was only in a regime of popular power that present framework of austerity and exploi-

[54] Which was joined by a section of ANTARSYA and by other organizations of the extra-parliamentary Left.

tation would be able to be abolished. Popular Unity focused on the demand for debt cancellation and exit from the EMU. Golden Dawn emphasized the responsibilities of all politicians from the fall of the dictatorship onwards, not to mention the harmful effects of increased immigration into Greece. It opposed the presence of the lenders, whom they saw as being linked to Zionist capital.

Although the climate that seemed to prevail in Greek was to all appearances a prelude to a ND victory and a big fall in support for SYRIZA, events took a different turn. SYRIZA won 35.46% of the vote, signifying only a marginal drop of 0.88%, and elected 145 MPs. Its allied party, Independent Greeks, scored 3.69%, down 1.06%, but with the 10 parliamentarians that were elected, a new SYRIZA-ANEL government became possible, and was indeed formed. By contrast, ND saw an infinitesimal + 0.29% rise in its vote; PASOK (which stood under the name Democratic Coalition, allying itself with a section of DIMAR) scored 6.3%, achieving a rise of 1.3% (which was however to a significant extent attributable to a renewed influx from KIDISO—which did not participate to these elections). The River, with its 4.1%, fell about 2%. On the Left, the KKE remained stationary at 5.5%, Popular Unity narrowly missed entering the Parliament (2.9%) and ANTARSYA rose marginally from 0.70% to 0.85%. As for the other parties, Golden Dawn increased its vote slightly by 0.7% to reach 7% and for the first time the Union of Centrists entered the parliament with 3.43% of the vote, which was a significant change (+1.64%) if compared to its performance in the January elections.

The September elections were characterized by a continuation of the trend towards an increase in the average age of SYRIZA voters. SYRIZA experienced a drop in its share in all age groups, with the exception of the 25–34 age scale, where the pre-existing fall was counterbalanced, with the result that there was no difference from the national rate, and with the exception of the 65 years where it rose by 1.5%.[55] At the same time, there was an increase of 1.9% among pensioners and a 4.4% decrease among students. It is perhaps significant that this trend coincided with a tendency towards de-urbanization of the SYRIZA electoral base and (re)urbaniza-

[55] The figures are taken from a Public Issue exit poll (September 2015).

tion of its ND counterpart. SYRIZA may have suffered losses in the popular strata but their extent was limited: −4.9% among public sector employees, −3.1% among private sector employees, −4.5% among the unemployed, with a 2% increase among the self-employed. By contrast, the losses in the bourgeois strata and sections of the petty bourgeoisie were very extensive: −9.6% among employers/entrepreneurs (where it had taken a total of 17.2% of the vote), −6.8% among employers/self-employed (out of a total 28.1%), −13.4% among professionals and people employed in light industry (out of a total of 23.3% overall). The only section of a potential popular bloc where SYRIZA experienced a large decline in its influence was among farmers (−14.0%). On the other hand, although the national average vote for ND was more or less at the January level (+0.3%), there was considerable strengthening in the bourgeois and petty bourgeois strata (+47.2%) (!), among employers/entrepreneurs (amounting to an impressive 68.7% of the total for this category), +7.7% among employers/self-employed, +5.3% for people professionally employed in light industry, +6.4% for the self-employed. However, among some popular strata there were losses: −3.2% among private sector employees (so that they comprised only 15.9% of the total). But it should be noted that both in the case of farmers (+12.3% and 39% of the total) and the unemployed (+4.7% and 19.4% of the total) there was a significant increase.

In conclusion, the September elections revealed a significant trend towards loss of bourgeois, petty bourgeois and rural strata, and a much lower tendency towards loss of labouring strata. And there was a rise in the average age of supportive voters. In contrast, ND re-established support in the bourgeois and petty bourgeois strata and strengthened its support among the agricultural strata and the unemployed.

As for the other parties, Golden Dawn was over-represented among entrepreneurs (10.6%), farmers (11.5%) the unemployed (11%), the River enjoyed particular support from private employees (6.4%), self-employed people (7.7%) and entrepreneurs (7.6%), the KKE among students (9.3%), the unemployed (6.9%), private employees (6.3%), the 18–23 age group (9.3%) and 24–29 age group (7.3%), PASOK—Democratic Coalition among farmers (10.7%) and pensioners (10.3%), the Union of Centrists among students (5.9%) and the 24–29 age group (6.5%).

A reading of the results suggests at first glance that SYRIZA achieved a major electoral victory, despite acceptance of a new Memorandum no part of which it would have accepted while in opposition. A victory despite a fierce internal controversy led to the departure of thousands of members, the great majority of the party's youth and dozens of parliamentarians, with a mood of mute frustration predominant throughout the country. The victory can be interpreted as bitter acceptance by the electorate that under the circumstances there was no better alternative and that it preferable for SYRIZA to manage the new situation rather than ND, with possible allies PASOK and The River. This is confirmed by the results for these parties as well as by the results for the parties to the Left of SYRIZA. The Memorandum parties were not able to exploit SYRIZA's failure to lift the country from the international surveillance or to convince the electorate that time had been wasted with the negotiations and that if it had followed the programme of the Samaras government the economy would be in better shape. And the three parties of the Left had no reason to be any happier. The KKE failed to win the larger share of the vote, which perhaps could have been interpreted as a sign of former voters returning. Popular Unity suffered a serious defeat, given that it succeeded in taking with it only 5% of the "No" voters, notwithstanding the fact that four former ministers had come over to it, the President of the outgoing Parliament, more than twenty MPs, a member of the European Parliament and a section of ANTARSYA, not to mention other groupings of the extra-parliamentary Left. ANTARSYA, finally, may like the fact that it has achieved slight growth but after so many developments and so much regroupment in the milieu of the Left, it still has not managed to attract even 1% of the vote. Of course, this is just one aspect of things, because there is also another consideration, which is that between the two elections in 2015 abstention grew by about 700,000 votes (or rather "non-votes"), that is to say from 35.13% it rose to 43.43% (+8.3%). And by comparison with the 2009 elections, abstention had already increased by 14.38% and by comparison with 2014 by 20%. SYRIZA lost 320,000 votes, New Democracy 192,500, Golden Dawn 9000, the KKE 37,000, The River 152,000 votes, and ANEL lost 93,000 votes. The Democratic Coalition vote rose by 52,000 but if from those votes one subtracts the greater part of the votes for KIDISO in January (152,000) and a section of the votes for the electoral coalition of DIMAR and the Greens (3000 votes), it is reasonable to conclude that this combination also declined in absolute terms. The only parliamentary formation to win more votes (+76,000) was the Union of Centrists.

All the above reveals the widespread discredit into which the political scene has fallen. A steadily growing proportion of the Greek population is opting to delegitimize parliamentary procedures. In this context, the skyrocketing vote for the Union of Centrists from 17,000 (0.28%) in June 2012 to 186,000 (3.43%) and nine deputies in September 2015 becomes explicable, the more so given that the party in question is highly popular with younger audiences: 5.4% in the 18–24 age group; 6.5% among those aged 25–29, 5.9% among those aged 30–34.[56] Regarded until 2014 as a party without roots in any social milieu, with an individual, V. Leventis, as leader who was generally considered to be lacking in seriousness, it was transformed into a staging post for voters who calculated that through this choice (abstention is negative) they were positively making a mockery of the Greek political system. In any case, the choice of abstention and the vote to Union of Centrists makes it clear that a significant section of the Greek people expect nothing from Greek political personages. Eurobarometer statistics are indicative: citizens' confidence in the Greek Parliament declined from 61% in the autumn of 2004 to 33% in the autumn of 2009 and 17% in the autumn of 2015. Correspondingly, confidence in the Greek government fell from 50% to 25% and 18%. Confidence in political parties came down from 17% to 15% and 8%.

The conclusion that emerges is that the outcome of the September elections can be read in two ways, without either of them being in a position to exclude the other. Given that elections are held so that a balance of power can emerge with the capacity to govern the country, SYRIZA managed to come out relatively unscathed from the impasse of the third Memorandum and the elections, without any other party, with the special exception of the Union of Centrists, being able plausibly to claim that it achieved anything at all, however, minor. On the other hand, dissatisfaction with SYRIZA and the rest of the political system, coupled

[56] According to a Kapa Research exit poll.

with inability to find an active outlet (supporting another Left party), led hundreds of thousands of voters to abstention (and secondarily to support for the Union of Centrists) a trend that had begun several years previously.

Beyond all that, in the period following the September elections, governance by the SYRIZA-ANEL coalition government can be said to have been characterized by four elements:

The first is implementation of the Memorandum commitments: privatization of the airports was completed rapidly, the Piraeus and Thessaloniki port authorities were sold off, the new insurance policy was enacted, including a raising of the retirement age, pension cuts, an increase in insurance contributions, VAT was increased on a number of basic necessities, the tax-free income threshold was lowered, a Privatization Fund was set up to which all public assets to be disposed of were transferred, primary residence auctions were held for debts to banks and bank accounts were seized for debts to the State. Above and beyond the special measures there was an agreement with lenders to establish an automatic cost-cutting mechanism so that when the targets for specific budget surpluses are not met, then new fiscal measures will be implemented, based mainly on wage cuts in the public sector and an increase in VAT. In contrast to the debt question, expectations for relief were transferred to the end of the third Memorandum, in late August 2018, and only on the assumption that Greece would have a net surplus of 3.5% from 2018 to 2022 (and 2% from 2023 to 2060) and would not cancel the reforms made during the Memoranda.

The second is the abandonment of most of the social component of the so-called parallel programme in response to reactions from lenders and its replacement by an attempt to introduce targeted services of limited economic range to specific categories of recipient, which, however, do not offset the overall losses to these social strata. These are benefits in the form of one-off payments and not structural changes (as, for example, a policy of increasing pensions could be). Other policies in the latter category would be free hospital treatment for uninsured persons, provision of free textbooks to students studying for a second degree, a lump-sum benefit to retired people in 2016 and to people on low incomes in 2017 and in 2018. To compensate for the new capitulation, additional emphasis was placed on certain improvements at the level of individual rights (e.g. the introduction of marriage between couples of the same sex, upgrading of cohabitation agreements) and, on the other hand, a shift in the focus of political confrontation to the institutional plane, with initiatives around the electoral law through introduction of a more proportionate system, a constitutional review and a framework for licencing television stations.[57] For television licences in particular it was clear that the government's attempt to introduce conditions into the broadcasting landscape meant nothing more than new deals with entrepreneurial centres and perpetuation of commercialized information and entertainment. Ultimately all three of these initiatives have yielded limited results. Given that it was approved but did not secure 180 votes, the new electoral law will be applied at the elections after next. The Constitutional Review also failed to win the required support and so will not proceed. As for the broadcasting licences, the government suffered a defeat following annulment of the relevant legislation by the Council of State and was obliged to co-manage the whole process with ND and PASOK through establishment of a new National Council for Radio and Television.

The third element was the gradual retreat from social mobilizations. It is a fact that adoption of the new policy on insurance triggered a nation-wide strike on February 4, 2016, with significant participation from the self-employed and the learned professions (doctors, lawyers, engineers), for whom the new reforms were particularly damaging. Increased taxation on farmers contributed to the launching of major agricultural mobilizations in the January of the same year, but in both cases, they were soon brought to a halt. The only relatively massive and certainly protracted form of mobilization to be pursued was the movement against the auctions of primary residences, but it too failed to act as a catalyst for wider developments. All in all, the people and the organizations involved in the collective action that had been dominant

[57] Although private television stations have been operating freely in Greece since 1989 (!) a procedure has never been established for regulating permanent licencing, with the result that private TV stations operate with temporary licences that expired more than ten years ago.

in the 2010–2015 period seemed to be trying to understand what had caused SYRIZA's retreat in 2015, what its consequences were and why it was not possible to relaunch such mass mobilizations.[58] The second year saw a retreat into private concerns, with the notion predominant that nothing could radically change, that the forces the anti-Memorandum movement had to confront were much stronger, with ultimate consequence the political demobilization.

The fourth has to do with a slight improvement in the economic indicators. Already in 2016, but much more strongly in 2017, the first signs of economic recovery emerged. Specifically, according to the most recent available data, the GDP for the fourth quarter of 2017 showed an increase of 1.9% over the corresponding quarter of 2016. There was a 2.6% fall in unemployment between December 2016 and December 2017. Private consumption expenditure increased by 2% in 2017, gross value added rose by 2%, gross fixed capital formation by 1%, receipts from tourism services by 7%. Of course, this does not mean that in other areas the negative trends did not persist: industrial production in 2017 was down to 2%, public debt in the third quarter of 2017 was two billion euros more than in the third quarter of 2016, income tax receipts in 2017 were €686 million less than expected. But the general conclusion that emerges is that the situation is not as it was in 2011, or 2014, and this is felt in Greek society as being a key element in the government's argument that the crisis is ending. In fact, the Greek government's stance is that the twofold strategy of resumption of economic growth and faithful fulfilment of the terms of the third Memorandum will lead Greek society back to a period of normality.

Of course, many questions arise concerning the future. Will this economic growth, albeit moderate, continue? How close will be the supervision by the lenders (a supervision that will continue until 75% of the loans to Greece have been paid off), but also more generally what will be the position of the Greek social formation in the international environ-

[58] In this connection, there has been a great contraction in the practices of social solidarity that had developed in previous years.

ment? How likely is it that there will be a return to the climate of radicalization in the country? (Something that would signify prior understanding of the factors that have led to the precipitate retreat from movement practices). These are issues to be dealt with in the next chapter of this book.

References

Antoniou V., 2014, "2014 elections, a first approach" http://www.iskra.gr/index.php?option=com_content&view=article&id=16486:antoniou-2014&catid=81:kivernisi&Itemid=198, accessed on 13/6/2014 (in Greek).

Belantis D., 2014, "The centre-left and the biopolitical administrative state" http://rednotebook.gr/2014/05/kentroaristera-aftodioikhsh/, accessed on 12/6/14 (in Greek).

Eleftheriou K., 2014, "Cracks in the Monolith: the KKE in the 2012 elections", in Voulgaris G. and I. Nikolakopoulos (eds.) *2012, the twofold electoral earthquake*, Athens: Themelio, pp. 151–184 (in Greek).

Gaitanou E., 2011, "Social and Political Resistance from Youth on the grounds of the crisis", *Ektos Grammis* no. 27–28, pp. 55–58 (in Greek).

Gemenis K., 2012, "The 2010 regional elections in Greece: voting for regional government or protesting the IMF?", *Regional and Federal Studies*, vol. 22 no 1, pp. 107–115.

Georgiadou B., 2014, "The electoral rise of golden dawn. Revenge vote of the insecure and new political opportunities", in Voulgaris G. and I. Nikolakopoulos (eds.) *2012, the twofold electoral earthquake*, Athens: Themelio, pp. 185–219 (in Greek).

Katsourides Y., 2016, *Radical left parties in Government. The cases of AKEL and Syriza*, London: Palgrave.

Kousiantas K. 2012, "The growth of fascism in Greece" http://aristeroblog.gr/node/897, accessed on 1/4/2014 (in Greek).

Koustenis P., 2014a, "Elections 2014: the electoral cycle of Golden Dawn", *Archeiotaxio* no. 16, pp. 89–108 (in Greek).

Koustenis P., 2014b, "Deconstruction and reconstruction of electoral identities. The sociological detection of Attica" in Voulgaris G.- I. Nikolakopoulos (eds.), 2012, *The twofold electoral earthquake*, Athens: Themelio, pp. 83–123 (in Greek).

Lialiouti Z. and G. Bithymitris, 2013, "Crisis, hegemony and media", *The Example of SKAI and Kathimerini, Greek Review of Political Science* vol. 40, pp. 139–173 (in Greek).

Mavris G., 2010, "Disapproval in two rounds", *Kathimerini* of 21/11/2010 (in Greek).

Mavris G., 2012a, "The elections of 6th May 2012 and the end of the post-junta two party arrangement" http://www.publicissue.gr/2005/ekloges-2012-telos-metapoliteftikou-dikommatismou/, accessed on 28/3/2014 (in Greek).

Mavris G., 2012b, "Greece's austerity election", *New Left Review* vol. 76, pp. 95–107.

Mavris G., 2013a, "From the fragmentation of the right to conservative disintegration. New democracy a year after the elections" http://www.mavris.gr/3496/2-katakermatismos-dexias/, accessed on 28/3/2014 (in Greek).

Mavris G., 2013b, "Where is SYRIZA going?" http://www.mavris.gr/3533/pou-vadizei-o-syriza/, accessed on 29/3/2014 (in Greek).

Mavris G., 2013c, "The PASOK of Evangelos Venizelos. What is the source of the party's continuous electoral decline?", http://www.mavris.gr/3549/pasok-venizelou/, accessed on 29/3/2014 (in Greek).

Mavris G. 2013d, "The rise and fall of the democratic left", http://www.mavris.gr/3572/anodos-kai-ptosi-tis-dimar/, accessed on 29/3/2014 (in Greek).

Mavris G., 2014a "The fluctuations in SYRIZA's influence in the 2012–2014 post-election period", *Efimerida ton Syntakton of* 25/2/2014 (in Greek).

Mavris G., 2014b, "The unseen aspects of the electoral war. Elections in two stages: the Greek electoral experiment", http://www.mavris.gr/3981/elliniko_eklogiko_peirama, accessed on 10/6/14 (in Greek).

Mavris G., 2015 "From 2012 to 2015: why new democracy lost the elections" http://www.mavris.gr/4599/why-nd-lost-the-elections/, accessed on 4/4/2018 (in Greek).

Mavris G., 2016, "The Greek referendum of 2015" http://www.mavris.gr/wp-content/uploads/2016/07/Mavris_GrRef2015.pdf, accessed on 6/4/2018 (in Greek).

Mavroudeas S., 2015. "On the programmatic statements of the SYRIZA-ANEL government" https://stavrosmavroudeas.wordpress.com/2015/02/09/, accessed on 4 4/2015 (in Greek).

Moschonas G., 2012, "The elections of May 2012: The rupture, the tendencies, SYRIZA", *Synchrona Themata* vol. 116, pp. 6–7 (in Greek).

Paraskeva-Veloudogianni D., 2012, "The contribution of official political discourse to the legitimation of golden dawn", *Ektos Grammis* vol. 31, pp. 41–43 (in Greek).

Pleios G., 2013, "The crisis and the Greek media", http://left.gr/news/i-krisi-kai-ta-ellinika-mme, accessed on 24/32014 (in Greek).
Public Issue, 2015, "Conspectus of no voters" http://www.publicissue.gr/11719/referendum-2015-no/, accessed on 8/4/2018 (in Greek).
Spourdalakis M., 2016, "Becoming Syriza again" https://www.jacobinmag.com/2016/01/syriza-memorandum-troika-left-platform-tsipras-austerity-government/, accessed on 4/4/2018.
Stathopoulos P., 2014, "The deregulation of the party system", in Voulgaris G. and I. Nikolakopoulos (eds.) *2012, the twofold electoral earthquake*, Athens: Themelio, pp. 61–81 (in Greek).
Touliatos C., 2012, "Have we said it all, finally, about Golden Dawn?", *Ektos Grammis* vol. 31, pp. 51–53 (in Greek).
Vernardakis C., 2011, "Regional and municipal elections 2010: the vote, parties and the party system", in VPRC Institute (ed.) *Public opinion in Greece 2008–2010. Parliamentary and regional elections, political parties, political communication, cultural practices*, Athens, pp. 55–64 (in Greek).
Vernardakis C., 2012a, "Elections in the new post-Junta period", *Avghi* of 13/5/2012 (in Greek).
Vernardakis C., 2012b, "The June 2012 elections in the context of the last days' tendencies" http://www.vernardakis.gr/uplmed/145_Hotdoc%20(2).pdf, accessed on 29/3/2014 (in Greek).
Vernardakis C. 2013a, "The 17th June elections and the new breaches in the party system" http://archive.avgi.gr/ArticleActionshow.action?articleID=697536, accessed on 30/3/2014 (in Greek).
Vernardakis C. 2014, "European elections 2014. The key dividing lines in the electorate" http://rednotebook.gr/2014/05/evroekloges-vasikes-diairetikes-eklogikou-swmatos, accessed on 16/6/2014 (in Greek).
Voulgaris G. and I. Nikolakopoulos, 2014, "Introduction: the 2012 electoral earthquake", in Voulgaris G. and I. Nikolakopoulos (eds.) *2012 the twofold electoral earthquake*, Athens: Themelio, pp. 9–31 (in Greek).

10

Assessing the Crisis and the Dynamics (?) of the Future

The Impossibility of the SYRIZA-ANEL Government's Cancelling the Memoranda

Among other things, the previous chapter showed the evolution of the events that led to the defeat of SYRIZA in the confrontation with the lenders, resulting in the imposition of the third Memorandum and the eighth package of measures, with a brief mention of the factors that contributed to this outcome. In this section, the issue will be treated in greater depth.

The position supported is that the choices of decades (political and ideological) that marked the course of the Greek Eurocommunist Left had suffocating after-effects that could not be overcome by SYRIZA in just a few days or even a few weeks. In the aftermath of the 1968 split in the KKE a pro-Soviet majority continued, holding the franchise, as it were, and retaining the name but a Eurocommunist minority also emerged, the Communist Party of the Interior, which in the first years following the end of the dictatorship adopted a favourable stance towards the then European Economic Community (EEC). When the question of Greece's accession was raised it came out in favour, judging that despite

S. Sakellaropoulos, *Greece's (un) Competitive Capitalism and the Economic Crisis*,
https://doi.org/10.1007/978-3-030-14319-0_10

its reactionary characteristics it could be transformed into "People's Europe". That stance was maintained over the following years and affected its orientation to the individual treaties but also the construction of the European Monetary Union. In this context the party of SYRIZA continues with the policies of the Greek Communist Party (of the Interior).[1] It is a fact that in 2010 SYRIZA's internal opposition demanded Greek withdrawal from the Economic and Monetary Union (EMU) and a change of currency. But, this never became the majority position in the party. As a result, when SYRIZA took over the country's governance, there was a well-established understanding that negotiations would not be able to lead to withdrawal from the European Monetary Union, let alone from the European Union (EU). In essence, the alternative that was put to the test was an amalgam of belief in the European idea that was not reconcilable with such hard-line policies and beliefs as the proposition that if there were "tougher" negotiations a different outcome could be expected from what had been seen with previous governments. The assumption was in essence that the articulation of rational discourse and invocation of the "European idea" could be catalysts for change. What was being overlooked was the basic parameter of the whole situation, namely the sense among European elites that a retreat in the face of Greek demands would lead to a wave of questioning of the "iron rules" of European construction. This development could exert a domino effect within larger countries, strengthening political players such as Podemos in Spain and the Mélenchon candidature in France, with unpredictable consequences for the overall European strategy. To put it somewhat differently, there were two things that were not understood by SYRIZA. One was that from the moment that the European elites and the International Monetary Fund (IMF) had refused to make any concessions to the conservative New Democracy of Antonis Samaras and to PASOK's neo-liberal social democracy, when they thought that the euro was being

[1] To be precise in Communist Party of the Interior made a majority decision to transform itself into a Left-wing non-Communist Party, the Greek Left (EAR). In 1989, EAR collaborated with the KKE and formed the Left Coalition (Synaspismos). In 1991, the pro-Eurocommunist section of the KKE broke away from the party and together with EAR established a united party under the name Coalition of the Left. (Synaspismos tis Aristeras). In 2004, the Synaspismos collaborated with certain groups of the extra-parliamentary Left, establishing the front called Coalition of the Radical Left (SYRIZA), which in 2013 became an integrated party.

properly shielded, they had no reason to do so for a party of the Left, which was indeed in the international spotlight at that time. The other was that there was no reason for the lenders to make concessions unless they were faced with the risk of sustaining damage. There were two kinds of possible damage: exit from the euro and suspension of payments. If there had been an exit from the euro at the beginning of the Memorandum period, in 2010, it would have unleashed a barrage of pressures on the economies of the EMU and the European Central Bank, given the uncertain economic climate of the period. Five years later the tremors had died away to some extent, but they were still there. On the other hand, the choice of rupture, regardless of its timing, would create for the Greek economy a framework for export support, import reduction, improvement in the current account balance, greater public investment and higher wages in the public and private sector. As a result there could be growth in domestic demand, possibilities for income redistribution, and a focus on efficient functioning of the public sector in tandem with the involvement of public servants in decision-making, for the benefit of citizens, as opposed to the orientation of having public sector competencies taken over by the private sector. At the same time suspension of payments could deal its opponents a powerful blow, the strength of which would be multiplied if it were implemented alongside exit from EMU, given that the borrowers would then be presented with the problem of when and to what extent repayment of the loans would take place, and what the economic and political consequences would be internationally and domestically.

Contrasting with these options was the conviction that some kind of solution could emerge through the negotiations which, as indicated in the previous chapter, was called "honest compromise". By this term the government meant an agreement whose content might counteract some aspects of the Memorandum policies. It could, for example, include reducing the interest rate for borrowing, increasing the minimum salary and resuming collective bargaining. But the creditor side, for the reasons indicated, was totally opposed to any such prospect. Bear in mind that while the Tsipras government was conducting its ineffectual, as it ultimately turned out, negotiations, the Greek elites, for their part, through their control of the virtual totality of the mass media, had launched a relentless war against the policies being pursued by the government, with outrageous accusations that "Greece is going to be transformed into the last Soviet republic" and that "economic and social armageddon is upon us". This extremism was not unrelated to the Greek ruling class's anxiety in the face of an "honest compromise", albeit truncated, because it would mean on the one hand a reduction in capital's share of the national product and on the other a more general political success of a party of the radical Left on a terrain where the bourgeois parties had failed.

Yet despite the clearest of indications that the lenders were determined not to proceed to any concessions, however minimal, and while the confrontation with the domestic establishment accelerated, SYRIZA not only failed to use the two aforementioned weapons but in essence neutralized a third weapon that was at its disposal, namely the dynamism of the people. As mentioned in Chap. 5, the social mobilizations of the period 2010–2013 and the solidarity movements that had developed at that time had generated a climate of "dynamic anticipation", which meant that a large section of the Greek people were primed for action, not only demanding abolition of the Memoranda but contributing to the establishment of the new institutions necessitated by the new reality that would be created by a break with the lenders. But for that to happen there were two indispensable preconditions—the first was that the government itself should be actively encouraging a climate of, and institutions of, popular mobilization and participation. The second had to do with elaboration of a concrete and clear alternative programme to be implemented in the event of a break (new international alliances, industrial reconstruction through targeted public investment, a new way of functioning for the public sector, involving both workers and citizens in its operations, reorganization of agriculture centred on products that can be cultivated in the country but also, for the time being, imported from abroad etc.). But, on neither of these fronts was there the slightest sign of movement on the part of the government, precisely because it was focused exclusively on the negotiation process, excluding the possibility of a break.

All that has been said so far concerns SYRIZA's responsibility for the fact that ultimately it too was forced to sign a Memorandum. But, they are not enough to explain why the signing of the third Memorandum did not lead to SYRIZA's massive defeat or to the strengthening of the other

Left-wing political parties (KKE, Popular Unity and ANTARSYA). Here too there is the question of the people (the subordinated classes) and the development of relations of trust/representation between them and a party of the Left. The popular strata, actually their majority, recognized in SYRIZA the political party that through formation of a Left-wing government would take the country out of the Memoranda and legislate measures of financial relief for them. The turn towards SYRIZA began in the spring of 2011 and was consummated after about three and a half years, in January 2015. Support for the new government steadily increased during the negotiations, reaching 45% (Mavris 2016–2017: 95). As a result, there was a relatively brief but real consolidation of relations of representation, with a dynamic that intensified in the first half of 2015. As for the developments within the few short few weeks (from the beginning of July, when the referendum was held until mid-August, when the Third Memorandum was voted in Parliament), it was no simple matter for there to be any spectacular erosion of this relationship of representation, and the view continued to prevail that with the parallel programme some limitations could be set on certain consequences of the Memorandum. The high popularity rating for Alexis Tsipras also contributed to this attitude, for up until the September 2015 elections it never fell below 50% (Mavris 2016–2017: 95).

On the other hand, the parties of the Left failed to convince the electorate that they could lead things in a different direction. And that is not to be wondered at. The KKE, a great historical force had from the outset of the crisis dissociated itself from any idea of participation in a scheme of government. Its view was that, given that the duty of communists was to overthrow capitalism, participation in a government that set itself the goal of overthrowing the Memoranda, would serve an integrative function in the capitalist system and tend to inhibit a socialist perspective. For this reason, the KKE did not embark on any electoral alliance either at the level of central politics, in the unions, or in the local government elections. It regarded the rest of the Left as opportunistic, complicit with the bourgeois political system. At the same time, it also either abstained from social mobilizations in which the rest of the Left participated or else opted for participation, but with a *cordon sanitaire* separating it from the others. For its part, Popular Unity (LAE), though displaying a momentum in the first weeks, when it became clear that SYRIZA was heading for agreement on a new Memorandum, subsequently experienced a downturn, and in the September elections did not manage to elect even one parliamentarian. A key role in this failure was played by the fact that while supporting the country's exit from the European Monetary Union and the writing off of the public debt, it was unable to present a coherent programme with the potential to persuade voters that a process of breaking with the lenders was something feasible. Another factor was that long-standing shared trajectory of most of its cadres with SYRIZA and the participation of four of its leading activists in ministerial positions in the SYRIZA-ANEL governments did not help it to achieve a profile as something entirely different from, and opposed to, SYRIZA. ANTARSYA, from its part, with its more limited forces, seemed to combine the weaknesses of the KKE and Popular Unity—on the one hand it did not desire political collaboration for the purpose of forming a Left-wing government and accordingly rejected the possibility of a joint ticket with Popular Unity, and on the other it was not able to present a convincing and fully elaborated programme for breaking with the lenders, with EU regulations and with the European Monetary Union. Faced with this situation, it is in no way surprising that the majority of Left-wing voters opted for continuing to support SYRIZA, though a non-negligible number preferred to abstain. In other words a considerable proportion of the electorate that had voted "no" in the referendum found that they could not see any convincing solution in the other formations of the Left and on the other hand felt that in the country after the referendum a huge gamble had been embarked upon which, to be answered successfully required guidelines that would mean a break with the central ideological schemata of the Western world and the politics that stemmed from them, which would lead to a full-scale confrontation with the most powerful forces on the planet. In the face of such a prospect, the notion gained ground that not only was there no well-thought-out plan for embarking on such a wide-ranging conflict but also no allies that would be inclined to offer material assistance in such an eventuality. The unknown horizon that opened up before the Greek population, though there was nothing sudden about it, frightened a great many people, influencing their electoral behaviour.

And all of this prompts us to venture certain theoretical reflections. For much of the Left, Greek and foreign, during the period 2010–2015, the perception took hold that Greece is likely to become the weakest link in the capitalist system, the rupture of which will usher in similar upheavals in other countries, entry—in other words—into a period where the Left internationally will overturn the power balance for the first time since 1989. This perception was not unrelated to the phenomenon of the great mushrooming of the Greek social movements, triggered by the policies of international organizations and institutions such as the EU, the EMU and the IMF, in conjunction with the theory of the weakest link, implying that the conflicts within the imperialist chain could become concentrated within a specific national formation, setting the scene for a revolution on an international scale, as occurred in Russia in 1917. This position has been attributed to Lenin and it is true that he did make clear references to the concept of the "link" in a number of his works.[2] But, there it was employed in the sense that in a given political conjuncture there is a demand that can embrace all the desires of the popular strata for social change and if the revolutionary party can focus on it, the correlation of forces can be modified rapidly. There are, of course, other texts such as "'*Left-Wing' Communism: an Infantile Disorder*" or the text "*On the Slogan for a United States of Europe*", which in some interpretations suggest that within that weak link all the contradictions possible within in this specific conjuncture can accumulate and be sharpened.[3] And Stalin indeed further deepened the analysis by indicating that the weak link is not always to be found where industry is most developed but rather where the imperialist chain is at its weakest, and this can occur in a country that is less developed (Stalin 1924).

Of course, in this connection issues are touched upon such as the construction of socialism in one country which cannot be fully dealt with in this book. Nevertheless, apropos of this subject it should be noted that the weak links, in the sense of their overturning the international correlation of power, have been three in number historically: (a) the Russian

[2] We could mention, by way of example, works such as *The Chain Is No Stronger Than Its Weakest Link* or the *Report On The Immediate Tasks Of The Soviet Government*.

[3] For this specific approach, see Althusser 1996: 95–96.

revolution; (b) the almost simultaneous integration of the Eastern European countries in the socialist camp and (c) the victory of the revolution in China. Points (b) and (c) occurred with some chronological distance between them and were decisively upheld by the existence of the USSR, at a time when the Second World War had just ended, with the realignments that had come in its wake and with the crisis of colonialism under way. All subsequent developments, such as the Cuban revolution, benefited from these very firm underpinnings. So, the weakest link was either a national formation which on account of its own specific weight could support a political course independent of international constraints or a smaller national formation with the ability to build international alliances capable of facilitating its independent course. In the case of Greece neither of these conditions applied. It would be difficult to argue persuasively that a demographically small country with a narrow economic base and a limited internal market could act with anything approaching autonomy when confronted by the pressures imposed on it by the lenders. But at the same time there was no basis for support internationally that might aid and abet such an orientation. There was no great power that had come out on the side of Greece, or even a coalition of smaller countries, and a range of issues that placed the country in chronic confrontation with neighbouring Turkey[4] remained unresolved. This was understood by the great majority of voters who supported the "no" in the referendum, which was why there was no turning against SYRIZA in favour of other parts of the Left.

Could things have turned out differently? Probably, but it would have meant fulfilling three conditions in advance. The first concerns timely, before SYRIZA's accession to government, public formulation of a programme of political priorities for implementation so as to extract the country from Memorandum austerity (e.g. wage increases, nationalization of important sectors of the economy, redistribution of income

[4] The Greek–Turkish conflict has to do with sovereign rights over the Aegean continental shelf, the boundaries of the territorial waters and the boundaries of Greek national airspace. It has been going on for decades. To this there must be added the Cyprus issue, especially after 1974 and the invasion and occupation by Turkey of 37% of an island 80% of whose inhabitants are of Greek origin (see footnote 3, Chap. 2).

through taxation and selection of specific productive sectors to be strengthened through increased public investment). At the same time, it would be clear that this programme would be implemented even if Greece needed to break with the lenders. Having a clear understanding of these general guidelines, the electorate would be informed of SYRIZA's intentions and prepared for the difficulties that would follow. It would also be aware of the prospect that was opening up. But, at the same time, immediately after SYRIZA's assumption of government, a regime of capital controls would have to be introduced. The second has to do with the need to elaborate a multidimensional foreign policy. This means good relations with all the neighbouring countries, including Turkey, and adoption of the notion that compromises will necessarily be made on outstanding Greek-Turkish issues, as well as selective alliances on specific issues with powerful countries no belonging to the lenders' club of the Western hemisphere (e.g. Russia, China and India). The third is linked to the policy of managing the State apparatus. Precisely because the State is not neutral but rather structured so as to reproduce the exploitative capital/labour relationship, any Left-wing government faces two problems: the first pertains to structures that are intrinsically hostile to Left-wing power (e.g. the role of heads of administration who, utilizing legal, administrative and practical objections, erect obstacles to the government's legislative initiatives, the mode of operation of legal and financial instrumentalities, and the activity of the overtly repressive mechanisms). The second is the personnel themselves, who have been trained to serve plans for furthering capitalist interests and consider this to be their duty. Given all this, it is necessary to create alliances within the public sector (improving wages and working conditions, allocating decisive competences to a larger number of persons, clarifying to the public servants the importance of the specific programme for the majority of the population), and on the other hand to establish parallel institutions of grassroots involvement that will implement aspects of government policy (building social solidarity structures, initiating co-operative productive units, recruiting a militia etc.).

Naturally, none of this was done in the first six months of SYRIZA government, and everyone knows the result.

The Strategy (?) of the Greek Ruling Class and Prospects for the Country

The second issue to be dealt with in this chapter concerns the effect of the Memoranda on the strategy of the country's ruling class. The position put forward in this book is that the Greek bourgeoisie was surprised by the intensity of developments in the 2009–2010 period. But in any case, it did not want to be cut off from the EU and the EMU and saw considerable potential for increasing profitability through implementation of the Memoranda, though aspects of the policies implemented, such as the overall increase in taxation, were not to its liking. But from a certain point onwards the severity of the measures that drastically reduced domestic demand, or the inability of banks to approve loans, not only made business difficult but had a disastrous effect on very many enterprises, reducing their activity or even curtailing it completely.

Nevertheless, the question is what is the strategy of the surviving businesses? And this brings the focus to the orientations of the economic elite, because at the political level it is being accepted that no government will escape the limits imposed by the agreement concluded so far (and in any case until such time as three-quarters of the loans have been repaid, supervision by the lenders will continue). In other words, unemployment will continue to skyrocket, underemployment will similarly remain at high levels, wages and pensions will continue to be extremely low, and the deregulation of labour relations will be established as the norm. In the same vein, a very significant proportion of the national wealth will have passed into the ownership of foreign business groups, while people who cannot repay their loans or taxes will suffer the consequences of eviction.

Given the narrow parameters of government policies and the absence of movement practices or convincing alternative proposals, with consequent consolidation of the existing correlation of power, the basic question posed for the country's future is whether the Greek ruling class is prepared to pursue a different economic strategy with the potential to transcend the chronic problems of Greek capitalism: the factors that have led to the protracted (years-long) crisis. The data so far reveals the following tendencies.

On the subject of domestic investment for the 2009–2015 period in the manufacturing sector, an orientation can be seen towards low-tech investments (investment variation +12.7%) and low to medium-level technology (investment variation +77.4%). In contrast, the medium to high-tech sectors and high-tech sectors experienced a decline of the order of −16% and 29.8% respectively. In the services sector, the picture is the reverse—among marketed services there is a very significant increase in knowledge-intensive investments (+63.8%), but a 12.8% decrease in corresponding low-knowledge-intensity investments (Institute of Labour—Greek General Confederation of Labour 2017: 73–74).

In direct foreign investment in terms of stocks purchase within Greece by non-residents[5] a significant reduction is to be observed between 2009 and 2016, from €28.2 billion to €23.8 billion (−15.6%). It should nevertheless be noted that whereas between 2010 and 2014 there was a steep and continuing decline (from €30.1 billion to €17.75 billion, (−41%), the last two years of data (2015 and 2016) show an increase of €22.1 billion and €23.8 billion respectively. This change is interpretable as a transition from a crisis of confidence to the acceptance by foreign capitalists of optimistic prospects for the Greek economy. That said, it is interesting that in a number of sectors there is evidence of a downturn (*food, beverages and tobacco* fall from €4.8 billion to €2 billion, *information and communication* from €5.2 to €3.9 billion, and *financial and insurance activities* from €5.5 billion to €4.2 billion), while by contrast there has been remarkable dynamism in other sectors (*agriculture-mining* from €0.07 to €1.4 billion, *metal products* from €0.6 to €1.4 billion, *other manufacturing activity* from €0.9 to €1.4 billion, *alternative forms of energy* from €0.4 billion to €2.8 billion, *transport and storage* from €0.6 billion to €1.2 billion and *real estate* from €0.2 to €2.3 billion).

On the other hand, there was also a great drop in direct investments by Greek residents abroad, but in this case with no signs of recovery. Specifically, from €29.7 billion in 2009 they would fall to €24.2 billion in 2014 and to €18.2 billion in 2016. This was largely due to a sharp decline in *financial and insurance activities* (from €22.2 billion to €8.2 billion) for the well-known reasons of the banking crisis, but there was also

[5] The data is from the Bank of Greece.

a decline in sectors such as *information and communication* (from €2.9 billion to €2 billion) and *food, drinks and tobacco* (from €0.69 billion to €0.25 billion). In contrast *trade and repairs* (increasing from €1.6 billion to €3.7 billion), and *other manufacturing industries* (from €0.7 billion to €2.5 billion) were on the rise. As for geographical orientation, it is to be noted that whereas 67.1% of Greek foreign direct investment went to Cyprus, Romania, Bulgaria Turkey, FYROM and Serbia in 2009, this fell to 55% in 2016 due to withdrawal of the presence of banking and finance. In contrast, there was a large increase in investment in the United States (from €1.3 billion to €2.3 billion).

As for exports, in terms of composition the major change was with petroleum products, which increased from 20.3% of total Greek exports in 2009 to 31.5% in 2017. By contrast, with industrial products there was a fall from 52.9% to 42.6% and with farm products a fall from 22.3% to 19.5%. In geographical terms, as we saw in Chap. 4, it is to be noted that exports to five strong industrial countries (Germany, Italy, the United Kingdom, France and the United States) fell from 36.04% to 29.3%. The same occurred with exports to the Balkans, which similarly fell from 22.2% to 19.7%, and to Cyprus (a fall from 7.2% to 6.1%). By contrast there was a notable increase in exports to the countries of the Middle East and North Africa, from 8.5% to 15%.

In the field of Research and Technology, Greece continued to lag far behind in expenditure in this area as a percentage of gross domestic product (GDP): 1.01% in 2016 against an EU28 average of 2.03%. This did indeed represent an increase over 2009, when the figure was only 0.63%, but it was constrained by the 20% fall in GDP during the same period. In any case the largest proportion of this expenditure was borne by the State (53%), with businesses accounting for only 31.4% (2015) or 0.3% of GDP, whereas the average figure for the Organisation for Economic Co-operation and Development (OECD) countries was 1.45%. The percentage of Gross Domestic Expenditure on R&D disbursed by the business sector was 41.7% for Greece in 2016, compared to 68.9% for the OECD countries.[6] In contrast, the government sector accounted for

[6] It should be noted that, contrary to the dominant neo-liberal narrative, which for all these years has been targeting the educational level of Greek universities so as to enable private universities to be established (something so far prohibited by the Greek Constitution), 32.8% of R & D has been conducted by the higher education sector (OECD average 17.8%).

24.7% (OECD average 10.9%). So, it is no surprise that R&D as a percentage of value added in industry is no higher than 0.77% (OECD 2.50%). Research and technology personnel in the private sector accounted for only 14.5% of the total in 2015 (OECD average 61.4%) in 2015, and only 1.6% of the total number employed in industry (OECD average 6.9%). Total business enterprise R&D personnel in full-time equivalent employment per thousand jobs in industry came to 2.6% in 2015 (OECD average 10.2%). Last but not least in 2015 in Greece only 0.05% of triadic patent families[7] were produced as against the EU28 figure of 24.84% and the figure for the OECD countries of 91.95%.

The conclusion that emerges is that there is no significant high-technology investment. In industry there has been limited direct foreign investment abroad, which has diminished even further following the crisis of the banks. Foreign investment has also declined, precisely because of the global crisis, with a recovery observable in 2015–2016, mainly in the sectors where, due to the provisions of the Memorandum, there has been a generalized sell-off to foreign capital (energy, airports and real estate). Although Greek exports show an increase in absolute terms, this is due on the one hand to the dynamism of petroleum products and on the other to reduced labour costs. In other words, the majority of Greek capitalists were trying to survive through utilization of their main weapon: wage reduction, in accordance with Memorandum policies. They have done this rather than attempting to introduce State-of-the-art technology. Greece has lagged far behind in R&D spending, which—when it occurs—is primarily in the public sector. The contribution to technological innovation has been minimal. The lack of competitiveness that comes with attachment to traditional forms and sectors of production can also be seen from the way that Greek exports tend to be limited not only to the powerful capitalist economies but also to corresponding destinations in the Balkans, choosing markets in North Africa and the Middle East.

To summarize, the long-standing Memorandum policies have not brought about any significant changes in the worldview of the Greek

[7] That is to say, patents certified as such in all three regions: North America, EU, Japan.

capitalists who managed to survive the crisis. The Memoranda were seen as a very good arrangement for restricting competition while at the same time increasing profitability through a reduction in labour costs. Beyond that, and the forced alliance with the political personnel of the lenders, there has been no other kind of strategy in evidence that might generate a different business model for operations above and beyond that of "non-competitive capitalism", reproducing all the resulting pathogens from the past.

The vast majority of Greek society suffered greatly in the years of the crisis and experienced sharp drops in income, cuts in social spending, skyrocketing unemployment, the proliferation of part-time employment and their businesses going bankrupt. From whatever viewpoint Greeks saw the crisis, they imagined that the end of it would mark the beginning of a new and better period. But, the crisis lasted too long, the losses were correspondingly great and the prevailing reaction was one of disillusionment. Finally, on the basis of the reasoning developed in the first part of this chapter, it seems that in the present phase of capitalist domination, any substantial reversals of neo-liberal policies, if they are to get off the ground, will start from the societies of the most powerful states of the West, as a result of the social resistance there.

References

Althusser L., 1996, *For Marx*, London: Penguin Press.

Institute of Labour—Greek General Confederation of Labour, 2017, *The Greek economy and employment. Interim report 2017*, Athens: Institute of Labour—Greek General Confederation of Labour (in Greek).

Mavris G., 2016–2017, "Rise and fall. The electoral influence of SYRIZA before and after the referendum of 5th July 2015", *Tetradia* vol. 66–67, pp. 93–104 (in Greek).

Stalin I., 1924, *The foundations of Leninism*, https://www.marxists.org/reference/archive/stalin/works/1924/foundations-leninism/ch03.htm, accessed on 28/4/2018.

11

Conclusion

The profound economic crisis which has convulsed Greek society since 2009 is linked to the global crisis of the international economy, starting with the collapse of Lehman Brothers in the United States in 2008. The global crisis is related to the fact that despite the various plans opted for (initially a continuation of Keynesianism, then the adoption of permanent wage restraint, an increase in public debt, introduction of flexible forms of employment, financialization), it did not become feasible for the—genuine—rise in profitability to be returned to the levels of the global crisis of 1973. On the contrary, the resort to financialization generated a series of bubbles which began to explode after the bankruptcy of Lehman Brothers, projecting crisis phenomena across a wide range of national and international transactions. The way the crisis was managed in the United States was more straightforward, given that it is a single State, so that they were able to purchase toxic bonds and proceed with provision of low interest loans to the banks by virtue of the liquidity made available to them through their ability to print new money. On the contrary, in the European Union (EU) and the European Monetary Union (EMU), of which Greece is a member, things were more difficult. It is not a single State, so that it was not possible to pursue exactly the same policy. The solution that was chosen was to provide liquidity to the

S. Sakellaropoulos, *Greece's (un) Competitive Capitalism and the Economic Crisis*,
https://doi.org/10.1007/978-3-030-14319-0_11

banks enabling them to get rid of the toxic bonds. But some of the money received by the banks, and this is what is different from the United States, was used to purchase collateralized debt obligations (CDOs), while at the same time limits were imposed on the ability of the countries of the European periphery to secure loans. This led to a rise in the profitability of State bonds and an explosive proliferation of CDOs. Greece, which faced the greatest problem with its current account balance, suffered the heaviest damage because of the difficulty it faced in borrowing to service its debt, with the result that it was obliged to seek the required sums through special agreements with the EU, the European Central Bank and the International Monetary Fund.

As for why Greece found itself in such an inauspicious position, the country's political and economic establishment developed narrative underlining factors such as high wages, the pronounced tendency towards private consumption, the low productivity of the Greek work force and the bloated public sector. But careful study of the empirical data leads to entirely different conclusions. Wages have always been lower than the corresponding European wage levels and no increase in them has been higher than the corresponding increase in the productivity of the economy. Public sector employment and civil servants' salary levels were of the same order of magnitude as European averages. Last but not least, the increase in private consumption did indeed result in expansion of private debt but fell far short of the European average. So, the reasons for the Greek crisis must be sought elsewhere.

For a start, the question of the increase in public deficits that was noted shortly before the appearance of the crisis, which in turn would lead to additional loan requirements, is not unrelated to the fact of the state's choice of lowering taxation for wealthy and medium strata. This was effected through instituting reduction either of tax rates on company profits or of the efficacy of controls by the regulatory mechanisms. This helped the business world to recover from the shock of Greece's entry into the Economic and Monetary Union, with the consequent tension from competition with international capital. And this, precisely, was the basic problem that the Greek economy was called upon to deal with.

The post-war development of Greek capitalism was based on low wages, a factor reinforced by the mass influx of migrants in the 90s, the enduringly powerful presence of shipping capital, an upgrading of the role of tourism and construction, devaluations of the national currency, development of the financial system and the availability of resources from European community funds. On the other hand, there was no provision for strengthening sectors manufacturing high-tech products, or introduction of the necessary infrastructures for doing so. This would continue up to the time of Greece's entry into the EMU, with the result that it lost a large section of its in any case limited share of the European markets. The consequence of this was reduction in exports and a higher deficit in the trade balance. The situation would worsen even further in the light of the parallel steady deterioration of a number of factors in the current account balance (the energy balance, the balance of payments for marine transport, tourist revenue, European subsidization). An attempt was made to bridge the gap primarily through investment in bonds and interest-bearing treasury bills. When this, because of the international crisis, ran up against its limits, Greece found itself confronted with bankruptcy.

The move by the Troika (EU, IMF, European Central Bank) to issue loans so as to avoid non-servicing of the Greek debt was made for the following reasons: (a) foreign banks and also foreign investors were heavily exposed to Greek debt, (b) a Greek bankruptcy would bring the European economy back into a state of crisis, (c) there was a danger of the crisis spreading to Balkan countries (Bulgaria, Romania) that were part of the EU and in which the Greek banking system was strongly present, and (d) an opportunity was being provided for creation of a new regime of accumulation with the potential to enhance overall levels of profitability.

The measures to be imposed on Greece were to be aimed generally at transferring wealth from the working people, the middle strata and non-competitive sections of capital to the most powerful monopoly interests and would make it easier for foreign investors to avoid loss of the capital they had channelled into the Greek economy.

In order to secure the loan money from the Troika, the Greek state was obliged to implement three Memoranda covering eight packages of measures. These measures focused on questions of reduction in earnings and pensions, changes in labour relations in the direction of deregulation and flexibilization, increases in direct and indirect taxation, staffing cuts in the public sector, extension of privatization and mortgaging of public property.

All the above triggered a series of changes in the economy of the country. The period between 2009 and 2016 saw a drastic contraction in a range of indicators: GNP, public and private consumption, the formation of fixed capital, production of added value, property values, the stock market index, direct foreign investment, salaries, pensions, employment, debt servicing, the number of active enterprises, overall company profitability and public debt. Nevertheless, there were certain parameters where improvement was evident: increase in exports in absolute terms, reduction in imports in absolute terms, revenue from tourism and the balance of current accounts.

At the same time, there was an observable continuity in the orientation of Greek exports and Greek direct investment abroad towards the countries of the Balkans, the Middle East, North Africa and Cyprus.

At the level of individual branches of the economy, the greatest slump in absolute terms (2008–2015) was to be seen in the banking sector, industry, construction, trade, other services, hotels and restaurants. On the other hand, an upwards trend was observable with electricity, gas and water supply and other financial services. As for subsectors (2009–2015), the most significant dynamic was evident in oil refining, air transport, auxiliary transport activities and tobacco products. Beyond that, almost all the other sectors registered absolute decline, with characteristic instances textiles, clothing, timber, publishing, pharmaceuticals, non-metallic products, electrical machinery, construction, sale of motor vehicles, telecommunications, health, recreation, culture and sport.

As far as companies are concerned, the crisis damaged small and medium enterprises and a section of the larger firms, a development registered in the reduction of overall profitability. But there are also specific entrepreneurial groups that have been strengthened in the crisis. They include the 500 largest firms and the five largest enterprises in the field of industry and commerce.

Implementation of the eight packages of measures had very significant social consequences. For a start, there was a dramatic fall (in the order of 20%) (2010–2015) in the real income of wage earners. Correspondingly, radical reductions were effected in the minimum wage and in pensions.

Overall, the average assets of Greek households fell by more than 50% (2009–2016). The official unemployment rate skyrocketed from 7.8% to 20.9% (2008–2017), but according to other calculations unemployment surpassed 27%. At the same there were cuts to the level of unemployment benefit and to the maximum period for which it continues to be paid. There was a significant widening of the gap between the rich and the poor, while the richest 20% of the population owned 6.6 times more than the poorest 20% of the population. In 2014, 576 people were in possession of a fortune equal to 50% of GDP. Correspondingly, on the basis of the consumption model of 2008, in 2010 just one-fourth of the population would be characterized as poor, whereas in 2016 this figure was approaching 50% of the population. There was also a doubling of the number of people experiencing material deprivation, a rise in the number afflicted with serious illness, a rise in the number of deaths and a fall in the number of births, with the result that within a space of eight years (2008–2016) the population fell by 3%.

Between 2009 and 2017, there were also significant changes in social stratification: the severity of the economic crisis led to a reduction in the number of firms with a staff of ten or more people, either because of bankruptcy or because of reductions in the number of employees. This amounted to a decline in the specific weight of the bourgeoisie and a corresponding increase of the traditional petty bourgeoisie. At the same time, both the crisis itself and heavy taxation of the self-employed induced a forced movement of numerous individuals to different types of employment, typically menial. These people are therefore now part of the working class, which is accordingly experiencing significant growth. In the agricultural sector, there has been an evident overall numerical contraction, which is, however, interpreted differently for each separate category; a section of the poor rural strata, not able to survive, are forced to sell their property and seek different employment as members of the working class. On the other hand, a considerable proportion of middle and wealthy farming people sell their property and are demoted into the category of poor cultivators. The prevailing assessment is that the cultivated land sold is purchased by very wealthy farmers, and there is a consideration that the average amount of whose is expanded.

There have also been notable changes in the functioning of the Greek state, a by-product of more general restructuring of the State. Everything starts, internationally, from the emergence in the 70s of the phenomenon of authoritarian statism. On the one hand, the economic crisis of 1973 and on the other the global explosion of 1968 induced the dominant bourgeois and imperialist circles to adopt a mutated form of the classical bourgeois representative state in which the institutions of representation are in the process of being downgraded.

With regard to changes, the abovementioned developments might be summarized as the gradual convergence of the policies of the conservative and social democratic parties. Such policies consist of the creation of the state as the headquarters of economic restructuring, a further shift of powers from the parliament and the executive branch to the heads of government and the administration, and to international organizations, and, last but not least, the increased hardening of the machinery of repression.

This, together with the sharpening of the recent economic crisis, serves to create a new reality where the dominant variable will no longer be a coalition of power between different fractions of capital underwritten by supporting classes. On the contrary, there will be almost exclusive predominance of the most powerful monopoly sectors, which will emerge strengthened from the crisis, whereas the role of the surviving non-monopoly sectors will be downgraded and the petty bourgeois strata will gravitate towards the working class.

It should be noted that for the countries belonging to the EMU and/or the EU, the developments just described will be even further exacerbated in the light of the relatively recent institution of regulatory frameworks such as the "Euro Plus Pact" or the "Stability Pact" in which extremely stifling obligations are placed on every member state for the fulfilment of economic performance criteria, irrespective of what each national audience can aspire to or what each national parliament wants to vote.

In the Greek case, all of the above have been aggravated through the imposition of the Memoranda. For a start, whichever government was formed, it was no different from its predecessor in anything concerning its obligations under the Memoranda. Moreover, the parliament suffered a process of continuous downgrading because, as in most cases, it was either required to make decisions under great time pressure or the decisions it made were considered to be outside of its remit. In addition to that, many of these decisions were regarded as unconstitutional (e.g. the Private Sector Involvement (PSI) or the seizure of the property of the Greek public sector) and there has also been an intensification of repressive measures. What is interesting is that above and beyond that there has been, in a number of cases, direct involvement of the mechanisms of the lenders in the functioning of State institutions: initiation of the Franco-German Council, establishment of the Hellenic Republic Asset Development Fund with the presence of representatives of the lenders on the board of directors, installation of foreign commissioners in the administration of every bank, participation of representatives of the lenders in the independent public revenue authority.

All of these developments have produced a situation whereby the Greek state in the period of the Memoranda has been transformed into a quasi-protectorate. We use this term, in contradistinction to that of the classical protectorate, because the basic orientations of its foreign policy remain unchanged but the levers for implementation of its economic policy have come under the control of the lenders.

The deeply reactionary policy that was implemented because of the content of the Memoranda encountered very significant reactions. The first period, which starts in May 2010 and continues until May 2011, bears the stamp of the great mobilization of May 5, 2010. But there was no corresponding continuation given that, even if privately, a sizeable proportion of the Greek population hoped that no new package of measures was in the pipeline. When it became clear that the country was in for even harsher austerity, the new phase of the movement began. This was the movement of the squares (summer 2011), with the central *plateia* of every prefecture in the country occupied for around two months with protest demonstrations and with something similar also taking place, albeit more unevenly in numerous Athenian neighbourhoods. At the same time, structures of solidarity were created in support of these mobilizations and many of them would continue functioning when the movement of the squares had petered out. Reactions against the new measures would escalate when, in the context of the movement of the squares, there were massive strike mobilizations with the participation of hundreds of thousands of people. They were followed shortly after by the third phase, characterized by occupations of ministries which went on day after day but also by mobilizations leading to interruptions of national ceremonies. Finally, the mass demonstrations of February 2012, when the second Memorandum was being signed, resulted in the fall of the Papadimos government and the calling of the May elections that would mark the end of the two-party rule of New Democracy/PASOK, along with the entry onto the scene of SYRIZA, a party of the radical Left. The Samaras government formed in June 2012 would be faced not only by the very significant mobilizations of the autumn of the same year but also by the movement in defence of public television (ERT) in the summer of 2013. Essentially after the emergence of the movement in defence of ERT, the Samaras government was to experience a pronounced deficit of trust, which would accompany it until its fall at the beginning of 2015. In other words, from the summer of 2013 to the summer of 2015, there was a lull in the movement, as if the popular strata were waiting for SYRIZA to come into power and start the confrontation; they judged that the government of the Left would initiate with the lenders. When the SYRIZA-ANEL government was formed, the negotiations did not succeed and the referendum was resorted to. The last mass manifestation of the dominated strata took place on the evening of the address by A. Tsipras in Syntagma Square, two days before the holding of the referendum. After that, following the capitulation of the Tsipras government, there were some mobilizations over taxation and pensions policy but in terms of mass participation they fell far short of the numbers mobilized in previous years.

As far as the party system is concerned, the first tremors were felt at the regional elections of 2010 when the then Prime Minister George Papandreou threatened elections in the event that the former PASOK parliamentarian G. Dimaras won election in the region of Attica. The fact that the PASOK candidate G. Sgouros was elected symbolized the fact that the necessary social support for such an overturn was not yet available. It was to take place at the elections of May 2012, with everything that had preceded them: the movement of the squares, the occupations, the demonstrations of autumn 2011 and the massive rallies of 5th February 2012 that would induce dozens of parliamentarians to resign from their—pro-Memorandum—parties. The primary characteristic of these elections was the downfall of the—until then—two most powerful parties, PASOK and New Democracy. The second most important phenomenon was the spectacular surge in electoral support for SYRIZA, a party of the radical Left. The third was the level of parliamentary support for the Nazi party Golden Dawn. The fourth phenomenon was the expression of widespread discontent both through abstention with spoiled and blank ballots, and through voting for many small parties which did not manage to win election to the parliament. The fifth was the comfortable success of DIMAR in acquiring representation, although it was only two years since it had broken away from SYRIZA.

Inability to form a government led to new elections (June 2012), which were, however, of a different character: they were not elections for the expression of protest but elections for the formation of a government. The pre-electoral period saw the appearance of a new element: a Right-Left polarization as opposed to the hitherto familiar contest between Centre-Right and Centre-Left. But at the same time, it also took the form of pro-European versus anti-European forces, despite the fact that SYRIZA never spoke clearly of exit from the Economic and Monetary Union, let alone from the euro. But the focusing of the discussion on the bipolar question of Memorandum versus anti-Memorandum was perceived by both the European and the Greek elite as objectively raising the issue of the county's relations with European institutions. Finally, New Democracy emerged as first party, but without an absolute majority in the parliament, with SYRIZA second and the two parties together increasing their vote by a total of 21%. The formation of the Samaras government with participation from New Democracy, PASOK and DIMAR and accession of the—until shortly before anti-Memorandum but clearly pro-European—DIMAR marked the point where all available reserves had been gathered into the Memorandum camp. It was a fragile coalition, weakened by two contradictions: on the one hand, the growing discontent over the social consequences of the Memoranda and on the other hand the difficulty that DIMAR had in accepting that it was participating in a pro-Memorandum government. The question of ERT was to liberate a social dynamic that would be channelled into the months-long occupation of the broadcasting studios, contributing to what would finally be DIMAR's departure from the government. After that, and given that the New Democracy-PASOK coalition was not offering any positive vision to the dominated strata, it was only a question of time before SYRIZA's exclusion from power would end. This became obvious from the result of the European elections of 2014, where SYRIZA would come first, almost four percentage units ahead of New Democracy.

The inability to elect a president of the Republic at the end of 2014 would lead to early elections in January 2015 and this election, in turn, led to the formation of a government of collaboration between SYRIZA and ANEL. The new government had this profile because the two collaborating parties had until then shared the anti-Memorandum orientation. The KKE, for its part, although theoretically it could have gone into a progressive anti-Memorandum government, did not wish to be embroiled in a governmental schema that would mean trying to manage the capitalist system. The first six months of government was characterized on the one hand by the conducting of negotiations between the government and the Troika and on the other hand by intense conflict, starting from the pre-election period, between Left and Right. What is interesting is that the negotiations were being carried out in the context of an attempt to "persuade" the lenders to consent to a moderation of the austerity of the Memoranda and not a call for a break with it (which would have meant suspension of payments and probably exit from the Economic and Monetary Union). The government was seeking to compromise with the financial establishment: they offered the election of former New Democracy minister P. Pavlopoulos to the position of President of the Republic, the placement of State people with a Centre-Right background in key positions in the apparatus, the assurance that Greece would remain in NATO, etc. Nevertheless, even though this is what was happening, PASOK, New Democracy and Potami behaved as if a socialist regime was being established in the country. The explanation we give is that they were not so much anxious about what was happening but rather what *could* happen. The truth is that they were afraid of the communist origins of the greater part of the cadres of SYRIZA (including A. Tsipras), which in conjunction with pressures from the popular base could lead to unpredictable circumstances from the viewpoint of the dominant players. These anxieties climaxed when it was announced that there would be a referendum.

But the previous governmental record of the SYRIZA-ANEL coalition did not justify any such fears. There were three reasons for this: (a) all the negotiating strategy was permeated by the notion of "honourable compromise". But in order for there to be compromise and for the opponent to proceed with concessions, the other side must be ready to injure him in some way. Otherwise the exercise degenerates, as indeed happened, into an attempt to persuade the lenders of the mistake they are making; (b) there must be clearly formulated directions for a breach; (c) the government will have encouraged the creation of institutions of parallel State power with the active participation of the dominated classes. Precisely because none of these conditions were met, let alone all three together, a breach did not seem to be in any way a realistic prospect. It was too difficult. And the referendum was carried out not after some unilateral action of Greece but after drastic contraction by the European Central Bank of the available liquidity. And the referendum question did not pertain to the country's participating or not participating in the Economic and Monetary Union but rather to acceptance or not of the specific agreement proposed by the lenders.

Nevertheless, in the interval been the proclamation of the referendum and its being held, the country seemed to have descended into a state of unarmed civil war characterized on the one hand by particularly sharp conflicts and on the other by the fear of the Greek ruling class that the Left was preparing to take revenge for the defeat it had suffered in the 1947 to 1949 civil war. Contributing to the sharpness was the reality of undisguised interference by all the European elite, which on the one hand came down on the side of "yes" and on the other, if "no" won, threatened the country with economic strangulation. In effect, two different faces of Greece clashed in this referendum. On the one hand there was the world of business, media, political personages who had governed the country for decades, and conservative social strata (such as housewives and pensioners). On the other hand there were wage earners, young people, the lower strata in the petty bourgeoisie, all of those who judged that they had nothing more to lose—because they had already lost a great deal—from a head-on collision between Greece and the lenders. The clash stemmed from fear on the part of the dominant strata and on the other hand from the hope of the dominated.

After the referendum, the government continued with the lenders along the path of retreat because it had never elaborated any alternative plan, which shows both that the economic elite did not have very much to fear and that the dominated classes did not have many reasons to be hopeful. In any case, in the elections that were called a few weeks later SYRIZA emerged again as first party and the SYRIZA-ANEL coalition retained governmental power. This hegemony was secured because the Memorandum parties (New Democracy-PASOK-Potami) had nothing different to propose and the parties of the Left (KKE, Popular Unity, ANT.AR.SY.A) had never prepared for embarkation on another course. Within that framework, SYRIZA, despite the haemorrhaging of parliamentarians and cadres that it suffered, managed to retain the strategic initiative.

Another conclusion that may emerge from all this is that although it may be said by many that Greece has been seen as the weak link of neoliberal capitalism, this in fact is not the case. A very large country with economic, political and military capacity of a high enough calibre to be able to make its own way in the world for any length of time could be a weak link, as could a smaller country that might forge an alliance with the larger country that has *already* extricated itself from imperialist influence. Greece fits into neither of these categories.

The first years after the Tsipras government's compromise would be characterized by the faithful implementation of the Memorandum obligations without any significant challenge to them. It was not feasible to implement any parallel relief programme for the subaltern strata, regardless of the relevant declarations of A. Tsipras. The economy, finally, would progress, albeit with low growth rates, without ceasing to be somewhat fragile and subject to perpetual challenge, both due to the international conjuncture and its own internal contradictions.

The above factors are accentuated further from the fact that the Greek economic elite did not proceed to adopt a strategy that could free the Greek economy from the pathogens of the past. Instead of an orientation towards strengthening the production of high-tech commodities, all the indications are that the pre-Memorandum policies have been continued: local investments have been directed primarily towards low- and medium-level products (2009–2015), and direct foreign investments by Greek entrepreneurs will be fewer (2014–2016) and on the other hand will continue to be oriented primarily towards Balkan states and Cyprus. And, last but not least, Greece continues to fall short in spending in the field of Research and Technology by comparison with the countries of the developed West.

Consequently, nobody can predict what the future has in store for the country, given the fixation of the indigenous elite on the determinants whose outcome is Greece's present position in the straitjacket of the Memoranda. The prospects of radical change through evolution of the movements of the dominated appear limited and it seems that whatever changes are on the agenda will have been preceded by transformations at the centre of developed capitalism.

Appendix

Table 11.1 Evolution of house prices

	Athens area	Country total
% change annually		
2000	15.1	10.6
2001	17.9	14.4
2002	16.2	13.9
2003	4.0	5.4
2004	3.0	2.3
2005	8.6	10.9
2006	11.3	12.2
2007	5.2	4.6
2008	2.7	2.8

Source: Pelagidis and Mitsopoulos (2010: 296–297)

Table 11.2 US mortgage loans 2001–2006 ($ billions)

Year	2001	2002	2003	2004	2005	2006
Total originations	2215	2285	3495	2920	3120	2980
Subprime	160	200	310	530	625	600
Subprime securitized	96	122	203	401	508	483

Source: Lapavitsas (2013: 272)

References

Lapavitsas C., 2013, *Profiting without producing, how finance exploits us all*, London and New York: Verso.

Pelagidis T. and M. Mitsopoulos, 2010, *The moment of the turn for the Greek economy. How progressive pragmatism can place it once more on a developmental course*, Athens: Papazisis (in Greek).

References

Agamben G., 2005, *State of exemption*, Chicago: Chicago University Press.

Althusser L., 1971, "Ideology and ideological state apparatuses" https://www.marxists.org/reference/archive/althusser/1970/ideology.htm, accessed on 5/5/2018.

Althusser L., 1996, *For Marx*, London: Penguin Press.

Althusser L., 2001, "Ideology and Ideological State Apparatuses" in L. Althusser, Lenin and Philosophy and other essays, London and New York: Monthly Review Press, pp. 127–186.

Antoniou V., 2014, "2014 elections, a first approach" http://www.iskra.gr/index.php?option=com_content&view=article&id=16486:antoniou-2014&catid=81:kivernisi&Itemid=198, accessed on 13/6/2014 (in Greek).

Argeitis G. and M. Nikolaidi, 2014, *Economic crisis and productive restructuring in Greece: the role of manufacturing industry*, Athens: Institute of Labour—Greek General Confederation of Labour (in Greek).

Argeitis G., G. Dafermos and M. Nikolaidi, 2011, *The public debt crisis in Greece. Causes and prospects*, Athens: Institute of Labour—Greek General Confederation of Labour (in Greek).

Asimakopoulos I, A. Karapappas, S. Brisimis, F. Symigiannis and N. Tsaveas, 2010, "Funding the current account balance: structure, developments and policy", in Economou G., I. Sambethai and G. Symigiannis (eds.) in *Greece's Current Account Balance: Causes of imbalance and policy proposals*, Athens: Bank of Greece, pp. 427–442 (in Greek).

S. Sakellaropoulos, *Greece's (un) Competitive Capitalism and the Economic Crisis*,
https://doi.org/10.1007/978-3-030-14319-0

Athanasoglou P., E. Georgiou and K. Bakinezou, 2010, "The Greek economy's export performance: the effect of competitiveness and of merchandises' composition", in Economou G., I. Sambethai and G. Symigiannis (eds.) *Greece's current account balance: causes of imbalance and policy proposals*, Athens: Bank of Greece, pp. 163–204 (in Greek).

Belantis D., 2011, "Legal and constitutional aspects of the 'new agreements'", *Outopia* vol. 97, pp. 13–16 (in Greek).

Belantis D., 2012a, "Weimar days" http://www.rednotebook.gr/details.php?id=5068, accessed on 11/11/2012 (in Greek).

Belantis D., 2012b, "On the parliamentary state of emergency and its connection with the fascist threat (8 theses on a question for discussion)" http://ektosgrammis.gr/index.php?option=com_content&view=article&id=1777:%2D%2D%2D%2D%2D%2D%2D%2D%2D%2D%2D%2D%2D%2D8%2D%2D%2D%2D%2D%2D&catid=117:ektosylhs&Itemid=516, accessed on 9/11/2012 (in Greek).

Belantis D., 2012c, "Theses on the contemporary "state of emergency"" http://rednotebook.gr/details.php?id=4701, accessed on 15/11/2012 (in Greek).

Belantis D., 2012d, *Towards the state of emergency: the weakening of legal forms*, mimeo (in Greek).

Belantis D., 2013a, "Neo-liberalism, fascism, and the "state of exception"" http://rednotebook.gr/details.php?id=10676, accessed on 12/2/2014 (in Greek).

Belantis D., 2013b, ""Why there is not going to be a dictatorship": aspects of the present day parliamentary state of emergency and exception" http://www.iskra.gr/index.php?option=com_content&view=article&id=14461:ektakth-anagkh-eksiresh&catid=81:kivernisi&Itemid=198, accessed on 12/2/2014 (in Greek).

Belantis D., 2014a, "Positive dynamic with serious contradictions" http://rproject.gr/article/thetiki-dynamiki-me-sovares-antifaseism, accessed on 11/6/2014 (in Greek).

Belantis D., 2014b, "The centre-left and the biopolitical administrative state" http://rednotebook.gr/2014/05/kentroaristera-aftodioikhsh/, accessed on 12/6/14 (in Greek).

Bensaid D., 1995, *Marx l'intempestif*, Fayard: Paris.

Bihr A., 1989, *Entre Bourgeoisie et Prolétariat*, Paris: L' Harmattan.

Bilias F., 2014, *Seeking an alternative productive model for Greek agricultural production*, mimeo (in Greek).

Bitzenis A. and V. Vlachos, 2011, "Outward FDI from Greece and its policy context", *Columbia FDI Profiles*, pp. 1–20.

Bogiopoulos N., 2011, *'It's capitalism, stupid.' The culprits for the crisis and the 'debt' that will bring them down. A polite answer to the praetorians of the MEMORANDA*, Athens: Livanis (in Greek).

Bouvier-Ajam M. and G. Mury. 1963, *Les classes sociales en France*, Paris: Editions Sociales.

Brenner R., 2009, "What is good for Goldman Sachs is good for America. The origins of the current crisis", pp. 1–76, file:///C:/Users/user/Desktop/spiros%20back-up/Spiros/epistimi/arthra/BrennerCrisisTodayOctober2009.pdf, accessed on 19/1/2018.

Bresia M., 2011, "Is all of Greece a town square?", in Giovanopoulos C. and D. Mitropoulos (eds.) *Democracy under construction. From the streets to the squares*, Athens: A/synechia, pp. 91–100 (in Greek).

Burgi N., 2014, "Introduction", in Burgi N. (ed.) *La Grande Regression. La Grece et l' avenir de l' Europe*, Lormont: Le Bord de l' Eau, pp. 15–52.

Burgi N., 2017, "Le démantèlement méthodique et tragique des institutions grecques de santé publique", *La Revue De l' IRES* vol. 91–92, pp. 77–110.

Carchedi G., 1977, *On the Economic Identification of Social Classes*, London: Routledge.

Charalambakis E., 2017, "How much has the crisis affected the situation of Greek households?", *Financial Bulletin of the Bank of Greece* vol. 45, pp. 37–54 (in Greek).

Charalambopoulos L., 2013, "Tax robbery and tax exemption: the fleecing of the weak and the 'I won't pay' of the strong", *Unfollow* vol. 13, http://unfollow.com.gr/print-edition/forolehlasia/, accessed on 31/1/18 (in Greek).

Chesnais F., 2016, *Finance capital today. Corporations and banks in the lasting global slump*, Leiden-Boston: Brill.

Chrysogonos K., 2013, *Getting around the constitution in the age of the memoranda*, Athens: Livanis (in Greek).

Croix de ste G., 1984, "Class in Marx's Conception of History, Ancient and Modern", *New Left Review* no 146, pp. 94–111.

Dafermos G. and C. Papatheodorou, 2011, *The paradox of social policy in Greece: why has the increased expenditure on social protection not reduced poverty?*, Institute of Labour—Greek General Confederation of Labour, pp. 1–6 (in Greek).

Drybetas E. and N. Kalogeridis, 2014, "The dynamics and the role of the banking system", in Roukounas S. and P. Sklias (eds.) *Greek political economy 2000–2010: from the EMU to the support mechanism*, Athens: Livanis, pp. 66–95 (in Greek).

Dumenil G. and D. Levy, 2011, *The crisis of neoliberalism*, Cambridge Massachusetts: Harvard University Press.

Economakis G., M. Markaki and G. Androulakis, 2014, "Extraversion and crisis of the Greek economy: a study", *Bulletin of Political Economy* vol. 8 no 2, pp. 175–204.

Economakis G., M. Markaki and A. Anastasiadis, 2015, "Structural analysis of the Greek economy", *Review of the Radical Political Economics* vol. 47 no 3, pp. 424–445.

Economou G., 2010, "Current account balance: conclusions from the analysis and policy proposals", in Economou G., I. Sambethai and G. Symigiannis (eds.) *Greece's current account balance: causes of imbalance and policy proposals*, Athens: Bank of Greece, pp. 3–74, (in Greek).

Eleftheriou K., 2014, "Cracks in the Monolith: the KKE in the 2012 elections", in Voulgaris G. and I. Nikolakopoulos (eds.) *2012, the twofold electoral earthquake*, Athens: Themelio, pp. 151–184 (in Greek).

Felkerson J., 2011, *$29,000,000,000,000: a detailed look at the Fed's bailout by funding facility and recipient*, Levy Economics Institute, Working Paper no 698, pp. 1–36.

Fine B., 2011, "Beyond financialization", in Vlahou A., N. Theoharakis and D. Mylonakis (eds.) *Economic crisis and Greece*, Athens: Gutenberg, pp. 19–36 (in Greek).

Fotopoulos T., 2010, *Greece as protectorate of the supranational elite. The need for immediate exit from the EU and a self-sufficient economy*, Athens: Gordios (in Greek).

Foucault M., 2008, *The birth of biopolitics. Lectures at the college de France 1978–1979*, New York: Palgrave Macmillan.

Gaitanou E., 2011, "Social and Political Resistance from Youth on the grounds of the crisis", *Ektos Grammis* no. 27–28, pp. 55–58 (in Greek).

Garganas P., 2010, "Crisis: from the banks to the whole economy, ideology and politics", in M. Stylou et al. *The Greek Capitalism, the Global Economy and the Crisis*, Athens: Marxistiko Bibliopoleio, pp. 38–50 (in Greek).

Gemenis K., 2012, "The 2010 regional elections in Greece: voting for regional government or protesting the IMF?", *Regional and Federal Studies*, vol. 22 no 1, pp. 107–115.

Georgiadou B., 2014, "The electoral rise of golden dawn. Revenge vote of the insecure and new political opportunities", in Voulgaris G. and I. Nikolakopoulos (eds.) *2012, the twofold electoral earthquake*, Athens: Themelio, pp. 185–219 (in Greek).

Giannitsis T., S. Zografakis, I. Kastelli and D. Mavri, 2009, *Competitiveness and technology in Greece*, Athens: Papazisis (in Greek).

Giannitsis T. and S. Zografakis, 2018, *Crisis management in Greece*, IMK Studies 58-2018, IMK at the Hans Boeckler Foundation, Macroeconomic Policy Institute.

Giannitsis T., 2013, *Greece in crisis*, Athens: Polis (in Greek).

Gogas P. and E. Takli, 2014, "The framework of the World Economic Crisis", in S. Roukounas and P. Sklias (eds.) *The Greek Economy from the EMU to the Bailout*, Athens: Livanis, pp. 321–338 (in Greek).

Gramsci A., 1972, The intellectuals. Athens: Stochastis (in Greek).

Hardouvelis G., 2008, "Macroeconomic management and the need for structural reforms following entry into the monetary union", in Giannitsis T. (ed.) *Greek economy: crucial questions of economic policy*, Athens: Alpha Bank Historical Archive, pp. 77–116 (in Greek).

Harvey D., 2010, *The enigma of capital and the crisis of capitalism*, New York: Oxford University press.

Hayek F., 2001, *The road to serfdom*, London and New York: Routledge.

Hellenic Statistical Authority (ESYE), 2009, Concise Statistical Yearbook, Athens (in Greek).

Hellenic Statistical Authority (ESYE), 2010, Census of Agricultural and Livestock Holdings, Athens (in Greek).

Hellenic Statistical Authority (ESYE), Labour Force Survey 2nd Quarter 2017, Athens (in Greek).

Hellenic Statistical Authority, 2010, *Research study on income and living conditions in households for the year 2010*, Athens (in Greek).

Hellenic Statistical Authority, 2016, *Research study on income and living conditions in households for the year 2016*, Athens (in Greek).

Hellenic Statistical Authority, 2017, *Research study on household budgets*, 2016, Athens (in Greek).

Iliou I., 1962, *The truth about the common market*, Athens (in Greek).

ICAP, 2009, *Greek financial guide 2013/Greece in figures/5*, Athens, http://dir.icap.gr/mailimages/e-books/GrFigures2013/index.html, accessed on 1/6/2014 (in Greek).

ICAP, 2011, *Greek financial guide 2011/Greece in figures/5*, Athens (in Greek).

ICAP, 2014, *Greek financial guide 2014*, Athens, http://dir.icap.gr/mailimages/e-books/GrFigures2014/index.html, accessed on 1/6/2014 (in Greek).

ICAP, 2016, *The six years of crisis 2008–2016*, Athens (in Greek).

ICAP, 2017, *Greece in figures 2017*, Athens (in Greek).

INE-GSEE (Institute of Labour—Greek General Confederation of Labour), 2009, *The Greek Economy and Employment. Annual Report 2009*, Athens: Institute of Labour—Greek General Confederation of Labour (in Greek).

Institute of Labour—Greek General Confederation of Labour, 2009, *The Greek economy and employment. Annual report 2009*, Athens: Institute of Labour—Greek General Confederation of Labour (in Greek).

Institute of Labour—Greek General Confederation of Labour, 2010, *The Greek economy and employment. Annual report 2010*, Athens: Institute of Labour—Greek General Confederation of Labour (in Greek).

Institute of Labour—Greek General Confederation of Labour, 2011, *The Greek economy and employment. Annual report 2011*, Athens: Institute of Labour—Greek General Confederation of Labour (in Greek).

Institute of Labour—Greek General Confederation of Labour (INE-GSEE), 2012, *The Greek economy and employment. Annual report 2012*, Athens: Institute of Labour—Greek General Confederation of Labour (in Greek).

Institute of Labour—Greek General Confederation of Labour, 2013, *The Greek economy and employment. Annual report 2013*, Athens: Institute of Labour—Greek General Confederation of Labour (in Greek).

Institute of Labour—Greek General Confederation of Labour, 2014, *The Greek economy and employment. Annual report 2014*, Athens: Institute of Labour—Greek General Confederation of Labour (in Greek).

Institute of Labour—Greek General Confederation of Labour, 2016, *The Greek economy and employment. Annual report 2016*, Athens: Institute of Labour—Greek General Confederation of Labour (in Greek).

Institute of Labour—Greek General Confederation of Labour, 2017a, *The Greek economy and employment. Annual report 2017*, Athens: Institute of Labour—Greek General Confederation of Labour (in Greek).

Institute of Labour—Greek General Confederation of Labour, 2017b, *The Greek economy and employment. Interim report 2017*, Athens: Institute of Labour—Greek General Confederation of Labour (in Greek).

Ioakeimoglou I., 2011, *Labour cost, profit margins and competitiveness in Greece 1995–2009*, Athens: Institute of Labour—Greek General Confederation of Labour (in Greek).

Ioannidis G., 2013, "The peculiar distributional character of the Greek taxation system (1995–2008) and the necessary reform which never happened", *Synchrona Themata* vol. 10, pp. 61–68 (in Greek).

Ioannidis G. and C. Pierros, 2015, *A proposal for 10% reduction in the rate of unemployment within three years*, Athens: Institute of Labour—Greek General Confederation of Labour (in Greek).

Iordanoglou C., 2013, *State and interest groups*, Athens: Polis.

Johnson T., 1977, "What is to be known?". *Economy and Society*, vol 6 no 2, pp. 194–233.

Kaltsonis D., 2014, *Law and Society in the 21st century*, Athens: Topos (In Greek).

Kappos T., 2004, *The social structure of the Greek modern society*, Athens: Alitheia.

Karakioulafis C., 2014, "Santé et éducation: victimes des politiques d'austérité", *Chronique internationale de l'IRES* vol. 148, pp. 83–103.

Katsourides Y., 2016, *Radical left parties in Government. The cases of AKEL and Syriza*, London: Palgrave.

Kassimatis G., 2010a, *The Loan Agreements of Greece with European Union and IMF*, Athens: Athens Bar Association, http://www.constitutionalism.gr/html/ent/817/ent.1817.asp, accessed on 10/11/2018 (in Greek).

Kassimatis G., 2010b, *Greece's loan agreements with the EU and the INF*, Athens: Athens Bar Association, http://www.constitutionalism.gr/html/ent/817/ent.1817.asp, accessed on 10/11/2012 (in Greek).

Kassimatis G., 2012a, "An outline of the illegal loan regime", *Pontiki* of 29/12 (in Greek).

Kassimatis G., 2012b, "A silhouette of the lawless lending regime", Pontiki 29/12/2012 (in Greek).

Kavoulakos K. and G. Gritzas, 2015, "Movements and alternative locations in the Greece of crisis. A new civil society", in Georgarakis N. and N. Demertzis (eds.) *The political portrait of Greece. Crisis and deconstruction of the political*, Athens: Gutenberg/National Centre of Social Research, pp. 337–358 (in Greek).

Kapaktsis A., 2012, *The 'Greek problem', origin, development, outcome*, Thessaloniki: iWrite (in Greek).

Kaplanoglu G., 2017, "Is it true that Greeks are overtaxed?", in Katsikas D., K. Filinis and M. Anastasatou (eds.) *Understanding the Greek crisis. Answers to crucial questions on the state, the economy and Europe*, Athens: Papazisis, pp. 59–78 (in Greek).

Katrougalos G., 2012, *The crisis and the way out*, Athens: Livanis (in Greek).

Katrougalos G., 2013a, "The legal exit from the crisis", *Outopia* vol. 102, pp. 174–180 (in Greek).

Katrougalos G., 2013b, "Memoranda, individual rights and democracy: the eclipse of the constitution", *Outopia* vol. 103, pp. 7–13 (in Greek).

Katsaganis D., 2014, "Five German ministries active in Greece", *Kefalaio* 29/3/2014 (in Greek).

Katsikas D., 2017, "Is it true that that way of handling the Greek crisis was dictated by the need for saving European banks?", in Katsikas D., K. Filinis and M. Anastasatou (eds.) *Understanding the Greek crisis. Answers to crucial questions on the state, the economy and Europe*, Athens: Papazisis, pp. 249–272 (in Greek).

Kazakos A., 2011, "From collective labor agreements to violence of individual employment contracts", in *Crisis and Labour*, Athens: ESIEA Cultural Foundation, pp. 20–32 (in Greek).

Klouri A. and A. Karapappas, 2010, "The tourist industry", in Economou G., I. Sambethai and G. Symigiannis (eds.) *Greece's current account balance: causes of imbalance and policy proposals*, Athens: Bank of Greece, pp. 205–220 (in Greek).

Kotzias N., 2013, *Greece, debt colony. European empire and German primacy*, Athens: Patakis (in Greek).

Kotios A. and E. Koutoulakis, 2014, "Economic policy and the consequences for access to international borrowing", in Roukounas S. and P. Sklias (eds.) *Greek political economy 2000–2010: from the EMU to the support mechanism*, Athens: Livanis, pp. 384–414 (in Greek).

Kousiantas K. 2012, "The growth of fascism in Greece" http://aristeroblog.gr/node/897, accessed on 1/4/2014 (in Greek).

Koustenis P., 2014a, "Elections 2014: the electoral cycle of Golden Dawn", *Archeiotaxio* no. 16, pp. 89–108 (in Greek).

Koustenis P., 2014b, "Deconstruction and reconstruction of electoral identities. The sociological detection of Attica" in Voulgaris G.- I. Nikolakopoulos (eds.), 2012, *The twofold electoral earthquake*, Athens: Themelio, pp. 83–123 (in Greek).

Kouvelakis Stathis, 2011a, "The invisible end of a winter. Towards the second phase of the politico-social confrontation", *Epochi* of 25/3 (in Greek).

Kouvelakis Stathis, 2011b, "Crisis hour. Six theses on the revolt", *Dromos tis Aristeras* of 11/6 (in Greek).

Kouvelakis S., 2011c, "Movement time, political time" http://anasynthesi.gr/index.php?option=com_content&view=article&id=324&Itemid=1, accessed on 20/3/2014 (in Greek).

Kouzis G., 2011a, "The labour landscape in Greece following the Memorandum" in *Crisis and Labour*, Athens: ESIEA Cultural Foundation, pp. 34–43 (in Greek).

Kouzis G., 2011b, "Labour in the vortex of the economic crisis and the memorandum: ten points", *Outopia* no 97, pp. 7–12 (in Greek).

Kouzis G., 2016, "The crisis and the memoranda flatten labour", *Social Policy* vol. 6, pp. 7–20 (in Greek).

Kouzis G., 2018, "Labour under attack during the period of crisis and austerity", in Sotiris P. (ed.) *Crisis, movement, strategy: the Greek experience*, London: Brill, pp. 88–95.

Labrianidis L. and N. Vogiatzis, 2013, "The mutually reinforcing relation between international migration of highly educated labour force and economic crisis: the case of Greece", *Southeast European and Black Sea Studies* vol. 13, no 4, pp. 525–551.

Labrianidis L., 2015, *Outward migration from Greece during the crisis.* Final report, http://www.lse.ac.uk/europeanInstitute/research/hellenicObservatory/CMS%20pdf/Research/NBG_2014_-Research_Call/LOIS%20 LAMBRANIIDIS_Outward%20migration%20from%20Greece%20 during%20the%20crisis%20.pdf, accessed on 7/3/2018.

Lapatsioras S. and G. Milios, 2008, "Financial Crisis and 'economic regulation'", Second Part, Theseis no 104, http://www.theseis.com/index.php?option=com_content&task=view&id=1042&Itemid=29, accessed on 23/1/2018.

Lapavitsas C. et al., 2010, Eurozone Crisis: Beggar thyself and beggar neighbor, Research on Money and Finance, http://eprints.uwe.ac.uk/23045/1/fullreport.pdf, accessed on 7/5/2018 and not Lapavitsas 2010.

Lapavitsas C. et al., 2012, *Crisis in the Eurozone*, London: Verso.

Lapavitsas C., 2013, *Profiting without producing, how finance exploits us all*, London and New York: Verso.

Laskos C. and T. Tsakalotos, 2012, *Without Return*, Athens: Kapsimi (in Greek).

Lenin V.I., 1916, *Imperialism, the highest stage of capitalism. A popular outline*, https://www.marxists.org/archive/lenin/works/1916/imp-hsc/index.htm, accessed on 23/12/18.

Lenin V. I., 1977, *A Great Beginning*, Peking: Foreign Languages Press.

Leventi C. and M. Matsaganis, 2016, *Estimating the distributional impact of the Greek crisis (2009–2014)*, OECD Economics Department Working Papers, no. 1312, OECD Publishing, Paris.

Marialiouti Z. and G. Bithymitris, 2013, "Crisis, hegemony and media", *The Example of SKAI and Kathimerini, Greek Review of Political Science* vol. 40, pp. 139–173 (in Greek).

Louka M., 2012, "Cassandra mines: when the gold does not shine", *Ektos Grammis* vol. 30, pp. 75–77 (in Greek).

Lykos M., 2012, "Research and technology in the Greek regions", in Maraveyas N. (ed.) *Exit from the crisis*, Athens: Themelio, pp. 146–185 (in Greek).

Lytras A., 1993, *Introduction to the Theory of Greek social structure*, Athens: Livanis (in Greek).

Manassaki A. and E. Koltsida, 2010, "The contribution of transfers from the EU to the balance of payments and economic development", in Economou G., I. Sambethai and G. Symigiannis (eds.) *Greece's current account balance: causes of imbalance and policy proposals*, Athens: Bank of Greece, pp. 235–260 (in Greek).

Manassaki A., C. Kaiforis and M. Vassardanis, 2010, "The international competitiveness and the Current Account Balance of Greece", in G. Economou, I. Sambethai and G. Symigiannis (eds.) *Greece's Current Account Balance: Causes of Imbalance and Policy Proposals*, Athens: Bank of Greece pp. 77–130 (in Greek).

Maniatis T., 2011, "The fiscal crisis and the social wage in Greece", in Vlahou A., N. Theocharakis and D. Mylonakis (eds.) *Economic crisis and Greece*, Athens: Gutenberg, pp. 206–226 (in Greek).

Maniatis T., 2013, "Accumulation of Capital and Crisis in Global and Greek Economy: a Marxist approach", in *Group of Marxist Researches, Marxism and the Greek economic crisis*, Athens: Gutenberg, pp. 42–87 (in Greek).

Markantonatou Maria, 2012, "The fiscal crisis state and the rhetoric of state of emergency, economic warfare and the retreat of sovereignty", *Theseis* vol. 118, http://www.theseis.com/index.php?option=com_content&task=view&id=1172&Itemid=29, accessed on 7/11/2012 (in Greek).

Marselou A. and G. Basiakos, 2013, *Over-indebted households and Greek economy*, Athens: Institute of Labour—Greek General Confederation of Labour (in Greek).

Mavris G., 2010a, "Disapproval in two rounds", *Kathimerini* of 21/11/2010 (in Greek).

Mavris G., 2010b, "Regional elections 7th November 2010: The anatomy of the election result", *Kathimerini* of 14/11/2010 (in Greek).

Mavris G., 2012a, "The elections of 6th May 2012 and the end of the post-junta two party arrangement" http://www.publicissue.gr/2005/ekloges-2012-telos-metapoliteftikou-dikommatismou/, accessed on 28/3/2014 (in Greek).

Mavris G., 2012b, "Greece's austerity election", *New Left Review* vol. 76, pp. 95–107.

Mavris G., 2013a, "From the fragmentation of the right to conservative disintegration. New democracy a year after the elections" http://www.mavris.gr/3496/2-katakermatismos-dexias/, accessed on 28/3/2014 (in Greek).

Mavris G., 2013b, "Where is SYRIZA going?" http://www.mavris.gr/3533/pou-vadizei-o-syriza/, accessed on 29/3/2014 (in Greek).

Mavris G., 2013c, "The PASOK of Evangelos Venizelos. What is the source of the party's continuous electoral decline?", http://www.mavris.gr/3549/pasok-venizelou/, accessed on 29/3/2014 (in Greek).

Mavris G. 2013d, "The rise and fall of the democratic left", http://www.mavris.gr/3572/anodos-kai-ptosi-tis-dimar/, accessed on 29/3/2014 (in Greek).

Mavris G., 2013e, "Conspectus of golden dawn", http://www.mavris.gr/3625/aktinografia-xa/, accessed on 31/3/2014 (in Greek).

Mavris G., 2014a "The fluctuations in SYRIZA's influence in the 2012–2014 post-election period", *Efimerida ton Syntakton of* 25/2/2014 (in Greek).

Mavris G., 2014b, "The unseen aspects of the electoral war. Elections in two stages: the Greek electoral experiment", http://www.mavris.gr/3981/elliniko_eklogiko_peirama, accessed on 10/6/14 (in Greek).

Mavris G., 2014c, "Conspectus of the vote in the European elections" http://www.mavris.gr/4110/aktinografia-tis-psifou, accessed on 15/6/14 (in Greek).

Mavris G., 2015a "From 2012 to 2015: why new democracy lost the elections" http://www.mavris.gr/4599/why-nd-lost-the-elections/, accessed on 4/4/2018 (in Greek).

Mavris G., 2015b, "The social forces of the anti-memorandum alliance" http://www.mavris.gr/en/621/the-social-forces-of-the-anti-memorandum-alliance, accessed on 4/4/2018.

Mavris G., 2016, "The Greek referendum of 2015" http://www.mavris.gr/wp-content/uploads/2016/07/Mavris_GrRef2015.pdf, accessed on 6/4/2018 (in Greek).

Mavris G., 2016–2017, "Rise and fall. The electoral influence of SYRIZA before and after the referendum of 5th July 2015", *Tetradia* vol. 66–67, pp. 93–104 (in Greek).

Mavroudeas S., 2015. "On the programmatic statements of the SYRIZA-ANEL government" https://stavrosmavroudeas.wordpress.com/2015/02/09/, accessed on 4 4/2015 (in Greek).

McKinsey and Company, 2011, Greece 10 years ahead. Defining the new growth model for Greece, http://www.sev.org.gr/Uploads/pdf/Greece_10_Years_Ahead_Executive_summary_Greek_version_small.pdf, accessed on 29/1/13 (in Greek).

Medjad K., n.d., "Legal and economic reform in today's protectorates: lessons from contradictions" www2.jura.uni-hamburg.de/le/Medjad%20Paper.pdf, accessed on 20/10/2006.

Meiksins P., 1986, "Beyond the boundary question", *New Left Review* no 154, pp. 101–120.

Melas K., 2009, *Befuddled Europe*, Athens: Exantas (in Greek).

Melas K., 2010, "A first evaluation of the Eurozone and the common currency", *Monthly Review* no 64, pp. 22–39 (in Greek).

Melas K., 2011, *Contemporary crises of the global financial system (1974–2008)*, Athens: Livanis (in Greek).

Melas K., 2013, *Small lessons in Greek economy. Peculiarities. The road to the memorandum. Hubris and nemesis*, Athens: Patakis (in Greek).

Metaxas G., 2016, *Crisis?*, Athens: Ekdoseis ton synadelfon (in Greek).
Milios, 2011, "The Greek crisis as a version of the global economic crisis and the crisis of the European Monetary System" http://www.rednotebook.gr/details.php?id=2075, accessed on 7/2/2014 (in Greek).
Milios G., 2002, "The question of the petty bourgeoisie. A single class or two discrete class aggregations?" *Theseis* no 81, pp. 59–80. [in Greek.]
Milios G., 2006, "A Marxist Analysis of Finance and the Question of Commodity Money", Theseis no 97, http://www.theseis.com/index.php?option=com_content&task=view&id=961&Itemid=29, accessed on 23/1/2019.
Mitrakos T., 2018, "Economic inequalities, poverty and social exclusion: international experience and the case of Greece in the recent crisis", *Social Policy* vol. 9, pp. 7–24 (in Greek).
Mitropoulos A., 2013, *Society in the gunpoint. The violent internal devaluation*, Athens: Livanis (in Greek).
Moschonas G., 2012, "The elections of May 2012: The rupture, the tendencies, SYRIZA", *Synchrona Themata* vol. 116, pp. 6–7 (in Greek).
Nikolaidis E., 2005, "The agricultural sector in Greece. A contribution to highlighting its true dimensions", in Argeitis G. (ed.) *Economic changes and social conflicts in Greece. The challenges at the beginning of the 21st century*, Athens: Gutenberg, pp. 87–125 (in Greek).
Nikolaidis E., 2011, "The agro-food system and the growth of the Greek economy", in Vlahou A., N. Theocharakis and D. Mylonakis (eds.) *Economic crisis and Greece*, Athens: Gutenberg, pp. 304–310 (in Greek).
Norfield T., 2012, "Imperialism by numbers" http://economicsofimperialism.blogspot.gr/2012/05/imperialism-by-numbers.html, accessed on 26/1/2013.
OECD, 2011, "Government at a glance 2011" http://www.oecd-ilibrary.org/docserver/download/4211011ec027.pdf?expires=1391032406&id=id&accname=guest&checksum=754DE0EB3673B1F2D74C139C1D4CE150, accessed on 29/1/2014.
OECD, 2014, "Social expenditure update" https://www.oecd.org/els/soc/OECD2014-SocialExpenditure_Update19Nov_Rev.pdf, accessed on 18/2/2018.
Pan-Hellenic Confederation of Agricultural Co-operatives, 2013, *Recent developments in the Greek rural economy*.
Panagiotou S. and Z. Bragoudakis, 2010, "Marine transport—seagoing shipping", in Economou G., I. Sambethai and G. Symigiannis (eds.) *Greece's current account balance: causes of imbalance and policy proposals*, Athens: Bank of Greece, pp. 221–234 (in Greek).

Panitsidis G., 1992, *Approaches to the class structure of our farm economy*, Athens: Synchroni Epochi (In Greek).

Papadimitriou, Dimitri and Anwar Shaikh, Claudio Dos Santos and Gennaro Zezza, 2005, How Fragile is the US Economy?, Strategic Analysis, February 2005, The Levy Economics Institute of Bard College as cited by Chris Harman, 2008, "From the Credit crunch to the spectre of the global crisis" International Socialism no 118, www.marxists.org/archive/harman/2008/xx/crisis.htm#f10, accessed on 10/3/2019.

Papatheodorou C. and S. Papanastasiou/Unicef, 2017, *The situation of children in Greece 2017: children of the crisis*, Athens: Unicef (in Greek).

Papanikolopoulos D., 2016, "The syndicalist dynamic 2010–2015", *Enimerosi* vol. 232, pp. 2–28 (in Greek).

Paraskeva-Veloudogianni D., 2012, "The contribution of official political discourse to the legitimation of golden dawn", *Ektos Grammis* vol. 31, pp. 41–43 (in Greek).

Pelagidis T. and M. Mitsopoulos, 2010, *The moment of the turn for the Greek economy. How progressive pragmatism can place it once more on a developmental course*, Athens: Papazisis (in Greek).

Pelagidis T. and M. Mitsopoulos, 2012, *Understanding the crisis in Greece*, Athens: Psychogios (in Greek).

Petropoulos D., 2013, "The public servants: victims of the memoranda policy", *Aristeri Syspeirosi* no 26, pp. 47–56.

Petropoulos D., D. Fatouros, G. Kyriazopoulos and D. Paschalidis, 2010, "Long-term development of the dimensions of external trade in agricultural products in Greece in the 1994–2008 period", in *Proceedings of the Hellenic conference on administration and economy*, Kavalla 4–6 June, pp. 320–332 (in Greek).

Pleios G., 2013, "The crisis and the Greek media", http://left.gr/news/i-krisi-kai-ta-ellinika-mme, accessed on 24/32014 (in Greek).

Poulantzas N., 1980, *State, power, socialism*, London and New York: Verso.

Poulantzas N., 1984, *State, Power, Socialism*, Athens: Themelio (in Greek).

Public Issue, 2015, "Conspectus of no voters" http://www.publicissue.gr/11719/referendum-2015-no/, accessed on 8/4/2018 (in Greek).

Roberts M., 2016, *The long depression: Marxism and the global crisis of capitalism*, Chicago: Haymarket Books.

Sakellaropoulos S., 2001, *Greece in the post-junta period 1974–1988*, Athens: Livanis (in Greek).

Sakellaropoulos S., 2007a, "Towards a declining state? The rise of the headquarters state", *Science and Society* vol. 71, no 1, pp. 7–32.

Sakellaropoulos S., 2007b, "On the new protectorate states", *Monthly Review* vol. 26, pp. 70–79 (in Greek).

Sakellaropoulos S. and P. Sotiris, 2005, "Returning to imperialism. An intervention on the views of Panich and Gindin concerning construction of the informal American empire", *Monthly Review* vol. 26, pp. 22–38 (in Greek).

Sakellaropoulos S., 2013, "Organization of state power in the Post-Junta period. A benign break in the capitalist continuity", *Ektos Grammis* vol. 34, pp. 39–43 (in Greek).

Sakellaropoulos S., 2014, *Crisis and social stratification in the Greece of the 21st century*, Athens: Topos (in Greek).

Schneider F., A. Buehn and C. Montenegro, 2010, "Shadow economies all over the world: new estimates for 162 Countries from 1999 to 2007" http://www.econ.jku.at/members/Schneider/files/publications/LatestResearch2010/SHADOWECONOMIES_June8_2010_FinalVersion.pdf, accessed on 8/2/2014.

Selcuk B. and N. Yilmaz, 2011, "The effects of global crisis into Euro region: a case study of Greek crisis", *European Journal of Economic and Political Studies* vol. 4 no 2, pp. 49–72.

Soros G., 2008, *The new paradigm for financial markets, the credit crisis of 2008 and what it means*, New York: Public Affairs.

Sotiris P., 2003, "Empire: new theoretical model or reproduction of old contradictions?", *Theseis* vol. 85, http://www.theseis.com/index.php?option=com_content&task=view&id=835&Itemid=29, accessed on 7/5/2018 (in Greek).

Sotiris P., 2011, "The age of post-democracy" http://aristerovima.gr/details.php?id=2939, accessed on 11/11/2012 (in Greek).

Sotiris P., 2012, "The age of insurrections and the left (thoughts on the "squares", politics and left strategy in a landscape of surprises and overturns", *Theseis* vol. 120, http://www.theseis.com/index.php?option=com_content&task=view&id=1193&Itemid=29, accessed on 20/3/2014 (in Greek).

Spourdalakis M., 2016, "Becoming Syriza again" https://www.jacobinmag.com/2016/01/syriza-memorandum-troika-left-platform-tsipras-austerity-government/, accessed on 4/4/2018.

Stalin I., 1924, *The foundations of Leninism*, https://www.marxists.org/reference/archive/stalin/works/1924/foundations-leninism/ch03.htm, accessed on 28/4/2018.

Stathopoulos P., 2014, "The deregulation of the party system", in Voulgaris G. and I. Nikolakopoulos (eds.) *2012, the twofold electoral earthquake*, Athens: Themelio, pp. 61–81 (in Greek).

Stasinopoulos G., 2005, "Entrepreneurship: the deficient developmental parameter in the Greek economy", in Argeitis G. (ed.) *Economic changes and social conflicts in Greece. The challenges at the beginning of the 21st century*, Athens: Gutenberg, pp. 127–168 (in Greek).

The Wealth Report, 2017, "*The global perspective on prime property and investment*", KnightFrank.com/WealthReport, accessed on 25/2/2018.

Tompazos S., 2010, *Centrifugal times. The global economic crisis 2007, 2008, 2009*, Athens: Papazisis (in Greek).

Tompazos S., 2018, *Global crisis 2007–2017 and patterns of capital reproduction*, Athens: Topos (in Greek).

Tompazos S., 2019, *Global crisis and reproduction of capital*, London: Palgrave.

Touliatos C., 2012, "Have we said it all, finally, about Golden Dawn?", *Ektos Grammis* vol. 31, pp. 51–53 (in Greek).

Toussaint E., 2017, *The public debt. Its history and importance in today's crisis*, Athens: Red Marks (in Greek).

Truth Committee on Public Debt, 2015, *Preliminary report*, Athens: Greek Parliament.

Tsakloglou et al., 2016, *Map for exit from the crisis. A new productive model for Greece*, Athens: Dianeosis (in Greek).

Tsiboukakis I., 2012, "The development of agricultural production in Greece", *Kommounistiki Epitheorisi* no. 6, http://www.komep.gr/2012-teyxos-6/h-ekseliksh-ths-agrotikhs-paragoghs-sthn-ellada, accessed on 17/2/2019 (in Greek).

United Nations, 2010, *World investment report. Investing a low carbon economy*, New York and Geneva.

Valavani N., 2016, *The third memorandum, overturning of an overturning*, Athens: Livanis (in Greek).

Varoufakis Y. and V. Missos, 2012, *Global Economic Crisis*, Athens: INE-GSEE (in Greek).

Varoufakis Y., T. Patokos, L. Tserkezis and C. Koutsopetros, 2011, *The economic crisis in Greece and Europe in 2011*, Athens: Institute of Labour—Greek General Confederation of Labour (in Greek).

Varoufakis Y., 2017, *Adults in the room. My battle with Europe's deep establishment*, ebook: Farrar Straus and Giroux.

Vassalos Y., 2018, "Consolidation of autocratic rule in the EU and opposition: the parallel processes of the Troika's emergence and the economic governance reforms and how they could be overthrown", in Sotiris P. (ed.) *Crisis, movement, strategy: the Greek experience*, London: Brill, pp. 68–87.

Vernardakis C., 2011, "Regional and municipal elections 2010: the vote, parties and the party system", in VPRC Institute (ed.) *Public opinion in Greece 2008–2010. Parliamentary and regional elections, political parties, political communication, cultural practices*, Athens, pp. 55–64 (in Greek).

Vernardakis C., 2012a, "Elections in the new post-Junta period", *Avghi* of 13/5/2012 (in Greek).

Vernardakis C., 2012b, "The June 2012 elections in the context of the last days' tendencies" http://www.vernardakis.gr/uplmed/145_Hotdoc%20(2).pdf, accessed on 29/3/2014 (in Greek).

Vernardakis C.2013a, "The 17th June elections and the new breaches in the party system" http://archive.avgi.gr/ArticleActionshow.action?articleID=697536, accessed on 30/3/2014 (in Greek).

Vernardakis C., 2013b, "La gauche grecque aux elections de 2012: le retour du vote de classe" http://www.vernardakis.gr/uplmed/149_FRANCE%20TRANSFORM%207-9-2012%20final.pdf, accessed on 30/3/2014.

Vernardakis C. 2014, "European elections 2014. The key dividing lines in the electorate" http://rednotebook.gr/2014/05/evroekloges-vasikes-diairetikes-eklogikou-swmatos, accessed on 16/6/2014 (in Greek).

Vlahou A. and G. Lambrinidis, 2011, "Crisis and uneven development in the context of the EMU: The External Trade Balance and the international competitiveness of the Greek Economy", in Vlahou A., N. Theocharakis and D. Mylonakis (eds.) *Economic crisis and Greece*, Athens: Gutenberg, pp. 229–255 (in Greek).

Voulgaris G. and I. Nikolakopoulos, 2014, "Introduction: the 2012 electoral earthquake", in Voulgaris G. and I. Nikolakopoulos (eds.) *2012 the twofold electoral earthquake*, Athens: Themelio, pp. 9–31 (in Greek).

Wolff R., 2011, "A Marxist analysis of the crisis", in Vlahou A., N. Theocharakis and D. Mylonakis (eds.) *Economic crisis and Greece*, Athens: Gutenberg, pp. 52–72 (in Greek).

Wealth X., 2014, *World ultra wealth report 2013–2014*, http://www.worldwealthreport.com, accessed on 10/4/2018.

Wealth X., 2017, *World ultra wealth report 2016–2017*, http://www.worldwealthreport.com, accessed on 10/4/2018.

Zisimopoulos G. and G. Economakis, 2013, "Labour relations in Greece. The impact of restructuring of the public sector", *Theseis* vol. 122, pp. 13–36 (in Greek).

Zografakis S. and P. Spathis, 2010, "Economic crisis and Greek economy: the end of budget gaps and the consequences", in Bank of Greece (ed.) *The Greek labour market: characteristics, developments and challenges*, Athens, pp. 13–42 (in Greek).

Zizek S., 2009, *First as a tragedy then as a farce*, London and New York: Verso.

Index[1]

[1] Note: Page numbers followed by 'n' refer to notes.

S. Sakellaropoulos, *Greece's (un) Competitive Capitalism and the Economic Crisis*,
https://doi.org/10.1007/978-3-030-14319-0